118993

D1572453

JOHN

LIFE ETERNAL

JOHN
LIFE ETERNAL

A devotional commentary

by

Roy L. Laurin

MOODY PRESS • CHICAGO

Library of Congress Catalog Card Number: 74-175497
ISBN: 0-8024-4350-8

Printed in the United States of America

Contents

Introduction

CHRISTOPHER MORLEY wrote in *Parnassus on Wheels*, "When you sell a man a book you don't sell him just twelve ounces of paper and ink and glue — you sell him a whole new life." This is true of the fourth gospel. It is a way of life — eternal life made available in the divine person of Jesus through His life and death. An old Quaker expressed it this way: "By God's grace I'm going to really live until I die, and then I'm going to live forever."

What is eternal life? It is not something that happens at death but something that those who are born again possess now. They obtain it by birth, not by death. It is the life Jesus has and imparts to us upon the exercise of our faith.

THE AUTHOR

John, not to be confused with the baptizer, was the son of Zebedee, a fisherman, and Salome, one of the women who followed Jesus until His crucifixion. His mother was probably a sister of the mother of Jesus, and therefore John was a cousin of Jesus (Jn 19:25). John, originally a disciple of the Baptist, and his brother Andrew became the first disciples of Jesus.

After the ascension and Pentecost, John continued to live at Jerusalem where he was one of the three pillars of the church (Gal 2:9). In later years he moved to Ephesus and lived there until he was very old. Finally he was banished to Patmos (Rev 1:9) where he wrote the book of Revelation.

John wrote his gospel in Ephesus toward the end of the first century. William F. Albright says, "The Dead Sea manuscripts and other recent discoveries show that the Gospel of John, believed to have been written 130 years after the death of Christ, was written at least 50 years earlier."

8   *JOHN: Life Eternal*

THE CONTENT

Words used most in John's gospel are:

Know or *knowledge,* occurring 142 times
Believe, occurring 99 times
Life, occurring 36 times
The Father, occurring 121 times
Love, occurring 54 times
Truth, occurring 25 times

John speaks of eight of Jesus' miracles — changing water into wine, raising the ruler's son, healing the impotent man, feeding the five thousand, walking on the water, healing the blind man, raising Lazarus, and the miraculous catch of fish. These constitute the credentials of Jesus as God.

The items reported by John which are common to the synoptics are the work of John the Baptist, the Last Supper, the anointing at Bethany, the passion and resurrection of Jesus, and two miracles — feeding the five thousand and walking on the water.

Items omitted in the fourth gospel but found in the synoptics are the birth, baptism, temptation and transfiguration of Jesus, the institution of the Lord's Supper, the agony in the garden, and the ascension of Jesus. John's purpose is to offer a devotional exposition in terms of faith, life and experience.

THE PURPOSE

The overall purpose of the gospel is to present Jesus as God. In this general purpose, John says, "Behold your God."

The specific purpose is the presentation of Jesus as Messiah by giving details of His life and work so that through faith in these things God might communicate eternal life to us. Of this specific purpose, John says, "Believe and live." "These are written, that ye might believe that Jesus is the Christ, the Son of God; and that believing ye might have life through his name" (Jn 20:31).

THE STRUCTURE

While John, like Acts, is narrative, it does have a structural framework which makes it a cohesive whole. In a devotional treatment the content must be broken up in edible portions, like slices of bread, for the convenience of the eater.

THE VERSATILITY OF JOHN

Here is a book which we instinctively give to sinner and saint alike, for it is suitable for both the uninitiated and the initiated. It is a handbook of truth for the young Christian, and a source of inspiration for the matured Christian.

THE VIRTUOSITY OF JOHN

Here is superlative and lofty philosophical truth. John exceeds the other gospel writers in his account of Jesus' life and sayings, showing remarkable skill in the smoothness of his narrative and choice of material.

THE VERITIES OF JOHN

More great truths are assembled in this single section of Scripture than in any other part of the canon. Here are the deity of Jesus Christ, the love of God, the life eternal, the light of the world, the Father's house and the way to it. Here is the greatest verse in all the Bible — John 3:16. Here are the greatest evangelistic texts in all of God's Word. And all of these great things are presented in the simplicity and sincerity of a man, once fisherman, who was the disciple closest to the Master.

THE OUTLINE

   I. Jesus and the Past — the eternal Word of life (1:1-18).
  II. Jesus and the Present — the source and sustainer of life (1:19—20:31).
 III. Jesus and the Future — the glory of life forever (21:1-25).

Acknowledgments

In his day, John had the synoptic gospels as sources of information and reference for the writing of the fourth gospel; today a modern commentator has multiplied sources of reference for his treatment of it. This author is indebted to two sources almost exclusively: Heinrich A. W. Meyer, *Critical and Exegetical Handbook of the Gospel of John* (New York: Funk and Wagnalls, 1884); and John C. Geikie, *The Life and Words of Christ* (New York: American Book Exchange, 1880). From the latter, material was sometimes drawn without immediate identification and woven into the warp and woof of the finished literary fabric. Without Geikie's excellent material, this devotional exposition would not have been possible. Also, the inspiration and help of a lifetime of reading and study have furnished the unseen background of knowledge for this work.

1

In the Beginning

1:1-13

THE BIBLE is a book of beginnings, processes and endings. Genesis records the beginning of time. Revelation records the beginning of eternity. John records the beginning of redemption. In Genesis God creates man. In John God re-creates man. In Revelation God dwells with man.

The beginning recorded in John is introduced by the profound statement, "In the beginning was the Word, and the Word was with God, and the Word was God." Three things are said about this Word:

1. "In the beginning was the Word." The Word is Jesus Christ who is the "Logos," the speech or philosophy of God. In the incarnation God is articulating Himself in a language of life. Jesus Christ is described as "Alpha" and "Omega," the first and last letters of the alphabet, which infer that He is the entire alphabet out of which is spelled the language of life. Men cannot know God except by that language of which Jesus Christ is every letter. He is God's thought expressed in word.

2. "The Word was with God." This refers to the eternal co-existence of Christ with God. He is not just a carpenter from Nazareth. What He is dates from the fact that He was "with God."

Some years ago a book appeared under the title *The Small Town Man*, inspired by the fact that Jesus was born in Bethlehem and reared in Nazareth, both small towns. But the uniqueness of Jesus does not come from either of these small towns. He was "with God," a man coming down — not rising up.

3. "The Word was God." He who was in the beginning with God "was God." The direction is not from man to God, but from God to man. Jesus Christ is Immanuel — God with us.

11

The Unbegun Beginning (v. 2)

"The same was in the beginning with God." This beginning preceded that of Genesis where it says, "In the beginning God created the heaven and the earth." It is the invisible behind the visible, the eternal behind the temporal. It is that beginning which the Bible elsewhere describes as the "foundation of the world."

The Creative Beginning (v. 3)

"All things were made by him; and without him was not any thing made that was made." Jesus Christ is Creator as well as Redeemer. He is the Architect of the universe as well as the Author of the new life, the Creator who made "all things," and the Redeemer who makes all things new.

The New Beginning (vv. 4-5)

The gospel of John with its redemptive beginning and the book of Genesis with its creative beginning stand in contrast to each other. In Genesis there is the account of creation, in John the account of redemption. In Genesis God spoke in edicts of divine power, in John in expressions of divine love. In Genesis creation came by God's spoken word, in John redemption came by God's living Word. In Genesis, when God had made galaxies, earth, oceans, fish, birds, plants, animals and man, God "saw everything that he had made, and, behold, it was very good." But what was "very good," man despoiled through sin and God had to redeem what man had corrupted. This required the coming of God in incarnation. We behold that incarnation in the gospel of John.

In the creative beginning God created the world out of nothing. In the redemptive beginning God created the new man out of nothing. The new man is not made out of the best things of the old man. He is a new creation: "Which were born, not of blood, nor of the will of the flesh, nor of the will of man, but of God" (v. 13).

In the creative beginning man was made in the image of God (Gen 1:27). In the redemptive beginning God was made in the likeness of men, for "the Word was made flesh, and dwelt among us" (Jn 1:14).

In the creative beginning God began the creative process with the world and ended with man as its crowning feature. In the redemptive beginning God began the new creation with man and will end it with "a new earth, wherein dwelleth righteousness" (2 Pe 3:13).

THE REDEMPTIVE BEGINNING (v. 4)

"In him was life; and the life was the light of men." The two redemptive instruments are life and light, man's essential and basic needs.

Man needs life. All men have life in its natural, human sense, but it is a corrupted and dying life. Jesus brought into the world a new form of life — eternal life — which is incorruptible and undying.

Faith in Jesus Christ will bring eternal life. "I give unto them eternal life; and they shall never perish" (Jn 10:28).

Man needs light. Man is not only spiritually dead; he is spiritually darkened. He is unable to communicate with God, for "the natural man receiveth not the things of the Spirit of God . . . neither can he know them" (1 Co 2:14).

With the redemptive elements of life and light, God fashions the new man and builds the new world which is the end and purpose of the kingdom of God.

THE REDEMPTIVE NEED (v. 5)

"The light shineth in darkness; and the darkness comprehended it not." So deep is the darkness in man that he does not recognize light when he sees it. He does not comprehend the extent of his own need nor does he comprehend the nature of God's salvation that will remedy his need. Only illumination through the life and light which is Christ can do this.

THE NEW WITNESS (vv. 6-9)

"There was a man sent from God, whose name was John. The same came for a witness, to bear witness of the Light, that all men through him might believe. He was not that Light, but was sent to bear witness of that Light. That was the true Light, which lighteth every man that cometh into the world."

This man came to tell the world that the light is turned on. He was John the Baptist, but his more important ministry was as a witness. Baptizing is secondary to witnessing, even as it is secondary to believing.

John did not tell his Palestinian friends that the sun was shining because they had physical vision and could see it for themselves. What they lacked was spiritual vision to comprehend a spiritual light. This is a universal condition, for all mankind lacks spiritual sight. Man is born into a world of darkness.

Men are not naturally the children of God. What is called the universal fatherhood of God is an original condition which was breached by sin when man repudiated God and became an alien living in darkness and death. There was murder among the first brothers, and successive civilizations were built on bloodshed and deceit. Not until man is restored to a new bond of fellowship with both God and man by the new birth will the original condition be restored.

John's mission was twofold: to introduce Jesus to men, and introduce men to Jesus. John did not claim to be the light; he only claimed to know the light was shining.

The New Man — Redeemed (vv. 10-13)

Man cannot get the light and life he so desperately needs at his first birth because he is born in darkness. There must be a second birth, which was Jesus' purpose in coming. But the tragedy is the contentment in which man continues in darkness, for "he was in the world, and the world was made by him, and the world knew him not. He came unto his own, and his own received him not" (1:10-11). Even today men are living in this self-chosen darkness. If men are not naturally the children of God, how can they become His children?

MEN MUST DO SOMETHING (v. 12)

"But as many as received him, to them gave he power to become the sons of God, even to them that believe on his name." The conditions governing salvation are believing and receiving.

To believe means to agree; to receive means to take. To believe is an act of mind; to receive is an act of will. To believe Christ is what you think of Him; to receive Christ is what you do with Him.

GOD MUST DO SOMETHING (v. 13)

"Which were born, not of blood, nor of the will of the flesh, nor of the will of man, but of God." What happens to the person who believes and receives Jesus Christ is described in the first three words of verse 13 — "which were born." The explanation of the process of birth is in four things:

"*Not of blood.*" This refers to heredity and tells us we do not inherit this new life. Men can and do inherit the disposition to sin, but they can never reproduce the life of God by natural processes.

"*Nor of the will of the flesh.*" This refers to reformation, an outward change of conduct without a corresponding inward change. Regeneration, however, is an inward change of which our Christian experience is the outworking.

"*Nor of the will of man.*" This refers to the efforts of others on our behalf. No ceremony or ritual can make anyone a Christian. Becoming God's child is not accomplished by man's will in any religious rite performed for us.

"*But of God.*" The new birth is the result of God's gift. When it says "of God" it does not exclude human responsibility. There is both our part and God's. Ours is the exercise of faith in the work of Christ, and God's is the spiritual application of this work of grace to our lives.

2

When God Had a Skin Face

1:14

A MOTHER ONCE SAID to her child, "There's nothing to fear in the dark, and besides, the angels are near you." "Mother, I don't want angels, I want a skin face," the child replied.

John describes God coming to man with a skin face. "God, who commanded the light to shine out of darkness, hath shined in our hearts, to give the light of the knowledge of the glory of God in the face of Jesus Christ" (2 Co 4:6).

The one who came was the Word, now "stepping down the staircase of time to become flesh." This will remain a profound mystery forever, but why He came will be understandable. An early church Father said, "God became what we are, in order that we might become what He is." This is the heart of the Christian message.

We cannot wholly understand how Jesus combined in His person two distinct substances: humanity and deity; or how Jesus, being truly God, was also truly man; or how, as God, He had infinite intelligence and power, while, as man, He had finite intelligence and power; or how, as God, He remained unchanging and without growth, yet, as man, He "increased in wisdom and stature, and in favour with God and man" (Lk 2:52).

But we can understand what men saw in Him as He lived and died in this interlude of time between His eternal existences. What they saw was God "made flesh" — God in terms of Companion, Comforter, Friend and Redeemer. There is no more beautiful picture of God than that which represents Him as the Companion of man in His experiences of sin, sickness, sorrow and toil. It was God who came to Adam when he had sinned and lost everything, and gave him hope. It was God who came to Abraham the night faith ran low and courage was gone, and gave him renewed faith. It was God who met Jacob as he faced the great wilderness, and who gave him courage to go on. When Moses, brokenhearted by Israel's faithlessness, pleaded for help and guidance, it was God who said, "My presence shall go with thee" (Ex 33:14). When Joshua stood on the fringes of the promised land, it was God who said to him, "Be strong and of a good courage; be not afraid . . . for the LORD thy God is with thee" (Jos 1:9). When Elijah was discouraged, wishing only to die, it was God who prepared his meal and gave him rest before sending him back to his prophet's work. And when man reached the end of his long struggle to find peace, forgiveness and salvation, it was God who "was made flesh and dwelt among us" as our Redeemer and Partner in the great enterprise of life.

Everything Jesus said or did was based upon who He was — the eternal Son of God. Other men before Him, like Socrates, had said, "I know truth," but only He could say, "I am . . . the truth." Other men could say, "I am a messenger of God," but only He could say, "I and my Father are one." Other men had to say, "I have sinned," but Jesus never shed a tear of repentance, never needed or asked divine pardon.

He who was with God is now with man. "The Word was made flesh, and dwelt among us, (and we beheld his glory, the glory as of the only begotten of the Father,) full of grace and truth" (v. 14).

Note four things:

CHRIST WAS "MADE FLESH"

In His incarnation, Jesus assumed both a physical body and a human personality. In the early church many false systems were current, among them Docetism, which said that Jesus Christ was without a real body and only appeared to have one. John refutes this in the plainest of language. Jesus Christ was clothed in the flesh of a real human body.

CHRIST "DWELT AMONG US"

The more accurate statement would be that Jesus Christ tabernacled among us or pitched His tent in our midst. The imagery is to early Old Testament days when a tabernacle or tent was used during Israel's transient years. There is remarkable correspondence between this Old Testament tabernacle and Christ's New Testament incarnation.

The tabernacle was a temporary provision to accommodate the unsettled years of Israel's national existence. Likewise, Jesus' life in the flesh was a temporary period — thirty-three brief years.

The tabernacle was covered with unattractive skins. In like manner, the glory of Christ was hidden beneath a veil of humanity. When Isaiah anticipated the Messiah's coming, he said, "He hath no form nor comeliness; and when we shall see him, there is no beauty that we should desire him. He is despised and rejected of men; a man of sorrows, and acquainted with grief" (Is 53:2-3).

The tabernacle was the place of God's presence among His people. In the same sense "God was in Christ" in the midst of His people.

The tabernacle was the place where God met with man in fellowship and communion. Here men came with their sins, sorrows, problems, sacrifices and praises. It is likewise true that men meet God in Jesus Christ. Through Christ they exchange sin for righteousness, trouble for peace, and despair for hope.

The tabernacle was the place where the high priest made atonement for the nation. In His person, Jesus Christ offered the divine provision for sin in a final and finished atonement.

MEN "BEHELD HIS GLORY"

Men saw something more than a man of flesh; they saw God's "only begotten." They saw Christ's glory when He changed water into wine at Cana where He "manifested forth his glory" (Jn 2:11). Men saw Christ's glory when He raised Lazarus from the dead, for He told His disciples, "This . . . is . . . for the glory of God" (Jn 11:4). Men saw Christ's glory when upon the mount of transfiguration "his face did shine as the sun, and his raiment was white as the light" (Mt 17:2). Men saw Christ's glory in the reflection of His character, the miracles of His power, and the display of His love.

Later in his first epistle, John said, "That which was from the beginning, which we have heard, which we have seen with our eyes, which we have looked upon, and our hands have handled, of the Word of life . . . that which we have seen and heard declare we unto you" (1 Jn 1:1-3).

Christ Was "Full of Grace and Truth"

Grace and truth are the two qualities of Jesus' life by which He manifested the glory of God and redeemed the world. Grace is what Jesus did; truth is what He said. Both grace and truth are essential experiences in man's redemption. It is "by grace are ye saved." But grace does not operate apart from truth. Divine truth proclaims God's grace and through it man appropriates the salvation God provides. Both these essentials are found exclusively in Christ.

Jesus possessed grace and truth in another sense. He possessed them fully in the actions of His life. He manifested grace truthfully, and He proclaimed truth graciously. He was dogmatic and positive without being offensive and intolerant.

Here is an area for the attention of modern Christians. While anxious to be apologists for our faith, we can defeat our purpose by holding correct opinions in an unchristian spirit. We cannot properly defend democracy with undemocratic acts, and we cannot defend the truth by unchristian tactics. We cannot keep the unity of the Spirit by ungracious tactics in defending the truth. Grace and truth must be held in a gentle balance that will preserve the integrity of both and provide the church with a united front in challenging the evil forces of this world.

3

What God Was Like

1:15-18

JOHN BORE WITNESS to someone coming who by all standards of measurement and evaluation was greater than he. In John 1:15-18 this coming one was described.

HIS PREEXISTENCE (v. 15)

"This was he of whom I spake, He that cometh after me is preferred before me: for he was before me." This refers to Jesus' preexistence. He lived before He was born, which sets Him apart from other men. John is saying that the one who lived before him and was preferred before him was God.

HIS FULLNESS (v. 16)

"And of his fulness have all we received, and grace for grace." Since Christ is "full of grace and truth," the experience of redemption in us means that we receive these things, of which Christ is full, in a continuous and progressive experience. Paul wrote something similar to the Ephesians: "Blessed be the God and Father of our Lord Jesus Christ, who hath blessed us with all spiritual blessings in heavenly places in Christ" (1:3). When John adds the phrase, "grace for grace," he seems to say that there is an inexhaustible supply of grace awaiting us in Christ.

Christian experience is progressive. It has a usual movement of growth which reflects maturity and advancement. We are expected to "grow in grace, and in the knowledge of our Lord and Saviour Jesus Christ" (2 Pe 3:18).

Companion texts match this statement of "grace for grace."

Romans 1:17 speaks of "faith to faith," which carries the idea of a progressive faith. Faith matures and develops just as any other element of our spiritual lives, and we are expected to move from one level of faith to another in our Christian experience. Psalm 84:7 tells of going from "strength to strength." Maturity and growth add to our strength. Finally, 2 Corinthians 3:18 speaks of being "changed into the same image from glory to glory." God's redemptive plan is to fashion men into the image of Christ. The process of this fashioning is grace, which changes us into Christ's image from "one degree of glory to another" (RSV).

"His fulness" is not something relative. A thimble can be full of water and an ocean can be full of water, but it could not be the same amount of water. The thimble is only relatively full when compared to the ocean. When you approach the fullness of Jesus Christ, it is not relative but absolute. It is an exhaustless and measureless fullness. Everyone can come to Him to be filled, and none will go away empty.

His Gift (v. 17)

"For the law was given by Moses, but grace and truth came by Jesus Christ." Here are two contrasting gifts — law and grace. The law served a good purpose, but when grace came the purpose of the law was finished. From the time of the appearance of Jesus, the law occupied a place of descending importance. The reason for this lies in the essential difference between law and grace.

The law reveals what is in man; grace reveals what is in God.

The law demands righteousness for the sinner; grace brings righteousness to the sinner.

The law tells us what men must do for God; grace tells us what Christ has done for men.

The law gives a knowledge of sin; grace brings forgiveness for sin.

The law brought God out to man; grace brings man unto God.

The law demands; grace gives. And "grace and truth came by Jesus Christ."

His Declaration (v. 18)

"No man hath seen God at any time; the only begotten Son, which is in the bosom of the Father, he hath declared him." We can *contemplate* God with wonder and awe while not being able to *comprehend* Him. We can understand what God has made without being able to understand the God who made it. Nor can we comprehend the fact that Jesus Christ is the "only begotten Son." This could properly read "God only begotten," making Jesus coequal and coexistent with God. We cannot comprehend this, but we must believe it.

Jesus Christ proceeded by eternal generation from the Father. His eternal beginning never began, for He always was what He always has been; and what He always has been, He always will be. Jesus Christ is the same yesterday, today and forever.

This profound matter is not left in this state of impossible comprehension. Our minds are not left dangling in suspense over the chasms of eternity, for out of eternity steps the Son of God to reveal what God is like.

"No man hath seen God at any time; the only begotten Son . . . hath declared him." No one has seen God in His unapproachable divine essence. Such a sight would destroy us, just as looking at the sun or looking at an atomic blast would destroy the eye. But now the apostle says that someone is coming out of the unbegun beginning into our world of humanity to reveal God's nature.

John uses a word which he never employs again: "declare," which means exegesis or exposition, interpretation or unfolding. Jesus is literally the exegesis of God; through Him we know what God is like.

We may partially understand this process of incarnation by considering the electrical transformer, an apparatus for transforming an electrical current from a high to a low potential, or from a low to a high potential, without changing the current energy. In the case of Jesus, He "stepped down" His divinity, transforming it into human terms without changing the nature of God.

Thus, John reveals the fact of God as man in the incarnation, and the further fact of God in man in the regeneration. This is the purpose of incarnation and regeneration, for Christ in history means nothing apart from Christ in experience.

Economists report twenty-five thousand ways of making a living in the United States, but there is only one way of making a life. Jesus Christ can show the way because He is "the way, the truth, and the life."

4

The Voice in the Wilderness

1:19-34

FOR SOME TIME a strange man had made quick, thrusting visits to the desert areas near the population centers of the Jordan Valley, saying, "Prepare ye the way of the Lord, make his paths straight" (Mt 3:3) and "Repent: for the kingdom of heaven is at hand" (Mt 4:17). This went on repeatedly until the man of unusual appearance and message became the sensation of his times.

This man, who became known as John the Baptist, had seen misery in the land: political and economic slavery to Rome, unjust taxation, heathen garrisons occupying the holy city, a succession of unjust governors and rulers, and an apostate national religious system. Amid such conditions, he proclaimed the coming of the long-expected Deliverer. John became "the voice of one crying in the wilderness" (v. 23), preparing an entrance for the Messiah, as Isaiah had prophesied.

John's rousing protests had broken four hundred years of silence which had begun when Malachi's prophetic voice ceased to speak in Israel. But John was more than a prophetic promiser and predicter of one yet to come; he was an introducer of one who was already here.

As John's influence spread, it became impossible to ignore him. Goaded by concern and fear, the Jewish leaders sent a deputation of priests and Levites to inquire concerning this provocative man.

John's dress consisted of a burnoose of camel's hair, a leather belt, a triangular headcloth and a pair of coarse sandals. His hair was long and uncut for thirty years, the mark of Nazarite consecration. His speech was biting, his spirit independent. These leaders meant to silence him.

So, they came and scornfully asked, "Who art thou?" (v. 19). Could he be Elijah? Could he be that prophet? "Tell us," they said, "who you are so we may bring an answer to those who sent us." Without a moment's hesitation, John gave his answer. Although he had amassed vast public support, and although the whole nation was under his influence, John repudiated his right to any of the designations his questioners had used. He was only a voice crying in the wilderness of human indifference, trying to get the people to make straight the way of the Lord.

The priestly deputation asked, "If you are not the expected Messiah, Elijah or that prophet, why baptizest thou then?"

At this point John made his formal introduction of Jesus: "I baptize with water: but there standeth one among you, whom ye know not" (v. 26). Here is the turning point of the whole narrative. Jesus was not coming; He was already there. He was not an idea in their religious literature; He was someone in the flesh. He was not a God in heaven; He was a man on earth. He was "one among you."

For thirty years Jesus had lived among them. Now He was about to step out of the shadows of comparative oblivion and stand upon the stage of world-shaking events. When John announced that Jesus was "one among you" he meant it literally, for Jesus was standing in the crowd that had gathered on the banks of the Jordan. Having shaken the dust from His carpenter's tunic forever, He now stood "one among" them, ready for the beginning of His redemptive mission.

But Jesus stood unrecognized, for they knew Him not. Here were men whose life business was the recognition of and preparation for the coming Messiah, but they did not know Him. They were religious but spiritually blind.

What may have been tragic for these religionists may be tragedy for us. We may be so busy running heavy religious juggernauts, spending millions, erecting buildings and directing organizations that we, too, may not know the personal reality of God. It is possible today that "there standeth one among you, whom ye know not" (v. 26).

Perhaps it was at this moment that Jesus stepped out of the crowd and, approaching John, asked to be baptized. With characteristic humility, John declined, saying, "I have need to be baptized of thee, and comest thou to me?" (Mt 3:14). And when he baptized Jesus, he beheld the Holy Spirit, dovelike, descending on the Son of God, and he heard God say, "This is my beloved Son, in whom I am well pleased" (Mt. 3:17).

This was John's authentic identity of Jesus as the Son of God: "He that sent me to baptize with water, the same said unto me, Upon whom thou shalt see the Spirit descending, and remaining on him, the same is he which baptizeth with the Holy Ghost. And I saw, and bear record that this is the Son of God" (vv. 33-34). Here are two important designations of Jesus: He is the Lamb of God (v. 29), and the Son of God (v. 34).

As the Lamb of God He would "take away the sin of the world"; as the Son of God He would "baptize with the Holy Ghost." As the Lamb of God He would redeem; as the Son of God He would sustain. As the Lamb of God the cleansing agent was blood; as the Son of God the enabling agent was the Spirit. As the Lamb of God it meant death; as the Son of God it meant life.

Jesus was not identified as a teacher to pass on information, or as a healer to pass on health, or as an example to pass on inspiration. He was identified as the divine Redeemer that He might communicate eternal life.

Two Outstanding Facts

THE NATURE OF JOHN'S WITNESS

John bridges an old and a new dispensation. As Paul would later announce, "The law was our schoolmaster to bring us unto Christ, that we might be justified by faith. But after that faith is come, we are no longer under a schoolmaster" (Gal 3:24-25). This foretold time had now come. It was no longer rituals, ceremonies and priests. Salvation is now related to a personal identity with Jesus Christ. Henceforth the salvation experience would be linked with faith, repentance and a new birth.

THE NATURE OF JOHN'S BAPTISM

John employed baptism as the mark of a new discipleship.

Linked with repentance, it was the sign of the need of remission of sins. When the Christian church later employed baptism as the mark of Christian discipleship, it became the sign of a finished redemption.

The old rites and ceremonies were meaningless in the presence of Jesus Christ. The washings, purifications and cleansings of the Old Testament were performed over and over again, whereas baptism was performed once, expressing the great change demanded in the life of a believer.

John's baptism gave way in later New Testament practice to a more meaningful baptism related to Jesus' death and resurrection. The water symbolized death and also was a sign of that purification by the Holy Spirit which is required before we are baptized.

As in John's baptism, no one could receive it until he had proved his sincerity by a public confession of sins. So in Jesus' baptism there had to be credible evidence of both repentance of sins and faith in Jesus Christ.

Jesus' baptism was His way of identifying Himself with man. Our baptism is our way of identifying ourselves with God — both an act of identification with Jesus' death, burial and resurrection, and an act of confession before the world.

In New Testament times, entry into the church was obtained by means of baptism with the laying on of hands. There were no church buildings, fonts or baptisteries. Baptism of new believers usually took place by the bank of a river, into which the candidates descended and were immersed; this represented their dying with Christ and their burial with Him. Their emergence from the waters represented their being raised with Christ, as sharers in His resurrection. The apostles and their successors then laid their hands upon the candidates in ratification of the baptism. The going down into the waters represented the washing away of the filth and stain of heathendom, and also the death of their old sinful self; the laying on of hands represented the giving to them of the gift of the Holy Spirit.*

The work of John the Baptist was now finished. He had

Crossroads (Mar. 9, 1952). Board of Christian Education, Presbyterian Church, U.S.A.

pointed men to "the Lamb of God, which taketh away the sin of the world." From now on he occupies a lessening place in life. Later he would say, "He must increase, but I must decrease" (Jn 3:30).

John had spoken as "the voice of one crying in the wilderness." But there is that greater and continuing wilderness of the human heart with its moral wastes, spiritual deserts and death. His voice cries out in this wilderness today — "Prepare ye the way of the Lord."

5

A Gracious Invitation

1:35-51

THE MISSION OF JOHN the baptizer was to reveal the Messiah, both in His person and work. As to His person, John had said that Jesus was "the Son of God." As to His work, he had said that Jesus was "the Lamb of God."

As the Son of God, Jesus was to be the regenerator of life. As the Lamb of God, Jesus had come to take "away the sin of the world." As the Son, Jesus came out of eternity to manifest God. As the Lamb, Jesus was the antitype of the Old Testament sacrificial system with its slain lamb. He was "the Lamb of God slain from the foundation of the world."

It would appear that the breathtaking announcement of John had been lost on the multitudes who stood beside the banks of the Jordan. But the next day (vv. 35-39) as John was standing with two of his disciples, Jesus again passed by and John again proclaimed Him as the Lamb of God. When John's two disciples heard this plain identification of Jesus, it was enough for them. That was it! They left the baptizer and followed Jesus.

The first two who attached themselves to Jesus were Andrew, the brother of Simon Peter, and John, the writer of this fourth gospel. Both were anxious to speak with Jesus. Hearing their approaching footsteps, Jesus turned and asked them, "What seek ye?" (v. 38). They countered with another question, "Where dwellest thou?" Jesus replied with this gracious invitation: "Come and see" (v. 39). These words are both an introduction and an invitation to a relationship between God and man that results in the greatest of all experiences – salvation.

When Andrew and John saw Jesus, what did He look like? We know that He must have been in the strength and vigor of early manhood, but there is not the slightest hint in the New Testament as to His physical appearance. Attempts so promiscuously made to describe Jesus are of little importance, for His excellency lay not in physical characteristics, marred later by suffering and death, but in the transcendent qualities of His divine nature that are not apprehended by our physical senses. Peter wrote one of the most important observations: "Whom having not seen, ye love; in whom, though now ye see him not, yet believing, ye rejoice with joy unspeakable and full of glory" (1 Pe 1:8).

Andrew is the first mentioned of the two disciples who came to Jesus, not only because of John's reticence to speak of himself, but primarily because Andrew had the rare distinction of bringing the first convert to Jesus. It was his own brother, Simon Peter.

What was it that persuaded Peter to follow Jesus? Andrew simply used the most persuasive thing anyone can use: his own personal experience. He said, "We have found the Messias" (v. 41). For Andrew it was the discovery of the ultimate, the greatest, the highest — "the Christ."

If living today, Andrew would make an ideal layman, a distinction that does not come by giving the most money, by being a gifted speaker or a clever organizer. It arises from the Christian's most important function — reproduction in another Christian. To bring another person to Christ is the greatest thing we can do and the highest honor we can achieve.

Andrew did not become a preacher, like Peter, nor an author, like Paul. He won fame by bringing his brother to Jesus.

Christianity needs Andrews as much if not more than it needs Peters or Pauls. Our generation can be won to Christ only by the method Andrew used — personal contact. It needs preachers and writers, but it needs witnesses more.

Jesus now had three men — Andrew, John the apostle, and Simon Peter. With this modest band He set out the very next day for His home in Galilee. On the way Philip joined Jesus. His attachment to Jesus was the result of another gracious invitation: "Follow me." The Bible's appeals are to the whole man, to the ears — "he that hath an ear let him hear"; to the eyes —

"Come and see"; to the mind — "Come now, and let us reason together"; to the will — "Follow me."

When Philip joined the small company he became so full of the joy of discovering the Messiah that he sought out Nathaniel, a friend who lived in Cana. There is no record of any sales resistance when Andrew witnessed to Simon; but when Philip sought out Nathaniel with his wonderful discovery of the Messiah, Nathaniel asked, "Can there any good thing come out of Nazareth?" (v. 46). No historical verification was offered; no prophetical proof was given. Philip just said, "Come and see." This is the standard by which anyone can judge Jesus.

Christianity demands faith, but not "blind faith." Faith does not say, "See and come"; it says, "Come and see." Many people are not Christians because they are waiting to see before they come. Their sequence is wrong; it is "come and you will see."

The lack of response in some is because they feel self-sufficient. They pride themselves with being self-made people and do not feel the need of outside help — even from God. A prominent man was being interviewed by a newspaper reporter who said, "I understand, sir, that you are a self-made man." The man replied slowly, "Yes, I guess I am what you would call a self-made man." Then he added ruefully, "But if I had it to do over again, I think I'd call in a little help." God is the help we need. "Come and see."

6

Doing the Impossible

2:1-11

THE MIRACLE AT CANA occurred on "the third day" (2:1). On
the first day John had introduced Jesus as "the Lamb of God"
(1:29). On the second day Andrew and John the apostle had
become Jesus' disciples (1:35). They were followed by Philip
and Nathaniel. On this "third day" Jesus and His disciples arrived at Cana in Galilee, where His mother told Him of a wedding to which they were invited.

A marriage in the East was a time of rejoicing. It consisted of
the nuptial ceremony, followed by an extensive feast provided
by the bridegroom and usually continuing for seven days with
great merriment.

THE MOTHER OF JESUS (vv. 1-5)

> And the third day there was a marriage in Cana of Galilee;
> and the mother of Jesus was there: and both Jesus was called,
> and his disciples, to the marriage. And when they wanted
> wine, the mother of Jesus saith unto him, They have no wine.
> Jesus saith unto her, Woman, what have I to do with thee?
> Mine hour is not yet come. His mother saith unto the servants,
> Whatsoever he saith unto you, do it.

The nuptial wine was exhausted and the feast was threatened
with tragedy. For this emergency Mary saw a remedy, not
through natural recourse to neighborhood wine cellars, but in
her Son.

Jesus, who had assumed what had been hidden since birth, the
prerogatives of the Godhead, stood now in the power and authority of the Son of God. And when Mary suggested that He

might remedy the situation at the wedding feast by supplying more wine, Jesus, by gentle rebuke, reminded her that the former human relationship of mother and son was gone forever. Jesus was now in the world as the Son of God and not the son of Mary. Mary said, "They have no wine." Jesus said, "Woman, what have I to do with thee? Mine hour is not yet come" (vv. 3-4).

This incident provides complete refutation of the idea of a cult of Mary which would later come into existence. At the very outset of Jesus' redemptive ministry, Mary is subordinated to religious insignificance. She still remains Jesus' mother, but she has nothing to say and nothing to do with His work of redemption.

When Jesus said to Mary, "Woman . . . mine hour is not yet come," He gently reminded Mary that henceforth their spheres lay apart and were never to meet again. Hitherto He had acted as the son of Mary; henceforth He would act as the Son of God. Hitherto He had obeyed Mary for human reasons; henceforth He would obey God for divine reasons.

Mary knew without further words what her place was and did not question it. She turned to the servants of the feast and said, "Whatsoever he saith unto you, do it" (v. 5). A new era had arrived. Mary stands forever in the shadows of the glory of the Son of God.

What Jesus subsequently does, He does as the Son of God and in obedience to His heavenly Father. He can no longer be commanded or controlled by any human relationship, for He is now before us as the divine Redeemer.

THE MIRACLE OF JESUS (vv. 6-10)

And there were set there six waterpots of stone. . . . Jesus saith unto them, Fill the waterpots with water. And they filled them up to the brim. And he saith unto them, Draw out now, and bear unto the governor of the feast. . . . When the ruler of the feast had tasted the water that was made wine . . . the governor of the feast called the bridegroom. And saith unto him, Every man at the beginning doth set forth good wine; and when men have well drunk, then that which is worse: but thou hast kept the good wine until now.

The six jars were brought and filled to the brim with fresh water. When, upon command by Jesus, the servants drew water from them and bore it to the governor of the feast, what they took out was the most wonderful wine the guests had tasted all evening. It was a custom in some of these homes that at the birth of a daughter a jar was filled with wine and, after being securely sealed, was buried. At the child's marriage this wine was placed before the bride and groom and later distributed to the guests. Perhaps this enlightens the assertion that "good wine" was always served first. It certainly enhances the greatness of the miracle. That which Jesus produced was found to be best of all — a sign that what He will do redemptively will never diminish; it will grow greater and better and more satisfying.

What takes place at Cana is described as "the beginning of miracles." There follows a succession of wonders that are to give credence to the Messiah's claims as the Son of God. Of the thirty-five miracles recorded in the four gospels, eight are in the gospel of John.

Jesus used two methods to teach: words and deeds. His words were often in the form of parables, while His deeds were sometimes in the form of miracles. Scroggie said, "His parables were miracles in words, and His miracles were parables in deeds." And Henry Norris Bernard wrote,

> The miracles of Christ formed part of that warfare which was ever waging between the Son of God and the power of evil which He was manifested to destroy. . . . The roaring wind and the surging waves seeking to engulf the fishers' boat, the sickness racking with pain man's body; the paralysis of the mental powers destroying man's intellect, . . . the death which shrouded him in the darkness of the tomb — these things were to the Saviour's vision but objective forms of the curse of sin which it was His mission to remove. . . . Man's infirmities and sicknesses, in the eyes of Christ, were the outward symbols of the sin which was their cause. . . . Every leper cleansed, every blind man restored to sight, every paralytic made to walk, . . . above all the dead recalled to life . . . furnished proof that a greater than Satan was here.

What is a miracle? To completely answer that question is impossible, for if we could explain a miracle it would cease to be miraculous. The closest we can come is to say that a miracle is something which transcends the operation of natural law. It is the visible working of the invisible God. As soon as we know the invisible laws which produce miracles, we will then know what is not possible now.

Jesus turns water into wine and we say, "It's a miracle." It is so and it will be so until we know the laws of God by which the water was changed into wine. I hold a book in my hand and then release it. At this instant the law of gravitation starts the book plunging to the floor. On its way downward, the law of my mind interposes my other hand and I stop the plunging book by catching it. Something like this happened in the miracle of Cana when Jesus stopped water from being water by the injection of a higher law. For centuries God had made water, soil and sun into grapes which wine-dressers made into wine. Jesus altered the time element. What took months, now took only moments. What took tools, now took only a look.

Skeptics say a miracle cannot happen because it changes the unchangeable laws of nature. But what kind of God would make a world He could not manage? It would be like making an automobile you could not steer. Let us allow God to be God and let us remain men. Godet said,

> To Jesus, miracles were not performed for the personal accommodation and comfort of the people. They were "Signs." . . . The true aim of these acts passed far beyond the relief of those who were the object of them. If Jesus was moved only by compassion for individual suffering, why, instead of giving sight to a few blind persons only, did He not exterminate blindness from the world? Why, instead of raising two or three dead persons, did He not annihilate death itself? . . . It was because the suppression of suffering and death is a blessing for humanity only as a corollary of the destruction of sin. . . . Miracles were "*Signs*" intended to manifest Jesus as the One by whom sin first, and then suffering and death, are to be one day radically exterminated.

The Manifestation of Jesus (v. 11)

"This beginning of miracles did Jesus in Cana of Galilee, . . . and his disciples believed on him." Jesus never performed a miracle to impress people with His ability, but rather to present His credentials as the Son of God. This was the result of this "beginning of miracles." First, He "manifested forth his glory"; second, "his disciples believed on him" (v. 11). John the Baptist had said, "This is the Son of God," and Jesus confirms this by His miracle.

Have miracles ceased to happen? Generally speaking, yes; specifically speaking, no. God can work a miracle any time He chooses, but generally speaking, as A. H. Strong writes, "Miracles have ceased not because of decline in faith or the withdrawal of divine power, but because the Holy Spirit has changed the method of His manifestation and has led the church to seek more spiritual gifts."

In addition to presenting the evidences of the deity of our Lord, miracles have typical significance. The setting of the Cana miracle is one of the happiest occasions of life — a marriage. It is a picture of salvation. Jesus later said, "Behold, I stand at the door, and knock: if any man hear my voice, and open the door, I will come in to him, and will sup with him, and he with me" (Rev 3:20).

7

The Home and the Church

2:12-25

AFTER JESUS PERFORMED His first miracle He went with His disciples, mother and brothers to Capernaum, which became the temporary home of His immediate family. Following a few days of rest there, they went to Jerusalem. It was Passover time and Jesus observed the profanation of the temple which He proceeded to cleanse by driving out its desecrators.

A number of practical lessons can be observed at this point:

THE AXIS

Jesus established the most important axis in human relations — the home and the church. He went from the house at Cana, by way of His home in Capernaum, to the temple. He went from the wedding to worship: from the house of man to the house of God.

The church is important to the home, for it supplies the ideals for the life of the home and it creates the climate in which our earthly lives are to be lived. If we had greater respect for the house of God, many of the tragic trends of tension, trouble, unhappiness and divorce which are found in our homes today would be reversed. God belongs in both places.

It was the temple Jesus cleansed, and it was the home where He performed a miracle. The temple was for contemplation, the home was for action. The beginning of miracles at the home of family friends at Cana, the healing of the paralytic let down into the house by helpful friends, the healing of Peter's mother-in-law, the raising to life of Jairus' daughter — these acts of Jesus indicate His intention to bring His greatest blessings to us in the home.

The Jews of Jesus' day made much of the home where discipline was applied and life training achieved. Psychologists believe that half the life training of a child is achieved at three years of age, and three-fourths at seven years of age. If this is true, then how important is the home.

The Directions

When Jesus and His party went from Capernaum to the temple at Jerusalem, their journey is described as going "up" (v. 13), for Jerusalem is situated on a hill and is "up" to every part of Palestine. But, no matter where the house of God is located, that place is always "up" because we reach a higher level when we worship God. We are on what the hymnist calls "higher ground." Therefore, we always go "up" when we seek God.

Men need the change of spiritual climate which comes from the spiritual elevation of God's house. Vision is always greater from the heights, for we can see farther and clearer when we get above the ground haze and the man-made smogs of our mechanized civilization. The Lord's Day is a pleasant experience in spiritual elevation. Let us go "up."

The Cleansed Temple

On His arrival at the temple, Jesus cleansed it by chasing out those who were misusing it. There were two such cleansings: one at the beginning of His ministry, and the other at the close. In both He indicated the importance of the house of God. Jesus did not cleanse the Roman Senate or the Jewish Sanhedrin, or the markets or the brothels. He cleansed the temple.

In its cleansing Jesus emphasized the things the temple stood for. He did not glorify stone and mortar, or invest buildings with His presence and His power; He did something greater: He invested human personality with Himself. It is through human personality, not through buildings, ceremonies or tradition, that Jesus works. In the New Testament we find a new temple replacing the old; it is the temple of our body, the habitation of the Holy Spirit. "Know ye not that ye are the temple of God, and that the Spirit of God dwelleth in you?" (1 Co 3:16).

Jesus' attitude to the house of God is described in the words of the psalmist, "The zeal of thine house hath eaten me up" (Ps 69:9). It is from "zeal" that we get our word *zealot* (an extremely ardent person). Another word for zeal is *enthusiasm.* While not a scriptural term, enthusiasm has a divine derivation, for its root meaning is "in God" (*en Theos*). Zeal and enthusiasm are really divine qualities which belong to God's house, yet we reserve them for the stadium, arena and playing field. Let us bring enthusiasm and zeal into the activities that surround God's house and be enthusiastic for God.

THE DIVINE SIGN

When Jesus as a young unknown man sought to avenge the desecration of the temple by cleansing it, He had no formal authority to interfere. And since at this time He had not troubled the Jewish authorities, they could take no violent measures against Him. They asked Him for some "sign" to justify His act.

Jesus' reply embraced the very heart of His mission, even though the Jews did not understand it at the time. His allusion to His ability to destroy the temple and raise it up again in three days was a reference to His body and its resurrection. He saw in "the temple a sacred type of His body" and with the image of the temple before Him, but with the knowledge of His crucifixion in mind, He made a prophetic announcement of His resurrection. This utterance would be used against Him by His accusers at the time of His trial, but it was also one of the guidelines by which He would carry out His divine mission to the world.

From what immediately transpires after this incident, as Jesus deals with Nicodemus, we see the basis of Jesus' answer to men's problems. He was not a mere philosopher in search of wisdom, or a counselor seeking to give good advice. He was a Redeemer giving men a new life.

THE RESULT

Although Jesus did not respond to the challenge of the Jews to produce an authenticating miracle, He did work many miracles which are unrecorded. No wonder "many believed in his name" (v. 23). But in spite of this response to His miracles, Jesus did not receive anyone into the circle of His friends. He "did not commit himself unto them, because he knew all men" (v. 24). He did not trust Himself to them, for He undoubtedly knew, according to Meyers, that "their faith in His name [as that of the Messiah] . . . was only an opinion, produced by the sight of His miracles." It was the faith of the curious, not the committed. They were impressed but they were not yet ready to follow Him.

This is where many modern men stand. They believe in Jesus because they cannot refute His claims. They have faith, but it is not saving faith. They are impressed, but not committed.

8

The World's Most Famous Dialogue

3:1-8

THIS CHAPTER is a dialogue between Jesus and Nicodemus and consists of His teaching concerning man's entrance into the kingdom of God. It puts the finger on man's most acute problem — himself.

The content of the dialogue has had far-reaching effects upon the spiritual lives of multitudes of people. Here is laid bare the fact that what is needed in the world is not a political revolution but a spiritual revolution in the hearts of men — the revolution of the new birth.

Nicodemus was a Pharisee, the strictest sect of the Jews; he was a member of the Sanhedrin and merited the title "a ruler of the Jews." He was educated, religious, wealthy, accomplished and in high position, which gave importance and dignity to his coming to Jesus.

The intent of his visit was to ascertain the exact status of Jesus and His teaching. It turned out differently, for it resulted in Jesus telling Nicodemus how he and others could enter the kingdom of God.

NICODEMUS SPEAKS (v. 2)

"Rabbi, we know that thou art a teacher come from God: for no man can do these miracles that thou doest, except God be with him." The psychology of Nicodemus is perfect. He began with a compliment, thus establishing good personal rapport. He understood that Jesus was not an ordinary teacher but one "come from God." He observed, "No man can do these miracles except

41

God be with him." But Nicodemus was not yet committed to belief in Jesus as the Logos of God.

JESUS SPEAKS (v. 3)

"Jesus answered and said unto him, Verily, verily, I say unto thee, Except a man be born again, he cannot see the kingdom of God." Jesus was not impressed by the stature of Nicodemus. He pushed on to the heart of His mission: getting men ready for the kingdom of God.

God has a kingdom which is as diverse from the human kingdom as the human kingdom is diverse from the animal, as the animal is from the vegetable, and as the vegetable is from the mineral. For the present, this kingdom of God is spiritual and moral. In the future it will have a political, social and physical manifestation and will be internationally visible.

There is but one entrance into the kingdom of God — its own kind of birth which is described as being born again, born anew or born from above. What this new birth meant was the equivalent of a moral transformation and a spiritual regeneration. It was necessary because all men are by nature sinful and therefore unqualified for God's kingdom.

Karl Marx in his "Theses on Feuerbach" said, "Philosophers have explained the world, our business is to change it." The Communists have set about to change the world by force, bloodshed, cruelty, military and economic domination. It is the Christian's business to change the world, but the method of this change is from within.

NICODEMUS SPEAKS (v. 4)

"How can a man be born when he is old? Can he enter the second time into his mother's womb, and be born?" Jesus was speaking of things Nicodemus did not understand. He was speaking of one kind of life and Nicodemus of another. He was speaking of one kind of birth and Nicodemus of another. Jesus was speaking of spiritual birth while Nicodemus was speaking of physical birth.

To Nicodemus, being born again meant to be born over again.

He asked, "Can he enter the second time into his mother's womb, and be born?" But to be born over again would solve nothing, for it would only repeat the conditions of the original birth, human sinfulness. To be born over again would mean giving man another chance — our favorite supposition. All we need, we think, is another chance and then everything will be different. This is not true, for another chance would only repeat the mistakes of the first. What we need is a change that will reproduce in us Christ's kind of life.

Nicodemus' idea of being born over again was a variation of the idea of reincarnation in which one either advanced or retreated in the scale of life by virtue of his behavior. Jesus was talking about regeneration, not reincarnation. It was the generation of a kind of new life and the creation of a new kind of person.

Where does this leave the idea of the fatherhood of God and the brotherhood of man? This doctrine is the idea that God is automatically the Father of all mankind by one birth, whereas Jesus said, "Ye must be born again." It is the idea that all religion is but a variation and extension of Christianity, whereas Christianity is unique as a way to God. Jesus Christ says He is "the way, the truth, and the life: no man cometh unto the Father, but by me" (Jn 14:6).

This doctrine is the idea that creation is the basis of our relationship with God, whereas the basis is the new birth, for "except a man be born again, he cannot see the kingdom of God." The common denominator is not brotherhood, but sin. All mankind are sinners, not sons of God.

Jesus Speaks (vv. 5-8)

Verily, verily, I say unto thee, Except a man be born of water and of the Spirit, he cannot enter into the kingdom of God. That which is born of the flesh is flesh; and that which is born of the Spirit is spirit. Marvel not that I said unto thee, Ye must be born again. The wind bloweth where it listeth, and thou hearest the sound thereof, but canst not tell whence it cometh, and whither it goeth: so is every one that is born of the Spirit.

Jesus is revealing both the nature and the manner of this new birth when He says, "That which is born of the flesh is flesh; and that which is born of the Spirit is spirit" (v. 6). Here are two realms of life: the realm of the flesh and the realm of the spirit. We enter the realm of the flesh by the first birth, which was a natural birth; we enter the realm of the spirit by the new birth, which is a spiritual birth.

What is this spiritual birth like? "Except a man be born of water and of the Spirit, he cannot enter into the kingdom of God" (v. 5). Here are two elements: water and Spirit. We cannot arbitrarily say that water does not mean water while Spirit does mean Spirit, for this would not be truthful exegesis. Jesus said in verse 6, "That which is born of the Spirit is spirit." Water could not mean a physical thing because a physical element cannot achieve a spiritual result. It must therefore be a spiritual equivalent of something used in achieving the new birth. If "water" meant baptism, then baptism is an absolute necessity for salvation. But this cannot be true because water cannot communicate life.

Because Jesus is talking about a change which is "of the Spirit," water has the same spiritual significance as "spirit." It is a spiritual representation of the Word of God which is used by the Holy Spirit in the new birth. Jesus said, "Now ye are clean through the word which I have spoken unto you" (Jn 15:3). Peter said, "Being born again . . . by the word of God, which liveth and abideth for ever" (1 Pe 1:23). The agent of cleansing and of regeneration is the Word of God. It is used by the Spirit of God, and together they produce the new birth.

The word "again" as used in verse 7 means "from above." When the Creator produced human life in the beginning, it did not come out of the earth. Life came from a source outside of the world, "from above."

The lower forms of life in the mineral, vegetable and animal kingdoms cannot become higher forms of life by an inherent power. Only when the life above reaches down into the life below is the lower transformed into something higher.

The lowest kingdom is the mineral kingdom, and only when the life in the vegetable kingdom reaches down into the mineral kingdom and transforms it can it live. Then the animal kingdom reaches down into the vegetable kingdom and transforms it. Then the human kingdom reaches down into the animal kingdom and transforms it. Thus the life "above" transforms the life beneath and lifts it to a higher level of experience.

One more kingdom remains: the spiritual kingdom or the kingdom of God. We can only enter it "from above" and never from beneath. Only when the life which is from above reaches down and transforms the life which is from below can a person have spiritual existence.

Jesus said, "Don't be astonished at what I am telling you, for this is as natural as it is spiritual and as spiritual as it is natural." All He said about the spiritual birth could be proved by the natural birth, as all that He said about the higher could be proved by the lower. "Don't be astonished! Believe me, for only by believing can you prove what I am saying."

At this moment perhaps a strong gust of wind blew into the room, for Jesus said by way of further illustration, "The wind bloweth where it listeth, and thou hearest the sound thereof, but canst not tell whence it cometh, and whither it goeth: so is every one that is born of the Spirit" (v. 8).

Wind is a reference to the nature of the operation of the Spirit. It cannot be seen in its operation, but it can be observed in its effect. We cannot tell the "whence" (the origin) or the "whither" (the destiny). Similarly, neither the origin nor destiny of the new birth is observable, but the effect is observable in that which is produced.

9

The Dialogue Continued

3:9-21

JESUS USED SUCH ELEMENTS as water, spirit and wind to explain His meaning. Water is the equivalent of the Word, spirit is a reference to the Holy Spirit, and wind refers to the invisible operation of the Holy Spirit in His work of regeneration.

When Jesus used wind as an illustration of God's operation in the new birth, He linked regeneration with creation. In the creation, God "breathed into his [man's] nostrils the breath of life." This "breath" of the first creation and the "wind" of the new creation refer to the same thing. Both are acts of God in introducing the life principle into man. One was physical and the other spiritual; one invigorates and energizes the body, while the other invigorates and energizes the spirit.

NICODEMUS SPEAKS (v. 9)

"How can these things be?" Nicodemus did not ask, How can I have this life? His question was, "How can these things be?" This sounds like a natural inquiry into the nature of the things involved in the new birth, but it was, in effect, ignorance born of a form of unbelief. This is indicated by Jesus' reply in the conclusion of the dialogue.

JESUS CONCLUDES (vv. 10-21)

"Art thou a master of Israel, and knowest not these things?" There was a touch of irony and indignation here. Nicodemus was one of the three officers of the Sanhedrin, either its president, vice-president or master teacher. As such, he was the source of knowledge for all manner of inquiries to the Sanhedrin. His ignorance was the ignorance of unbelief. He was willfully rejecting the highest witness to truth.

The basic fault of all humanity is not lack of knowledge, but the willful lack of faith. None will ever be lost because he does not know, but only because he will not believe.

Gilbert K. Chesterton once took a train trip and on the way became so engrossed in his reading that he forgot where he was going. At a station stop, he called up his wife and asked her, "Where was I going?" She replied, "Look at your ticket." The irony of so much life today is not only that people do not know where they are going because of the ignorance of unbelief; they do not even have a ticket.

Jesus says, "We speak that we do know, and testify that we have seen; and ye receive not our witness" (v. 11). He is saying that He was telling only what He knew and saw as the heavenly witness of God concerning the great mystery of the new birth. Nicodemus' fault was not in his inability to understand the mystery, but in his rejection of God's witness.

"If I have told you earthly things, and ye believe not, how shall ye believe, if I tell you of heavenly things?" (v. 12). Jesus is saying that if Nicodemus cannot believe and accept what He revealed about the new birth which is to be experienced as an "earthly thing," how can he expect to believe and accept Jesus' word when He tells him "the higher truths of the kingdom" which are yet to come?

Jesus speaks again: "And no man hath ascended up to heaven, but he that came down from heaven, even the Son of man which is in heaven" (v. 13). There is no other source from which Nicodemus can expect to know the heavenly things Jesus is speaking of, because no man has ever ascended to heaven to learn them and returned to tell them. Only the one now speaking to Nicodemus could be a witness to these things since He had come down from heaven.

But the greatest of all questions is: How can I have this life? The conclusion of the dialogue between Jesus and Nicodemus says three things which answer the question:

LIFE IS BY DEATH (vv. 14-15)

"And as Moses lifted up the serpent in the wilderness, even so must the Son of man be lifted up: that whosoever believeth in him should not perish, but have eternal life." Jesus' death is set forth in an Old Testament incident which was well known to every Jew: the story of the brazen serpent. When the children of Israel sinned, God sent a plague of serpents whose bite was fatal. When Moses interceded with God for the lives of his people, he was instructed to raise a serpent of brass in the midst of the camp. Whenever one of these serpents bit any man, he had only to look at the brazen serpent and he would be healed. This became a type of Jesus' death upon the cross, the divinely appointed manner of our salvation. Men had but to look in faith and live.

The idea of Jesus' death by crucifixion was alien to the Jews, who looked for a reigning sovereign who would deliver them from bondage and elevate them to international prominence. It would be difficult for Nicodemus to think of Messiah in terms of crucifixion.

When Jesus spoke of His death, He used the word "must" (v. 14). It is imperative that Jesus die, for salvation can only come by life out of death. There are three "musts" in the text: the *sinner's imperative* (v. 7), the *Saviour's imperative* (v. 14), the *saint's imperative* (v. 30).

It is not only imperative that men be born again, but if they are ever born again it is imperative that Jesus Christ die, for life can only come by death. "Except a corn [kernel] of wheat fall into the ground and die, it abideth alone: but if it die, it bringeth forth much fruit (Jn 12:24).

LIFE IS BY LOVE (v. 16)

"For God so loved the world, that he gave his only begotten Son, that whosoever believeth in him should not perish, but have everlasting life." These words deal with:

the greatest Person — God
the greatest concern — love
the greatest extent — the world
the greatest sacrifice — gave His only begotten Son
the greatest condition — whosoever believeth in Him

the greatest result — should not perish but have everlasting life

There is an alternative to eternal life — perishing. There is also an alternative to savation — condemnation. It is to save us from these alternatives that God "so loved the world" and "gave his only begotten Son."

LIFE IS BY FAITH (vv. 18-21)

"He that believeth on him is not condemned: but he that believeth not is condemned already, because he hath not believed in the name of the only begotten Son of God. And this is the condemnation, that light is come into the world, and men loved darkness rather than light, because their deeds were evil."

As great as are the facts of Christ's death and God's love, they are not enough until we believe them and receive them in personal faith and experience. Faith is a choice — man's choice of Jesus Christ as God's way to life. Salvation is not forcibly or automatically thrust upon us, nor is it arbitrarily demanded of us. It is offered to us in the realm of our consciousness. The medium of participation in this life is faith, for salvation is to him "that believeth."

The alternative to faith is unbelief, which may be either passive or active, negative or positive. It can be either the positive unbelief of skepticism or agnosticism, with their rejection of Jesus Christ, or it can be the negative unbelief of neglect and indifference in which a person may agree with all the facts of the gospel, yet never take the active step of faith that embraces Christ.

Condemnation as the alternative to salvation is the natural state of all life. He who believes escapes being condemned, while he who does not believe is "condemned already." This "already" is the condition of life into which we were born, just as the state of physical life into which we were born is death.

A person need do nothing in order to die — just be negative to life and not eat, drink or breathe. Similarly, a person need do nothing to be lost — just be what he already is and not act upon the gospel.

Spiritual condemnation as the normal condition of life into which all men are born can be demonstrated by a law of nature known as "the law of reversion to type." Henry Drummond said:

> Suppose a bird fancier collects a flock of tame pigeons. . . . They are of all kinds, of every shade and color, and adorned with every variety of marking. He takes them to an uninhabited island and allows them to fly off wild into the woods. They found a colony there, and after the lapse of many years the owner returns to the spot. He will find that a remarkable change has taken place in the interval. The birds have all become changed into the same color. The black, the white, and the dun, the striped, the spotted and the ringed, are all metamorphosed into one — a dark slaty blue. Two plain black bands monotonously repeat themselves upon the wings of each, and the loins beneath are white; but all the variety, all the beautiful colors, all the old grace of forms have disappeared. These improvements were the result of care, of domestication, of civilization; and now that these influences are removed, the birds themselves undo the past and lose what they had gained.

This "law of reversion to type" runs through all creation. "If a man neglects himself for a few years, he will change into a worse man. If it is his body that he neglects, he will deteriorate into a wild savage. . . . If it is his mind, it will degenerate into imbecility. . . . If he neglects his conscience, it will run off into lawlessness and vice. Or, lastly, if it is his soul, it must inevitably atrophy."

Unless there is conversion to a higher type, there is reversion to a lower type. Conversion is God's process of regeneration which puts the higher life of Christ within us. Reversion is nature's process of degeneration and condemnation which causes us to die.

The natural world is not full of life; it is full of death. It is not natural for a flower or an animal or a man to live. These forms of life are only kept from dying by a temporary endowment of life which gives them a day by day dominion over the elements. Withdraw the temporary endowment and death results.

The biblical view of life is the same as the scientific view.

Man is conceived in sin and shapen in iniquity. The natural condition into which he is born is death. To counteract this natural condition, God introduces a new principle of life which reverses the process of death and results in eternal life. This is salvation.

Jesus is saying to Nicodemus, "You seek eternal life. The only way you can have it is by believing on Me." This is the unchangeable condition for entrance into the kingdom of God — then and now.

10

The New Order

3:22-36

THE NARRATIVE MOVES from the immediate environs of Jerusalem to the farther reaches of Judea, from the lesser mission of John to the greater mission of Jesus. "After these things" (v. 22) refers to all that transpired during Jesus' first visit to Jerusalem, including the cleansing of the temple, the many unrecorded miracles of Jesus, and the dialogue between Jesus and Nicodemus.

Jesus now moves out into Judea, which extended from the wilderness on the south to Samaria on the north. Here He circulated for an undescribed period of time, from village to village and town to town. In this area He preached and taught, and "tarried" in place after place while His disciples baptized the converts.

The narrative discloses four things of interest:

THE NEW BAPTISM (vv. 22-24)

"After these things came Jesus and his disciples into the land of Judaea; and there he tarried with them, and baptized. And John also was baptizing in Aenon near to Salim, because there was much water there: and they came, and were baptized. For John was not yet cast into prison."

The baptism is not new in mode, but new in administration and meaning. It is no longer administered by John the Baptist, but by the disciples of Jesus. It is no longer a baptism of repentance and spiritual renewal in expectation of the coming of Messiah. Now it has acquired the far greater significance of a profession of faith in Jesus as the Messiah already come. Giekie says, "John's baptism had implied a vow to live in the strict and painful asceticism of washings, fasts and legal observances; that

52

of Jesus transformed this life into one of divine liberty and loving joy."

Although verse 22 seems to indicate that Jesus did the baptizing of new converts in Judea, it turns out to be only a form of expression, for in John 4:2 we are told that "Jesus himself baptized not, but his disciples." Exactly why Jesus deferred to His disciples in this matter is not plain. Perhaps He avoided anything bordering on rituals, rites and ceremonies so His mission could not be misunderstood.

While the baptism of Jesus was performed in the same distinctive manner as that of John, it was new in its meaning. It symbolized the operation of the Spirit of God and the Word of God for the accomplishment of the new birth. Thus it stood for a new life which would henceforth be called eternal life.

THE NEW ORDER (vv. 25-30)

> Then there arose a question between some of John's disciples and the Jews about purifying. And they came unto John, and said unto him, Rabbi, he that was with thee beyond Jordan, to whom thou barest witness, behold, the same baptizeth, and all men come to him. John answered and said, A man can receive nothing, except it be given him from heaven. Ye yourselves bear me witness, that I said, I am not the Christ, but that I am sent before him. He that hath the bride is the bridegroom: but the friend of the bridegroom, which standeth and heareth him, rejoiceth greatly because of the bridegroom's voice: this my joy therefore is fulfilled. He must increase, but I must decrease.

At this point John the Baptist, having accomplished his mission, began to occupy a subordinate place. As Jesus moved into the foreground, John receded into the background. When John's disciples became agitated over Jesus' increasing prominence, John reminded them that it was not his purpose to do what Jesus was doing because he was not the Christ.

John alluded to a figure familiar to his disciples when he referred to himself as the friend of the Bridegroom (v. 29). Jesus is the Bridegroom, the new community of believers is the bride, and John is the friend who waits on the Bridegroom. As such, his position is subordinate, and when the bride and Bridegroom are brought together he disappears from the scene.

John's greatness is reflected in his humility and gentleness. He plainly says, "I am not the Christ, . . . I am sent before him." Then he concludes with a self-effacing statement: "He must increase, but I must decrease" (v. 30).

This is John's greatness. He goes up by going down; he becomes greater by becoming lesser. In this lies a practical lesson for all modern followers of Jesus — the lesson of self-effacement in the presence of Jesus. What a sad picture is often presented by modern leaders of the Christian faith who scramble frantically for frontline places in the passing religious parade. Their chief interest seems to lie in personal success and popularity rather than in the advancement of the kingdom of God and the glory of Jesus Christ. None of this activity is worthy of anyone who serves the cause of Christ. All personal promotion pales before John's magnificent statement: "He must increase, but I must decrease."

During General Sherman's campaign from Atlanta to the sea, he had promoted General O. O. Howard to lead a special division. On the night before the great review in Washington, Sherman sent for Howard and said, "The political friends of the man you succeeded are bound that he shall ride at the head of his corps, and I want you to help me out." "It is my command," replied Howard, "and I am entitled to ride at its head." "Of course you are," replied Sherman. "You led them through Georgia and the Carolinas; but you are a Christian and can stand the disappointment." "Putting it that way, there is but one answer. Let him ride at the head of the corps," was Howard's reply. "Let him have the honor," said Sherman, "but you will report to me at nine o'clock, and ride by my side at the head of the whole army." So it happened that the great Christian soldier, with his empty sleeve, rode at Sherman's side at the head of the army.

John the Baptist is now at the head of the army beside Jesus. It is in keeping with Jesus' statement that whosoever abaseth himself shall be exalted. The crown is gained by way of the cross.

THE NEW WITNESS (vv. 31-35)

He that cometh from above is above all: he that is of the earth is earthly, and speaketh of the earth: he that cometh from heaven is above all. And what he hath seen and heard, that he testifieth; and no man receiveth his testimony. He that hath received his testimony hath set to his seal that God is true. For he whom God hath sent speaketh the words of God: for God giveth not the Spirit by measure unto him. The Father loveth the Son, and hath given all things into his hand.

John leaves no doubt about the nature and stature of Jesus. He described Him as "he that cometh from heaven" as "above all." What He says is what He has seen and heard, whereas what John said is what he heard from someone else like the prophets. Jesus speaks with the authority of one "whom God hath sent"; therefore He speaks "the words of God."

Though born a Jew, He speaks as the Lawgiver of a new theocracy which He has come to found. As Giekie says, He lays down conditions to an entrance into the new community He is establishing, though He has nothing to offer but privation and self-denial. He promises eternal life to all who accept His claims and believe in Him. He claims to be the light to which all men, without exception, must come. He calmly announces that His home is heaven, that He knows the counsels of God from eternity, and that He is the only begotten Son of God. This is God's witness and it is from Him that John recedes as he presents Him as the voice of God.

John said of Jesus, "He whom God hath sent speaketh the words of God: for God giveth not the Spirit by measure unto him" (v. 34). The proof of Jesus' unique character and qualification as God's Witness is His possession of the Holy Spirit without measure and limit. This was not true of John or any other witness.

When did Jesus receive the Holy Spirit and become the accredited Witness of God? At His baptism when the Spirit was seen like a dove descending upon Him? Not at this or any other observable time, for, as Meyers says, God "must have endowed Him when He sent Him from heaven." Thus He was always the Son of God.

Surely one to whom God "hath given all things" would be gladly accepted by all who heard Him. But it was not so. Though Jesus was worthy of all homage and confidence, John observed that "no man receiveth his testimony." This is hyperbolic and undoubtedly refers to the few believers in comparison to the vast number of unbelievers. Let us be sure we are among the believers, for dire is the consequence of unbelief.

THE NEW LIFE (v. 36)

"He that believeth on the Son hath everlasting life: and he that believeth not the Son shall not see life; but the wrath of God abideth on him." At this early date in His career Jesus had laid down conditions for entrance into the kingdom of God. One condition was faith: Men must believe in Him as the Son of God and as the sin-bearer. Jesus says that unless we receive Him, we reject Him. To receive Him means life, while to reject Him means wrath.

Those who believe have life and begin to live eternally now. John says, "He that believeth on the Son hath everlasting life." It is not a hopeful expectation, but a joyful possession. It is not something he finds out at death, but something he knows assuredly and confidently in life.

But the opposite is also true. If believers have life, so unbelievers suffer an opposite condition which is described as "the wrath of God." The Word says, "And he that believeth not the Son shall not see life; but the wrath of God abideth on him." Wrath, Meyers says, "is not originated by the refusal to believe, but already exists, and through that refusal remains." It is a continuing condition in which man was born and now continues because of man's unbelief.

Here is a solemn thing. Let no one suppose that he is in a favored position because he has kept the law, performed good works, or lived an exemplary life. None of these things can abrogate the condition of wrath in which he was born. This can only be done by being born again.

11

Inexhaustible Resources for Life

4:1-15

AFTER JESUS' BRIEF MISSION to Jerusalem, He spent nine months in Judea, which had been chosen for His first extensive campaign of preaching and teaching. So successful was this first campaign that Jesus attracted great crowds and won disciples far in excess of those being won by John the Baptist, who was also preaching in Judea. Also, He threatened to draw the whole nation away from the religious leaders in Jerusalem. This prompted them to send an embassage to John to seek to arouse John's jealousy. This is when John revealed his loyalty to Jesus by saying, "He must increase, but I must decrease."

It seemed wise after nine months in Judea, and with the increasing animosity of the Jewish leaders, that Jesus change the scene of His operations. He left Judea and moved northward into Galilee. The direct road to Galilee from Judea led through the half-heathen country of Samaria which was occupied by a people who hated the Jews. While most Jews preferred the more circuitous road that skirted Samaria, Jesus resolved to take the direct road. It took Him straight to a village named Sychar which was near a famous well built by the Jewish patriarch Jacob.

It was noon on that December day when Jesus reached Sychar and approached the well. Finding its shade convenient, He rested while His disciples went to the village for food.

While He was resting there, a Samaritan woman came with a water jar on her head and a long cord in her hand with which to let the jar down into the well. Here was a propitious meeting — Jesus and a woman with a built-in need. It resulted in another famous conversation, second only in importance to that of Jesus and Nicodemus. The need in both cases was the same, but the subject matter was different.

Nicodemus and this woman were worlds apart. One was a Jew, the other a Samaritan. Nicodemus was a religious perfectionist; the woman was a mongrelized Jew.

While the Samaritans held a faith quite similar to the Jews and even expected a Messiah, their history was filled with idolatry and alien gods. For this reason they were shunned by the Jews. Here then is Jesus sitting with a hated Samaritan, but she was not hated by Him.

Notice how different the subject matter of this second conversation was from the one with Nicodemus. With Nicodemus it was technical and mystical, involving the mysteries of the origin and destiny of life, birth and the Spirit. But with the Samaritan it was about water, satisfaction and the inexhaustible resources of life. It was about a well built by Jacob, the common ancestor of both Jew and Samaritan. A water jar was in the hands of a thirsty woman. But Jesus had something the well could not supply — satisfaction. There are two problems here:

A RACIAL PROBLEM (v. 9)

"Then saith the woman of Samaria unto him, How is it that thou, being a Jew, askest drink of me, which am a woman of Samaria? For the Jews have no dealings with the Samaritans."

Ordinarily a Jew would not have dealings with a Samaritan. No Samaritan was allowed to become a convert of the Jews. A Jew might be friendly with a heathen, but never with a Samaritan. Here were sharp racial segregation and prejudice of the worst sort.

But Jesus was above these unworthy strifes and prejudices. To prove it He had sent His disciples into the Samaritan village to procure food, although this was a practice forbidden among the Jews. Furthermore, He deliberately engages a woman of this proscribed race in conversation.

Here is divine love in action. Love knows no barriers and can breach what barriers already exist between races and peoples. Love will do what law cannot do. Law cannot fully settle any racial issue, for people cannot be forced to abandon age-old prejudices and antagonisms. Law cannot change colors. But the example of Jesus reveals that a predominant love can surmount the bitterest racial and religious barriers.

A Personal Problem (vv. 10-15)

> Jesus answered and said unto her, If thou knewest the gift of God, and who it is that saith to thee, Give me to drink; thou wouldest have asked of him, and he would have given thee living water. The woman saith unto him, Sir, thou hast nothing to draw with, and the well is deep: from whence then hast thou that living water? Art thou greater than our father Jacob, which gave us the well, and drank thereof himself, and his children, and his cattle? Jesus answered and said unto her, Whosoever drinketh of this water shall thirst again: But whosoever drinketh of the water that I shall give him shall never thirst; but the water that I shall give him shall be in him a well of water springing up into everlasting life. The woman saith unto him, Sir, give me this water, that I thirst not, neither come hither to draw.

Jesus completely ignored the racial problem. He did nothing to justify the Jewish position or apologize for it, nor did He attempt to ameliorate the bitter situation by excuses or explanations. As an example of perfect technique for a Christian witness, Jesus began with this woman's present interest — water, not Himself or His claims. He did not relate what had happened in Jerusalem with Nicodemus. Jesus did not say a word about Himself or what He had done, because the interest of this Samaritan woman was not in that direction. She was interested in water.

When one goes fishing he begins with the interests of the fish: first, where they are; second, what their food habits are. He goes to the fish and doesn't expect them to come to him. Neither did Jesus expect a Samaritan to come to Him, a Galilean; He went to her. Fish do not care what you look like or how you are dressed. They are interested in only one thing — what you have got to offer.

Jesus ignored the racial and religious differences that separated Him from the Samaritan and said, "Give me to drink." His strategy of asking a favor was to establish rapport, communication and interest, and to disarm her of any tensions created by racial prejudice.

People are not won by being forcibly preached to but at the point of their interest and need. The strategic place to begin our witness to others is with their interest in themselves. They are not won on the level of theological debate. The woman said, "How is it that thou, being a Jew, askest drink of me, which am a woman of Samaria? For the Jews have no dealings with the Samaritans." Jesus was well aware of the great racial and religious antipathy of the Samaritans, but He did not engage in debate.

Jesus did not give a hint that He heard her question and said, "If thou knewest the gift of God, and who it is that saith to thee, Give me to drink; thou wouldest have asked of him, and he would have given thee living water" (v. 10). Thinking that Jesus meant well water, the woman said, "Sir, thou hast nothing to draw with, and the well is deep: from whence then hast thou that living water?" (v. 11).

But Jesus was speaking of another kind of water — the water of divine grace which only He could give, and which could satisfy the thirst of the soul. The satisfaction that Jesus was talking about is described as "living water." Just as He is the "living bread," so He is the "living water."

Someone has said, "Life is an everlasting struggle to keep the money coming in, and the teeth, hair and vital organs from coming out." But the struggle is more basic than this, and our needs are more imperative than these financial and physical problems. There is a human thirst for simple basic satisfactions. These are not the physical satisfactions because, as Jesus said to the Samaritan, they are never permanently satisfied: "Whosoever drinketh of this water shall thirst again." "This water is no doubt good," said Jesus, "but anyone drinking of it will have to come back again. I have access to water of which when one drinks he will never thirst again." These are His words: "But whosoever drinketh of the water that I shall give him shall never thirst; but the water that I shall give him shall be in him a well of water springing up into everlasting life" (v. 14).

Here are satisfactions of which Jesus Christ is the only source. This water will satisfy, not only because it was from a source that is never abated, but because it is suited to the inner spiritual need of the individual. This "living water" would come as the result of an encounter with the Son of God that would result in the new birth.

Physical water is a compound of hydrogen and oxygen, two parts to one. Being gases they are invisible, but when put with the catalyst of heat they combine to become a liquid called water. "Living water" is likewise a compound of two elements: grace and truth. Put these with the catalyst of faith and they become soul satisfaction.

The Samaritan now realizes that this "living water" is received upon request. None of us have it naturally; it is acquired by request, for the woman said, "Give me this water."

We need not argue whether she fully understood the nature of this "living water," any more than we need to argue whether a sinner needs to fully understand the nature of salvation. He does not. He need only to desire, to request and to receive it. This is the equivalent of faith.

12

The New Worship

4:16-42

JESUS HAD ASKED a Samaritan woman for a drink. She countered with the objection that Jesus was asking a favor of a Samaritan with whom the Jews had no dealings. Jesus ignored this religio-racial problem, saying that if she only knew who it was that was asking her this favor, she would have asked of Him and He would have given her living water. She raised another objection, saying that He had nothing to draw water with, and Jesus told her that He was talking about another kind of water that did not require waterpots. She then asked, "Give me to drink."

Here are two resistances to God's overtures. One of the most common is the religious rebuttal: Men justify themselves by saying, "I am religious." But religion is not the issue; the issue is "living water." Whether it is the moralist Nicodemus or the immoralist Samaritan, the need is life, and the way to life with its "living water" is the new birth.

The other resistance is the question of procedure: Men question the methods of God, doubting the efficacy of faith or the reliability of revelation or the reality of salvation. This was the problem of Nicodemus, for just as the Samaritan woman thought in terms of natural water, he thought in terms of natural birth. But the spiritual processes of God's work of grace are beyond human scrutiny. They are like the wind, invisible as to origin and destiny, but observable in its effects.

When these soul resistances were swept away, the woman was responsive and asked, "Give me this water." But she was not ready for this experience.

> Jesus saith unto her, Go, call thy husband, and come hither. The woman answered and said, I have no husband. Jesus said

unto her, Thou hast well said, I have no husband: for thou
hast had five husbands; and he whom thou now hast is not thy
husband: in that saidst thou truly. The woman saith unto him,
Sir, I perceive that thou art a prophet. Our fathers worshipped
in this mountain; and ye say, that in Jerusalem is the place
where men ought to worship (vv. 16-20).

This woman's condition had to be exposed as a step toward
an awakening of a sense of guilt that would lead to repentance.
None of God's provisions of salvation are predicated on the old
life with its sins; they require repentance as a preparation for
receiving God's grace. Thus, to expose this woman's immoral
condition was necessary to ultimate repentance.

Repentance must be real and thorough, not perfunctory and
hypocritical. A pilgrim was once ordered, as a means of pen-
ance, to walk a great distance with peas in his shoes. Being more
clever than conscientious, he took the liberty of making his task
easy by first boiling the peas. While fulfilling the letter of the
requirement, he did not fulfill the spirit of it. Boiled peas may
be all right for soup, but not for getting to heaven.

The Samaritan woman avoided the issue by appealing to her
traditions. She said, "Sir, I perceive that thou art a prophet. Our
fathers worshipped in this mountain; and ye say, that in Jerusalem is the place where men ought to worship" (vv. 19-20). Her
tradition, and that of her people, was associated with Mount
Gerizim, to them the most sacred spot on earth. Every Samaritan turned his face toward Gerizim when he prayed, for he believed the Messiah would appear on its summit.

But tradition was no substitute for repentance. All this trust
in sacred places, rituals and ceremonies would henceforth be
obsolete, for one stood in this woman's presence who was God
incarnate. Hitherto it had been places and things; now it was
to be a Person, the Son of God.

When the Samaritan woman pointed to her sacred mountain
as the meeting place between God and man, Jesus pointed to
Himself. He was the personal place of salvation. He would later
say, "I am the way, the truth, and the life: no man cometh unto
the Father, but by me" (Jn 14:6).

Jesus said, "Woman, believe me, the hour cometh, when ye shall neither in this mountain, nor yet at Jerusalem, worship the Father. Ye worship ye know not what: we know what we worship: for salvation is of the Jews. But the hour cometh, and now is, when the true worshippers shall worship the Father in spirit and in truth: for the Father seeketh such to worship him. God is a Spirit: and they that worship him must worship him in spirit and in truth" (4:21-24).

According to Geikie, Jesus was saying that "the worth of a man's homage to God does not depend on the place where it is paid. The true worship has its temple in the inmost soul, in the spirit and heart. It is spiritual and moral, not outward and ritual, springing from the great truth which Jesus had first uttered, that God is a Spirit."

The Samaritan woman used her worship of God as a cover for her immoral life. But when we understand true worship, it will create a sense of responsibility that will not permit this kind of irregularity. It was said of Job that he was "perfect and upright, and one that feared God, and eschewed evil" (Job 1:1). Job's fear of God gave Him a corresponding fear of evil — the true effect of true worship of God.

We have only partially conceived an act of worship in terms of sermon, music and ritual which are performed by someone other than the worshiper. Worship is something the individual must do; it is the communion of his spirit with God's Spirit.

We think of worship too often in terms of who is going to sing and who is going to preach, or what kind of a building will be used. But these things only satisfy personal and selfish whims. Worship is the soul's communication with God.

Worship is not a matter of location or ritual, of which the Samaritans boasted when they faced their holy mountain. Rather, it is a matter of personal relationship with God.

The dual revelation to Nicodemus of the way into the kingdom of God and to the Samaritan of the worship of God constitutes the foundation of the New Testament teaching of man's new relation to God. To Nicodemus it was the new birth as the beginning of the new life. To the Samaritan it was the new worship as the expression of that new life.

What Is an Act of Worship?

IT IS PERSONAL

An act of worship involves personal commitment to God. What tended to be a national group experience had now become an individual personal experience.

IT IS SPIRITUAL

To worship "in spirit" distinguishes between the senses and the spirit. True worship is not directed to or by the five senses but, rather, to and by the spiritual nature of man. The actual beginning of this new spiritual worship was seen in the destruction of the temple veil and the obsolescence of sacrifices, feasts and observances which involved the senses.

IT IS RESPONSE TO TRUTH

Worshiping God is responding intellectually and emotionally to the truth being proclaimed at the worship service. The sacrifice is no longer present in the new worship, therefore the altar is obsolete. Now the center of worship is truth, which calls for a pulpit instead of an altar.

IT IS GIVING

Worship is giving oneself to God through adoration, praise, love and commitment. Worship is the expression of the whole being.

Here was a matter too perplexing for a simple woman who could understand worship only in terms of what she could see. "The woman saith unto him, I know that Messias cometh, which is called Christ: when he is come, he will tell us all things" (v. 25). All men need the Messiah because the ultimate resolution of problems, perplexities and difficulties lies in His manifestation.

A remarkable thing happened then. Jesus revealed His identity as the Messiah: "I that speak unto thee am he" (v. 26). This is the first recorded disclosure of Jesus as Messiah — made not to Nicodemus of the Sanhedrin, but to a sinful Samaritan. It was like the first disclosure of Jesus as Saviour which was not made to religious leaders but to shepherds. In both cases the leaders are bypassed, not because they are religious but because of their haughty and hypocritical spirit. It is "the meek" who shall inherit the earth, and here was a woman with a modest and docile spirit revealing an honest desire to know the truth.

The response that this woman made was to leave her waterpot and go to the village and say, "Come, see a man, which told me all things that ever I did: Is not this the Christ?" (v. 29).

The first thing she did was to leave her waterpot. She left it for something greater and more satisfying — "living water." This must be true of all, even as Peter left his boat, Matthew his tax-gatherer's office, and Luke his scalpel.

While all this was taking place at Sychar's well, the disciples were buying food. Returning, they were astonished to find Jesus talking to the woman. Two counts were against her: first, she was a Samaritan; second, she was a woman and therefore considered inferior.

Women owe their emancipation from social slavery and marital inferiority to the lofty principles which Jesus brought into human life. In a large measure women have responded to that fact by their regard for Him. They are in the vanguard of those who love and follow the Saviour. It is to their eternal credit that nowhere is it recorded in the Bible that a woman was ever an enemy of Jesus.

The returned disciples offered Jesus the fruit of their bargaining, but He rejects it, saying, "I have meat to eat that ye know not of." What was this strange food of which Jesus ate with lasting satisfaction? It had nothing to do with any market produce; it was of the soul. His satisfaction was not of getting something, but doing something. It was "to do the will of him that sent me."

What was doing the will of God? For one thing, it was witnessing to the Samaritan — the perfect food for spiritual growth. Only those who have told another the story of Christ can know what a sweet morsel this is.

The disciples were not wholly committed to this concept of the will of God, and they certainly did not believe the Samaritans were ready to know about God. The field was too difficult; the crop had to mature. But Jesus, sensing their objections and excuses, said, "Say not ye, There are yet four months, and then cometh harvest? Behold, I say unto you, Lift up your eyes, and look on the fields; for they are white already to harvest" (v. 35).

In this harvest the sowers are not always the reapers: "And he that reapeth receiveth wages, and gathereth fruit unto life eternal: that both he that soweth and he that reapeth may rejoice together. And herein is that saying true, One soweth, and another reapeth" (vv. 36-37). We have different duties, but when the final harvest comes, God will reward us for our faithful labor, whether it was the labor of sowing or reaping.

Great glamor and excitement are involved in the work of the reaper (v. 38). But behind the reaping is the tedious work of plowing and preparing the soil, casting in the seed, and caring for the plants as they grow to maturity.

There was a great harvest at Samaria. Following the woman of Sychar was a host of townspeople who "believed." Their belief was not now because of the woman's testimony, because they too could say, "We have heard him ourselves, and know that this is indeed the Christ, the Saviour of the world" (v. 42).

13

Jesus, Healer of Souls

4:43–5:47

THE EVENTS of Jesus' life recorded in the gospel of John are a series of circumstantial providences which lead to the fulfillment of His redemptive ministry. For instance, when Jesus was in Samaria, His ministry to the woman at Sychar resulted in many of the Samaritans believing on Him. Then follows Jesus' return to Galilee, for His primary mission was to the Jews. On His way He skirted Nazareth because "a prophet hath no honor in his own country," and pushed on into Cana, the scene of His first miracle.

THE MIRACLE IN GALILEE (4:43-54)

To the north of Cana, on the shores of the Sea of Galilee, lay Capernaum. Here in a magnificent mansion lived a highly placed officer of the court of Herod Antipas. It was what every home can be, the scene of tragedy and sorrow. The nobleman's son was stricken with a grave illness and was "at the point of death." The father asked Jesus to come and heal him.

Jesus understood the superficial concept the nobleman had of His mission, based on what he had heard of miracles Jesus had performed. No doubt he had concluded that Jesus was a wonderful teacher and a miracle-worker. Was this all Jesus was, a wonder-worker? Would He be one thing to the Samaritans, whose souls He healed, and another thing to the Galileans by healing their bodies?

Jesus could not allow a superficial concept to prevail, for miracles were not an end in themselves. He had come to heal souls, not bodies, and when we elevate the healing ministry of Jesus above the redemptive ministry, we do Him disservice.

"How is it," said Jesus to the nobleman, "that you come to me to perform a physical wonder and believe on me only as a worker of signs and wonders?" Jesus was endeavoring to open the man's eyes to a greater need — the need to be healed of sin.

None should lose sight of this need today. We could be tempted to believe that in the super and ultramodern world which science is building for us, gadgets can substitute for godliness, and material things can satisfy the soul. But, in spite of all these, "men and women will still struggle for happiness, which will continue to lie within themselves." The problems do not yield to the inventions of science. It will always be true that "man shall not live by bread alone."

Whether or not he understood this fully, the distraught parent could only think of his dying boy. He pleaded, "Sir, come down ere my child die" (v. 49).

Jesus gave the nobleman a simple directive: "Go thy way; thy son liveth" (v. 50). This meant that the nobleman could believe before the miracle was performed, rather than after it happened. Jesus knew he would believe in Him if his son were healed. This would have been an inferior faith. Immediately, without question and without hesitation, the nobleman "believed the word that Jesus had spoken unto him, and he went his way" (v. 50).

It was about twenty miles to Capernaum from Cana and it required travel through the next day. In the morning one of the nobleman's servants came with the good news, "Thy son liveth." When the father inquired the time of his son's recovery, he found it to be at one o'clock the previous day, the very hour when Jesus told him that the boy would live. It confirmed the nobleman's faith, and he "believed, and his whole house." Thus, one by one, family by family, group by group, Jesus added to the growing number of His disciples.

Jesus remained in Cana for some time. Many events were crowded into this period — the preaching of the Sermon on the Mount, the healing of many sick, the performance of numerous miracles, the choice of the twelve disciples.

After these months in Galilee the season of the great feasts returned and Jesus went to Jerusalem, the place of the temple and its ark of the covenant. The hopes of a spiritually sensitive people rested here.

THE MIRACLE IN JUDEA (5:1-9)

As Jesus arrived in Jerusalem He passed by the Pool of Bethesda, believed to possess curative powers which were most effective when its waters were "troubled" by an angel. Consequently, the pool attracted a multitude of unfortunates who hoped to be healed of blindness, lameness, palsy and various other ailments by bathing at the right moment.

Among these unfortunates Jesus encountered a helplessly crippled arthritic who had been in his pitiable plight for thirty-eight years. In desperate hope he had come to test the curative powers of Bethesda's waters, but he had no friends to put him into the pool. This man's condition was both helpless and hopeless. He could not help himself and there was no one to help him.

Nothing in the record shows that this man appealed to Jesus for healing, or that he even knew who Jesus was. It was Jesus who asked the question, "Wilt thou be made whole?" (v. 6). Without waiting for the man to answer, Jesus gave him a simple directive, "Rise, take up thy bed, and walk" (v. 8). His "bed" was a sleeping mat which for thirty-eight years had carried him; now he was to carry his bed.

That which took place in this man's life required two things: first, Jesus' word, "Take up thy bed, and walk"; and second, the paralytic's faith. In this case he believed Jesus' word and then put that faith into action. Faith is not mere acquiescence; it is action — in this case, walking.

THE VINDICATION OF JESUS (5:10-47)

The healing of the paralytic created a crisis. It stirred the Jews, not as it should have — with feelings of compassion and rejoicing because a sick man had been made well — but to hatred, animosity and murderous intent. Their anger was not because a man had been healed, but because he had been healed on the Sabbath.

The Jews surrounded the seventh day of the week with all

kinds of regulations: what kind of knots could be legally tied, the distance one could travel, the amount of food that could be carried. Even to kindle or extinguish a fire was a desecration of the day.

All of this hopeless regulation was now being challenged by Jesus and declared useless and obsolete. The price He would have to pay for this challenge would be death, for it would only be a matter of time until the spies who followed Him would complete their reports to the religious authorities.

Here in all its naked significance religion stood in its own light. Ritual and regulation stood in the way of mercy, love, truth and salvation. Conversely, Jesus stood forth against this background to proclaim the great truth that man's relationship to God was not established by externalities, but by a new life. For the first time Jesus is called upon to make His defense and to declare the nature of His mission (vv. 17-47).

JESUS CLAIMED EQUALITY WITH GOD

Jesus made His defense by identifying His cause as God's cause and by standing before them in the equality of God (vv. 17-18). It was for claiming this equality with God that they ultimately put Him to death.

JESUS EMPTIED HIMSELF

Jesus made His defense by stating the nature of what we term the *kenosis* (vv. 19-20, 30). Philippians 2:7 says Jesus "made himself of no reputation," or emptied Himself. Here He reveals the depth of that emptying, for "the Son can do nothing of himself" (Jn 5:19).

JESUS CLAIMED RESURRECTION POWER

Jesus made His defense by claiming the ultimate, which was resurrection power (vv. 21, 25, 28).

JESUS MADE HIS WORD EQUAL WITH GOD'S WORD

Jesus made His defense by making His word the equivalent, in authority and power, of God's word (v. 24). The verbs are in the present tense. The experience is now; the assurance is immediate.

Jesus made His defense by appealing to an unimpeachable Witness to His claims (vv. 32-38). God was His Witness. John was also Jesus' witness and he was "a burning and a shining light" (v. 35). But Jesus had a greater witness than John (v. 36). If these very Jews had understood their own Scripture, they would have recognized Jesus because "they are they which testify of me" (v. 39). This put the Jews in the awkward position of seeming to disbelieve both Jehovah and the Scriptures.

Jesus now stood vindicated. He was vindicated by God (v. 37), vindicated by the works which He came to do (v. 36), and vindicated by the Word of God (v. 39).

The paradox of this situation is that by the very things Jesus appealed to, He sentenced Himself to death. All of these sources of justification pointed to the cross, for only by the cross could Jesus accomplish His work and fulfill the Scripture.

Now Jesus stands in the shadow of the cross, irrevocably committed to die. But even this was vindication, for out of that death would come life and salvation. From this point Jesus moves on to Calvary.

On a certain bus line in London is a crossroads where there is a pub called "World's End." Next door is a Salvation Army hall. As the bus approaches, the conductor cries out, "World's End! Salvation next door!" This is the way it is in life; life and death walk close together. World's end is just around the corner, but next door is salvation.

14

The Presence of Christ in Human Affairs

6:1-14

TWO YEARS of Jesus' public ministry had passed before the feeding of the five thousand. All four gospel writers record it. When John wrote his account toward the close of the first century, the other three gospels had been written. John probably had access to them, although he was an eyewitness to the event.

The main difference between John's account and those of the other writers is the historical connection which John establishes. By this time in Jesus' ministry a great many things must have transpired, including the calling of His disciples, the miraculous catch of fish, the healing of the leper, the resurrection of the widow's son, the teaching of the parables, and the raising of the daughter of Jairus.

The importance of this miraculous feeding lies in its emphasis upon God in human affairs. Many remove God as far from human life as they dare in order to be consistent with the idea of God, but the New Testament idea of God is one identified with life. A number of elements make this incident important:

THERE WAS A MULTITUDE

John says "great multitude." This is later described as a "great company" (v. 5) and finally numbered as "five thousand" (v. 10), exclusive of women and children.

IT WAS A TRUTH-HUNGRY MULTITUDE

The only kind of people who find God are hungry people. "Blessed are they which do hunger and thirst after righteousness:

73

for they shall be filled" (Mt 5:6). And akin to this is Jesus' word, "Seek ye first the kingdom of God, and his righteousness; and all these things shall be added unto you" (Mt 6:33).

IT WAS A MULTITUDE NEAR THE SOURCE OF BLESSING

As only those who followed Jesus over the Sea of Galilee were fed, we too must be near the source of blessing if we are to be helped. Only those following Christ will experience the blessing of His presence.

CHRIST AND THE DISCIPLES WERE THERE

Two different ideas are represented by Christ and His disciples in their attitudes toward the needs of the multitude.

JESUS' ATTITUDE WAS COMPASSION (vv. 5-6)

"When Jesus then lifted up his eyes, and saw a great company come unto him, he saith unto Philip, Whence shall we buy bread, that these may eat? And this he said to prove him: for he himself knew what he would do."

In Mark's account he says that Jesus "saw much people, and was moved with compassion" (Mk 6:34). Here are sympathy, concern and deep personal feeling. Jesus' immediate reaction to human need was to meet it, for this was the purpose of His mission. But Jesus saw a deeper need than the satisfaction of physical hunger; He knew that men needed something more than food.

THE DISCIPLE'S ATTITUDE WAS EXPEDIENCY

"Philip answered him, Two hundred pennyworth of bread is not sufficient for them, that every one of them may take a little" (v. 7). In Mark's account, the disciples said, "Send them away." They were thinking of the circumstances and not of the one who could control the circumstances. Faith sees beyond the immediate circumstances to the possible achievement. It is not limited by what we have or by what we do not have, for faith works on what God can do.

When, according to Mark's account, Jesus said, "Give ye them to eat," the disciples complained that "two hundred pennyworth of bread is not sufficient for them." Looking at their plight in terms of what would be needed, the disciples saw only an impossibility. But since Jesus "knew what he would do," He was not thinking of what they needed to satisfy the hunger of the people, but what they already had.

A Lad and His Lunch (vv. 8-9)

"One of his disciples, Andrew, Simon Peter's brother, saith unto him, There is a lad here, which hath five barley loaves, and two small fishes: but what are they among so many?"

Andrew discovered a lad, a mere boy, with a lunch consisting of five barley loaves — the food of the poor — and two small fish. This was insignificant in man's eyes, but not in God's. It represented what they had, not what they needed. God always works with what we have, not with what we need. We say, "Lord, increase our faith." Jesus says, "If ye have faith as a grain of mustard seed . . ." (Mt 17:20). We say, "Lord bless me"; God's Word says we are already blessed "with all spiritual blessings in heavenly places in Christ" (Eph 1:3). We say, "Lord, give me the victory"; God says, "Take it, for in Christ you are more than conquerors."

Miracles are wrought with the things we have right now. Jesus' miracle of feeding was wrought by the meager resources of five loaves and two fish. Notice on how small a hinge such a large door is swung. The lad and his lunch are the hinge; the feeding of the multitude is the door. God's instruments are often insignificant, for He chooses "the foolish things of the world to confound the wise; and . . . the weak things of the world to confound the things which are mighty" (1 Co 1:27).

The most effective hinge is the noiseless one. Translated into human terms, this means that the squeakless Christian is the most effective. He is not complaining or quarrelsome. D. L. Moody told about a certain man's well: "It was a good well with two exceptions: it froze up in winter and dried up in summer." Effectiveness means being available in time of need. This is the virtue of a hinge, and when that hinge is a Christian it means just that: availability in time of need.

Jesus' interest in human affairs. Jesus can identify with our daily life. This means the fellowship of prayer, strength for each day, and counseling in perplexity. Has Jesus ever broken bread for you?

This situation was not critical, for people can go without food for many days. It teaches us that there is nothing in life too small for Christ's sympathetic interest.

Jesus' solution in an impossible situation. For the disciples this was an impasse, but for Jesus an impossibility is the beginning of a miracle. The disciples could not take so little and make so much, but Jesus did not expect them to. He expects us to give what we have to Him, for it is in His hands that bread multiplies, not in ours.

WE WILL SEE THE MIRACLE OF BROKEN BREAD IN OUR EXPERIENCE

When we recognize the partnership between God and us. Paul describes this partnership as being "workers together with God." This existed between Jesus and the twelve, and it continues between the Saviour and us.

When we are obedient to the divine will. Jesus told the disciples to arrange the people in orderly platoons and prepare to feed them. The miracle hinged, at this point, on their obedience.

Israel's King Jeroboam and Judah's King Jehoshaphat, plus the king of Edom, went out to a battle in which they faced a water shortage. They called in God's prophet Elisha who said, "Ye shall not see wind, neither shall ye see rain; yet that valley shall be filled with water" (2 Ki 3:17). They were instructed to "make this valley full of ditches." Before the rain, ditches had to be dug in order to conserve the water. First there had to be preparation (obedience) and then there would be fulfillment.

When we fully consecrate our human ability for divine use. The human ability this day was a lad's lunch. In Jesus' hands it would become enough to feed a multitude. The difference was consecration, giving what he had to Christ.

Many in the church today have only five loaves and two fish. It is when our little gift is in His hands that multiplication takes place. This is consecration — what the lad did when he gave what he had to Christ.

Suppose some morning a carpenter picked up his saw as he prepared for his daily task, but the saw said, "No sir, I'm tired of being squeezed between boards and biting sawdust with my teeth." Suppose his hammer said, "No sir, I'm tired of hitting nails on the head." Suppose the chisel, the plane and the screwdriver engaged in similar rebellions. No work could be done that day by the carpenter.

What if the brush of the artist Sargent had refused the master's hand? What if the chisel of Michaelangelo had refused the master's use? What if Peter had refused the Spirit at Pentecost? What if Paul had refused the Macedonian's call? What if Luther, Carey, Moffatt and Livingstone had said no to God?

Perhaps the most interesting thing in this whole affair was what happened to the twelve baskets which were left over. The conjecture is that Jesus sent them home to the mother who packed the boy's lunch in the morning. What abundant return for giving so little.

The arithmetic of the circumstance tells us that five loaves plus two fish minus five thousand Jewish mouths equals twelve basketsful. God "is able to do exceeding abundantly above all that we ask or think" (Eph 3:20).

15

Peace for Troubled Waters

6:15-25

WHEN JESUS BROKE five small loaves of barley bread and two little fish until they became enough to feed a large gathering of people, He performed what the Bible calls a "miracle."

Those who were there said, "This is of truth that prophet that should come into the world" (v. 14). This recognition of Jesus was the prime purpose of the miracle. Jesus had not come to feed people. Anyone who tries to repeat the miracles of Jesus, even the miracle of healing, just for the sake of getting well, has missed the meaning of Jesus' mission to the world. If Jesus had come for such purposes as are suggested by this feeding and by healings, He would not have died. Jesus was showing His power to meet their higher needs by His ability to meet their lower needs. His real mission was to the higher needs — the spiritual.

The Jews' reaction to the miracle of bread was both good and bad. It was good, for they said, "This is of a truth that prophet that should come into the world" (v. 14). It was bad, for they thought to "take him by force, to make him a king" (v. 15). Their ideas of making Jesus king were outward and political, since they were thinking in terms of material power rather than moral preparation. Visions of national splendor dazzled the Jews, and their Messianic hopes blossomed anew, for they had seen Jesus doing wonderful things. This was their chance to get glory, power and wealth.

As far as Jesus was concerned, what Israel and the world needed was not a day of glory, but a day of humiliation. It was His intention to lead them to this day of humiliation in preparation for the day of glory. He would lead them down the lowly valleys until at last He faced a cross where He would hang in shame and ignominy. All that Jesus would do for Israel and the world had to be done by the cross.

As soon as Jesus perceived the intent of the people to force Him to act as their leader, He left them and went into the hills where He could be alone with God. There in quiet meditation He could prepare His soul for the ordeal ahead. He saw the cross, not the crown. He saw the humiliation, not the glory.

It is alone with God that we can most clearly see our purpose and place in life and gather the strength with which to fulfill it. Each of us is an individual facing life before God, and we can only know what to do with life when we are in communication with Him. The secret of this understanding is illustrated by Jesus getting alone with God.

While Jesus was in seclusion, His disciples waited for Him. They waited until night fell and when He did not come they set off across the Sea of Galilee without Him. As they rowed, a sudden squall caught their boat in its turbulent grip. Although it was only six miles across the sea, they made only two-thirds of the distance after rowing all night. Suddenly in their weariness, discouragement and despair, they saw a human form walking on the sea. Before they had time to cry out in their fears, there came the reassuring words, "It is I; be not afraid" (v. 20). It was the Lord, and with Him in the boat it meant new strength. So with easy sweeps of the oars they quickly arrived at the other shore.

VALUABLE LESSONS

THE LESSON OF TROUBLED WATERS

Life is often likened to a voyage. Frequently jeopardized by rough waters, it is not a trouble-free experience characterized by smooth sailing. This is true for the Christian as well as for the non-Christian. The disciples experienced troubled waters when they faced what Matthew describes as a "contrary wind." So will we. But how?

THE LESSON OF A PRAYING CHRIST

Our place on life's troubled waters is safeguarded by the praying Christ who went to be alone with God. Here is a picture of the present intercessory ministry of Christ as our High Priest. While we are on the sea, He is in the mountain. While we are in peril, He is in prayer. While we are on earth, He is in heaven. While we are struggling at the oar locks, He is interceding at the right hand of God. He is alive, making intercession for us. He is the living, praying, interceding Christ, watching over our perilous transit of life's sea.

THE LESSON OF QUIET WATERS

The miracles which Jesus performed can be put in three classes: first, those of physical nature, such as healings; second, those of human nature, such as demoniacs; third, those of the material world, such as changing water into wine. In this third class is placed the miracle of Jesus walking on the water.

The incident of the quieted waters is not only a confirmation of Jesus' mission; it is also a symbol of spiritual truth — peace for troubled waters. This peace can be applied two ways. *Individually* is one way. Men are constantly seeking peace for life's problems. Such peace will be found by a life lived with Jesus; it is something personal and individual. *Internationally* is another way. In every generation the world has had to cope with troubled times. Today atheism seeks to dominate the world through Communism. The immediate deterrent may seem to be an Atlas missile, but the ultimate deterrent is the praying Christ and the coming Christ.

When day broke after the eventful night on the lake, great numbers of people sought and found Jesus (v. 24). What troubled Jesus about these people were their motives. "And when they had found him on the other side of the sea, they said unto him, Rabbi, when camest thou hither? Jesus answered them and said, Verily, verily, I say unto you, Ye seek me, not because ye saw the miracles, but because ye did eat of the loaves, and were filled" (vv. 25-26). Jesus then commences one of His great discourses, of which fourteen are in the gospel of John.

In giving this discourse on the Sustainer of life, Jesus responded to the wrong motives of the people. The incident of the previous day should have raised desires for the higher spiritual food which even the rabbis taught them to expect from the

Messiah. But they wanted to see more miracles and also were anxious to confirm their hopes that Jesus would lead them against Rome. To these things Jesus turned a deaf ear and launched into His great discourse on the Sustainer of life (vv. 26-59).

16

The Sustainer of Life

6:26-40

WHAT SUSTAINS LIFE? With the danger of oversimplification, the answer is the relation of heredity to environment. Heredity gives us the start; environment gives us the continuity. Heredity invests us with qualities; environment develops those qualities.

The most important implications are in the moral and spiritual realm of life. Jesus is dealing with this as He presents Himself to the Jews as the Sustainer of life.

Having incited the wonder of the people by the miracle of the loaves and fishes, and having observed their interest in this lower level of satisfaction instead of the higher level of spiritual satisfaction, Jesus urged them not to set their hearts on the perishable food of the body. He told them to seek that food which both secures and sustains eternal life: "Verily, verily, I say unto you, Ye seek me, not because ye saw the miracles, but because ye did eat of the loaves, and were filled. Labour not for the meat which perisheth, but for that meat which endureth unto everlasting life, which the Son of man shall give unto you: for him hath God the Father sealed" (vv. 26-27).

The contrast between meat that perishes and meat that endures is in its source — "which the Son of man shall give you." This makes Christianity the exclusive source of eternal life and spiritual satisfaction. Jesus gave this food. "For him hath God the Father sealed" (v. 27). Seals were used to authenticate documents and, in this sense, by the miracle just performed, Jesus Christ was authenticated as the exclusive source of this life.

It might be wrongly implied from the injunction "labor . . . for that meat which endureth unto everlasting life" that salvation might be of works and not of faith. But this is not true. Here the activity of striving consists of a genuine struggle of faith. We must believe in Him, follow Him, deny ourselves and take up the cross. We must demonstrate our desire to have it before it will be bestowed upon us.

This immediately evoked a question from the Jews. "Then said they unto him, What shall we do, that we might work the works of God?" (v. 28). They were steeped in a life of religious effort, thinking of their relationship to God on the basis of performing special works appointed by God. Perhaps they even thought of miraculous works like the miracles of Jesus.

It was quite natural for the Jews to think of special works for God because their religious system involved manifold religious duties and observances. But Jesus had come to do away with all this and inaugurate a new day. Consequently, He startled and shocked them by announcing that a place in the new order He had come to establish only required faith — just believing on Him. "Jesus answered and said unto them, This is the work of God, that ye believe on him whom he hath sent" (v. 29).

When one has true faith, then all the necessary works for God will spring from it. Faith is not only the *source* of this new life; it is the *force* of this new life. Therefore, when men today ask, "What shall we do, that we might work the works of God?" the answer is simply and everlastingly, "Believe."

But is this just as binding in the twentieth century as it was in the first? Is not life different? Is not the world better? Has not man improved over his counterpart of Jesus' day? These things are true in a general sense, in such things as physical science, material progress and secular education. But the world is not essentially different in terms of the moral and spiritual aspects of individual man. Although he has created better surroundings, when the checks and balances of modern society are removed, he has the same potential for evil.

A remarkable prophecy was written in 1780:

> The rapid progress true science now makes, occasions my regretting sometimes that I was born so soon. It is impossible to imagine the height to which may be carried, in a thousand years, the power of man over matter. We may perhaps learn

to deprive large masses of their gravity, and give them absolute
levity. . . . Agriculture may diminish its labor and double its
produce; all diseases may by sure means be prevented or cured.
. . . O that moral science were in as fair a way of improvement,
that men would cease to be wolves to one another and that
human beings would at length learn what they now improperly
call humanity!

When Jesus urged His contemporaries to "labour not for the
meat which perisheth, but for that meat which endureth unto
everlasting life" (v. 27), He was saying what a modern writer
wrote: "Life with Christ is an endless hope; without Him, it is a
hopeless end."

> They said therefore unto him, What sign shewest thou then,
> that we may see, and believe thee? What dost thou work? Our
> fathers did eat manna in the desert; as it is written, He gave
> them bread from heaven to eat. Then Jesus said unto them,
> Verily, verily, I say unto you, Moses gave you not that bread
> from heaven; but my Father giveth you the true bread from
> heaven. For the bread of God is he which cometh down from
> heaven, and giveth life unto the world (vv. 30-33).

Perhaps some critic in the crowd demanded a proof of Jesus'
claims. He may have been one who had not witnessed the breaking of the bread, or perhaps he was reflecting the general rabbinical teaching that when the Messiah came He would repeat
Moses' miracle of the manna. Perhaps he thought that if indeed
Jesus was the Messiah, let Him produce this sign. But, from Jesus' standpoint, the manna of Moses was not the ultimate. It was
only a prefigurement — at best something material and perishable, for it was temporary. When the true and real bread came,
it would not fall from the visible heavens; it would be from the
invisible presence of God. It was this bread which God was giving now in Jesus. He was not only the water of life of which
one drank with everlasting satisfaction; He was also the bread
of life of which one ate never to hunger again.

But Jesus is bread — not cake. The metaphor is well taken.
Bread is basic to existence. This bread is heavenly in its source
and life-giving in its effect. When men try to live on a purely

material and secular level, theirs is not the highest or best life. When Jesus said, "Man shall not live by bread alone, but by every word that proceedeth out of the mouth of God" (Mt 4:4), He was talking of the material and secular in contrast to the bread that sustains and satisfies.

Bread, not cake, is what we give the needy and the hungry. Is there anything more elementary than bread? Is there anything more essential? Anything more satisfying? Transfer all of these to the spiritual realm and apply them to Jesus, and you will have the answer. Jesus is a necessity, not a luxury.

The response of the people to Jesus was like that of the Spaniards in the company of Ponce de Leon who went in search of the fountain of unfading youth. Clamoring to have this new benefit, they said, "Lord, evermore give us this bread" (v. 34).

The Jews still did not understand the full implication that this bread was Christ. No doubt they were caught up in the feeling of that day of anticipating the grandeur and majesty in the Messiah's kingdom. They were still hungering, too, for loaves and fishes. At this juncture Jesus says, "I am the bread of life: he that cometh to me shall never hunger; and he that believeth on me shall never thirst. But I said unto you, That ye also have seen me, and believe not" (vv. 35-36).

In the face of much unbelief, Jesus then presented one of the Bible's most blessed truths: the election of grace. "All that the Father giveth me shall come to me, and him that cometh to me I will in no wise cast out" (v. 37).

In saying that election is God's decree to save, we are on trouble-free ground; but if we say that it is God's decree to save an arbitrary number of people, we are in trouble. Let us therefore content ourselves with as simple an observation as is consistent with so great a matter.

Jesus was saying, "No man can be saved without God, but it is also true that there is no man whom God is not willing to save." All men are candidates for salvation because the work of Christ was for the whole world, and the gospel invitation is to "whosoever will."

The believing are not a select group of people whose number is arbitrarily predetermined by God, or whose act is foreknown by divine omniscience. They are those who are moved by the efficacious influence of divine grace to accept salvation. The unbelieving are those not thus moved.

God has elected all men in the sense that "whosoever will may come." He has elected some men in the sense that they alone of these "whosoever" have yielded to the influence of divine grace.

God is sovereign in His offer of salvation; man is sovereign in his choice of salvation. Whenever a man exercises his sovereignty of choice to accept God's sovereign offer, he is saved. God is sovereign in an absolute sense, while man is sovereign in a relative sense. Although God is sovereign, He will not save a man who is not willing to be saved. Likewise, no man can be lost if he wills to be saved, for "him that cometh to me I will in no wise cast out" (v. 37).

Why does Jesus not cast out those who come to Him? The answer is in the will of God:

> For I came down from heaven, not to do mine own will, but the will of him that sent me. And this is the Father's will which hath sent me, that of all which he hath given me I should lose nothing, but should raise it up again at the last day. And this is the will of him that sent me, that every one which seeth the Son, and believeth on him, may have everlasting life: and I will raise him up at the last day (vv. 38-40).

God will not cast out those whom He wills to save, and He wills to save whoever wills to be saved. When a seeking sinner meets a seeking Saviour, the result is salvation. It is eternal, not conditional, because "this is the Father's will which hath sent me, that of all which he hath given me I should lose nothing, but should raise it up again at the last day" (v. 39). God will never cast off (v. 39) those whom He has not cast out (v. 37). God who does the saving will also do the keeping.

Salvation is not something initiated by God and continued by man, for the God who does the initiating in election, predestination and regeneration also does the continuing, keeping and finishing. "For whom he did foreknow, he also did predestinate to be conformed to the image of his Son, that he might be the firstborn among many brethren. Moreover whom he did predestinate, them he also called: and whom he called, them he also justified: and whom he justified, them he also glorified" (Ro 8:29-30). "Being confident of this very thing, that he which hath begun a good work in you will perform it until the day of Jesus Christ" (Phil 1:6).

Salvation stretches from the past of divine election to the future of human glorification. Paul said,

> What shall we then say to these things? If God be for us, who can be against us? He that spared not his own Son, but delivered him up for us all, how shall he not with him also freely give us all things? Who shall lay anything to the charge of God's elect? It is God that justifieth. Who is he that condemneth? It is Christ that died, yea rather, that is risen again, who is even at the right hand of God, who also maketh intercession for us. Who shall separate us from the love of Christ? Shall tribulation, or distress, or persecution, or famine, or nakedness, or peril, or sword? As it is written, For thy sake we are killed all the day long; we are accounted as sheep for the slaughter. Nay, in all these things we are more than conquerors through him that loved us. For I am persuaded, that neither death, nor life, nor angels, nor principalities, nor powers, nor things present, nor things to come, nor height, nor depth, nor any other creature, shall be able to separate us from the love of God, which is in Christ Jesus our Lord (Ro 8:31-39).

17

The Living Bread

6:41-59

JESUS SAID in the synagogue at Capernaum, "And this is the will of him that sent me, that every one which seeth the Son, and believeth on him, may have everlasting life: and I will raise him up at the last day" (v. 40).

This caused a great sensation. Here was a man talking about raising people from the dead and about coming down from heaven. The people thought it was fantastic and ridiculous. They said, "We know His father and mother. How can He have come from heaven?" They thought He was mad or that He had a devil.

Is it possible to understand all that we believe? Or is there a place where reason and faith separate and we have to consider them apart? Or is there a place where they unite so that faith makes the irrational rational? According to Giekie, Jesus is saying that natural sense "will never help you to understand how I am the true Bread come down from heaven. If you wish to know how I can say so, you must submit yourself to the teaching and influence of God; must hear and learn what God says, for it tells us in the prophets — 'They shall be taught of God'; only those thus taught come to me or believe in me. The yielding your souls to God and your rising thus to communion with Him by spiritual oneness, can alone lead to the faith that recognizes the truth respecting one." There is, indeed, a spiritual perception involved here which goes beyond natural sense.

How shall we resolve these things? To begin with, we cannot reconcile reason and revelation any more than we can reconcile the sovereignty of God and the free will of man. There are some things eternally irreconcilable.

Science and the Bible are reconcilable because the Bible is a finished revelation while science is a continually unfolding story. Science has been described as "an orderly arrangement of what at the moment seems to be facts." But what seems to be facts at this moment may be otherwise the next moment.

There is no conflict between science and revelation. There may be conflicts between interpretations of Scripture and understandings of science, but what God has written in His Word never conflicts with what God has written in His world.

The apostle Paul recognized a distinction between the wisdom of this world and the wisdom which is of God as found in the Bible. "Has not God made the wisdom of this world look foolish? For it was after the world in its wisdom had failed to know God, that he in his wisdom chose to save all who would believe by the 'simplemindedness' of the gospel message" (1 Co 1:20-21, Phillips).

There is a wisdom of this world which is to be respected, but it is still the wisdom of the world and for this world only — not for the world to come. The man of faith does not affirm the uselessness of the wisdom of this world; he only says it is useless when it seeks God. At no time has man by this world's wisdom ever been able to know God. Without the gospel, God is always the "unknown God," as Paul discovered among the Greek philosophers.

There was great and respected wisdom in the old worlds of Babylon, Egypt, Persia, Greece and Rome. In Babylon

> there were walls seventy feet high, on which war-chariots might be driven four abreast; there were hanging gardens filled with flowers and birds; there were temples of polished marble, overlaid with ivory and gold; there were highways, firm and hard, stretching from Rome to all the ends of the known world, it was all of this world, and of this world only; it was outward, material, transient. But this old world with all its acumen, genius and military prowess "knew not god."

Today the world has grown wiser and more knowledgeable. In the last decade the amount of scientific knowledge has more than doubled. But it is still true that though we live in a world of great electronic wonder, the wisdom with which we have acquired this knowledge is not the wisdom by which we can know God.

If and when man acquires a faith that sustains him in a world of injustice and suffering and provides him with eternal life, he will not get that faith from either philosophy or science. Science tries to make man comfortable in a world of suffering. But in spite of science and because of science, our age is the most brutal in human history. Science has killed more people than were ever killed before. Science has caused more suffering in the past several generations than was ever true before. Science is not the answer.

If I were not a Christian I would be an agnostic. Like every person who inquires into the meanings of life, there are philosophic problems that can only yield to the wisdom of the Bible. There is only one answer — faith. I cannot quarrel too much with the Jews who tried to reconcile Jesus' statement about being bread from heaven with the fact that His mother and father were known to them. There is no reconciliation of the eternity of Jesus with the paternity of Jesus.

Jesus came with truth that none had heard before. Pilate later asked, "What is truth?" Goethe said, "Truth is what man is meant to know." Truth is what man is meant to know in order to make him a better man. This truth — not machines — makes man supreme. Today we are producing an age of automation from which we get only what machines can do. It is the regenerated personality of man that is the key to a new world, not slide rules, drills, desks or kitchens.

Perhaps someone at Capernaum raised the objection of believing in a God that could not be seen. No one, said Jesus, but God's only begotten Son who was in heaven and has come down from heaven has seen God and now reveals Him to man (v. 46). Then He quickly added, "He that believeth on me hath everlasting life" (v. 47).

How can anyone by just believing have everlasting life? Jesus gives the answer, "I am that bread of life. Your fathers did eat manna in the wilderness, and are dead. This is the bread which cometh down from heaven, that a man may eat thereof, and not die. I am the living bread which came down from heaven: if any man eat of this bread, he shall live for ever: and the bread that I will give is my flesh, which I will give for the life of the world" (vv. 48-51). Believing is an act of will as well as an attitude of mind. As their forefathers accepted God-provided manna and lived, so they must accept the bread of life and live.

How would Jesus give everlasting life? He would do it by dying (v. 51). The Jews are very persistent: "How can this man give us his flesh to eat?" (v. 52). How can we live forever? How can faith be enough? How can mere believing bring salvation? Jesus replies by revealing the unique nature of His salvation. He would do it through death.

> Then Jesus said unto them, Verily, verily, I say unto you, Except ye eat the flesh of the Son of man, and drink his blood, ye have no life in you. Whoso eateth my flesh, and drinketh my blood, hath eternal life; and I will raise him up at the last day. For my flesh is meat indeed, and my blood is drink indeed. He that eateth my flesh, and drinketh my blood, dwelleth in me, and I in him. As the living Father hath sent me, and I live by the Father: so he that eateth me, even he shall live by me. This is that bread which came down from heaven: not as your fathers did eat manna, and are dead: he that eateth of this bread shall live for ever (vv. 53-58).

What did Jesus mean by "eating His flesh and drinking His blood"? At the communion service of the Lord's Supper, does the bread become the actual corporeal flesh of Jesus and the cup become His blood? Is it in this sense that we eat the body of Jesus? The only proper answer is an emphatic *no!*

It is seriously doubted that Jesus had in mind any reference to the Last Supper when He spoke of eating His flesh and drinking His body. When the assumption was made later by some theologians, they built up the cannibalistic theory of eating and drinking corporeal substances, whereas Jesus' reference was only to believing by accepting a spiritual provision.

In verse 47 Jesus said, "He that believeth on me hath everlasting life." In verse 54 He said, "Whoso eateth my flesh, and drinketh my blood, hath eternal life." The confluence of the two streams of truth says that whoever believes on Jesus has the same everlasting life as whoever eats His flesh and drinks His blood. Believing and eating are the same thing. It is not corporeal flesh but the words of Jesus which are to be accepted and assimilated for their life-giving value. Eating is done with the heart and mind, an appropriation by faith of the life of Jesus Christ.

As bread quickens the body, so truth quickens the soul. As one brings temporal life, so the other brings eternal life. The compelling fact of this discourse on eternal life is our personal involvement by faith. We do not bake the bread; we only eat it. We need not even know or understand the recipe for this bread; all we need to do is eat it. This is faith, and this faith brings everlasting life.

18

What Is the Alternative?

6:60-71

SOONER OR LATER we must consider the alternative to Christ and His scheme of life. We face this when Peter says to Jesus, "Lord, to whom shall we go? Thou hast the words of eternal life" (v. 68).

Jesus had spoken of Himself as the bread of life which came down from heaven. When His auditors asked how they could eat and have eternal life, Jesus revealed that this was related to His death and that men had to eat His flesh and drink His blood. The eating and drinking were an act of faith, for they were hearing and acting upon Jesus' word.

In emphasis of this great truth, Jesus closed His discourse by repeating the original figure of the message: He is the bread from heaven and "he that eateth of this bread shall live forever" (v. 58).

The reaction of the people, particularly to Jesus' concluding statement, was general incredulity. "Many therefore of his disciples, when they had heard this, said, This is an hard saying; who can hear it?" (v. 60).

This was another turning point in Jesus' career. He was in effect announcing His death because henceforth He faced the cross. But it was also a turning point in the lives of many of His disciples, for when Jesus went on, many of them went back. He went on to achievement; they disappeared from the scene.

The cross, not the crucifix, would forever be the symbol of the Christian faith. The crucifix, with Christ embraced in death, does not signify a finished redemption, for the true symbols of Christianity are an empty cross and an empty tomb. Now Jesus raises the symbol of the cross before His disciples. Later He would say, "If any man will come after me, let him deny himself, and take up his cross daily, and follow me" (Lk 9:23). This made the cross and following Jesus synonymous.

The cross in the redemptive life of Jesus constituted a great surprise to many of His followers. At this juncture, "many of his disciples went back, and walked no more with him" (v. 66). Oh, yes, men want to be saved, but they want salvation on their own terms.

One reason why there are so many varieties of religion is man's effort for a convenient way to be saved. Invariably it is a cross-less way. On the other hand, we are content with crosses on our churches, but not in our lives. We are proud to be cross-wearers, but not crossbearers. This is because it is easy to wear the cross but a different matter to bear the cross. Religion is all right until you get to the cross, and then it begins to lose its glamour.

An incident in history is highly illuminating. We have all heard of Marco Polo, his travels in China, and his description of the court of Kublai Khan. What we often forget is that his father, Niccolo Polo, and his uncle, Maffeo Polo, had already made a trip to China when Marco was a boy. When they were about to return to Italy, the Khan gave them letters to the pope, asking that the pope send one hundred learned men to teach Christianity in his domain. What an opportunity! What a chance for the gospel to reach those who had never heard it! Yet, when this request arrived, only two men — Dominican monks — could be found to answer it. They left for China with the three Polos. But long before they reached their destination, the monks became frightened by reports of a war along the way, and they returned home. The Polos went on, for the attraction of gold was enough to cause them to complete a trip too perilous for those entrusted with the souls of a continent. And this occurred during what has been called "the Thirteenth — Greatest of Centuries"!

Jesus' discourse in the synagogue had been interrupted at several places, but now at its close a low whispering and murmuring rose in rapid crescendo. These camp-following disciples observed that what Jesus had said was "an hard saying; who can hear it?" (v. 60). And as Jesus made His way out of the synagogue, He turned and said to the disciples,

"Doth this offend you? What and if ye shall see the Son of man ascend up where he was before? It is the spirit that quickeneth; the flesh profiteth nothing: the words that I speak unto you, they are spirit, and they are life. But there are some of you that believe not. For Jesus knew from the beginning who they were that believed not, and who should betray him. And he said, Therefore said I unto you, that no man can come unto me, except it were given unto him of my Father" (vv. 61-65).

It was difficult for these quasi-disciples to reconcile Jesus' references to Himself with their religious presuppositions about a kingdom of earthly glory. But if they could not comprehend the nature of His redemptive mission, how could they understand the resurrection and ascension? (vv. 61-62).

Salvation is not an experience resting upon one's natural observations; it is a matter of faith. To become a member of God's kingdom requires a spiritual process. And then to explain what He meant, Jesus said, "It is the spirit that quickeneth; the flesh profiteth nothing: the words that I speak unto you, they are spirit, and they are life" (v. 63).

This is what Jesus meant by eating His flesh and drinking His blood: He was talking about men believing His word. It is not His flesh they were to eat, but His words they were to believe.

The Word of God is spirit and life. This reveals the difference between the Bible and all other books, between God's Word and man's word. The Bible not only has life but is life-giving. For this reason salvation depends on one's acceptance of the Word of God, a life-giving seed-plot of life.

Salvation is not the improvement of the old life; it is the impartation of a new life. The instrument of impartation is the Word of God.

In every generation there have been those who did not believe, and some who stood in Jesus' midst did not believe (v. 64). Lest Jesus' auditors misjudged the acceptance of salvation as something which was left to their discretion and convenience, Jesus said, "Therefore said I unto you, that no man can come unto me, except it were given unto him of my Father" (v 65).

Some think they can do as they please with the gospel invitation to be saved. They presume to repent or not repent, believe or not believe, at their own discretion. They think salvation is something which is in their own power of choice. However, this is not so, for we can be saved only when the Holy Spirit draws us.

While this drawing is usually associated with the presentation of the gospel, it is not something which is synonymous with an invitation to accept Christ. The invitation or altar call is a purely human device, only one of the media by which men may respond to the inward drawing of the Holy Spirit. When it is used, we should understand that no one is saved in response to an invitation, but only because of the inward drawing to Christ of the soul convicted of sin.

Because Jesus says, "No man can come unto me, except it were given unto him of my Father" (v. 65), does not take away man's responsibility. If anyone is lost, it is his own fault. It is the individual who "loses his own soul" (Mk 8:36).

There are two aspects of salvation: the divine and the human (v. 65). The human aspect is found in the word *come,* for our coming depends on the human will and the exercise of faith. The divine aspect is found in the word *given* and refers to the divine will and the provision of faith.

By this time the effects of what had transpired took on a tragic proportion. John says, "From that time many of his disciples went back, and walked no more with him. Then said Jesus unto the twelve, Will ye also go away?" (vv. 66-67). He was giving His disciples — many of whom had false enthusiasm, shallow devotion, and material hopes — a chance to reevaluate their position with respect to their hoped-for Messiah. They wanted to see wonders, to eat bread that would protect them from dying, and to get places of power and wealth in the new kingdom they hoped the Messiah would set up. They were interested in the miracles of healed bodies rather than in saved souls. So the crowds began to disappear.

What was it that changed the minds of the defecting disciples? It was the promise of the cross. Put the same test to men today and some of them will "walk no more with him." This is what Paul calls "the offence of the cross" (Gal 5:11). While this was the first time it became a public fact, it was not the last time, for it continues today as a major consideration of many.

Jesus then turned sorrowfully to the twelve and asked, "Will ye also go away?" Peter's bold and discerning answer was "Lord, to whom shall we go? Thou hast the words of eternal life" (v. 68). What is the alternative to Christ? Where can one go for forgiveness, peace, hope and salvation?

There are many alternatives — agnosticism, materialism and secularism — but there are no solutions in those alternatives. There are many substitutes for Jesus — mental pursuits, social relations or material possessions — but none holds the promise of satisfaction. Jesus has many competitors but no surpassers.

The alternatives to Jesus are despair, hopelessness, sorrow and loss. "Lord, to whom shall we go? Thou hast the words of eternal life."

Three Important Things About the Incident

The Choice of Salvation Is Not Optional

"To whom shall we go? Thou hast. . . ." People often say that one way is as good as another; it is not. There are not many ways, only one.

The Form of Salvation Is Settled

"Thou hast the words. . . ." Salvation is not anything you think it is or want it to be. It is what God says it is — something final, settled and completed.

The Character of Salvation Is a Life

"Thou hast the words of eternal life." This is a life different from that inherited as a consequence of natural birth. It is divine, eternal and sinless, transcending all other experiences and satisfying all human desires.

In the light of these things, "To whom shall we go?" While there was a great stream of defectors, there were also those who stood at the side of Jesus in the shadow of the cross. Peter led them and made his magnificent confession: "And we believe and are sure that thou art that Christ, the Son of the living God" (v. 69).

It is either confession or defection; it is either acceptance or rejection. There is no middle ground of neutrality.

19

Rivers of Living Water

7:1-53

FOR NEARLY HALF A YEAR Jesus had been little better than an outlawed fugitive, hiding from His enemies in unsuspected districts and not daring to enter Jerusalem for extended periods. The reason for this was stated often by Jesus: His hour had not yet come. Now, however, He was about to be thrust into the heart of the vortex that would draw Him at last to the fateful hour of the cross.

It was Tishri, the seventh month of the Jewish year, part of our September and October. This was the month of full streams and full harvests, and on its fifteenth day was the first of the great harvest feasts — the Feast of Tabernacles, a time all the more joyous because it came only four days after the Day of Atonement.

At that time Jesus was in a great dilemma because Galilee, where He was at that particular moment, was no longer open to Him. The only other alternative was Jerusalem, the headquarters of Jewry. He knew that to go there would be, sooner or later, to die. And now He calmly and dispassionately determined to transfer the sphere of His activity from the secluded security of northern Galilee to the center of official hatred and plotting. Since He had come into the world as the Lamb of God to bring salvation to all mankind, that salvation had to be sealed with His blood at Jerusalem.

There was plainly before Him a solitary object — the cross. With this decision made, Jesus did not throw Himself rashly into the embrace of death, for He knew that much had to be accomplished to fulfill the divine purpose before He died.

While Jesus was still at Capernaum, a great caravan of feast-bound pilgrims had begun to move toward Jerusalem. Jesus, however, was not among them because a great wave of hostility had built up against Him. No doubt the people clung to what they had been taught by the rabbis: that the Messiah would restore Israel to national glory and would transfer the scepter of universal power from Rome to Jerusalem.

Jesus' attitude was expressed in these words: "After these things Jesus walked in Galilee: for he would not walk in Jewry, because the Jews sought to kill him" (v. 1). Even His disciples failed to grasp the full intent of His attitude and purpose. They wanted Him to go up to Jerusalem at once so that all the people might see His miracles and thus be constrained to support Him (vv. 2-9). But Jesus knew that the proper moment had not yet arrived. While the Jewish hierarchy did not hate His disciples, it hated Him.

Jesus waited at Capernaum until things were quiet (v. 10). Then He started toward Jerusalem with the twelve and a number of lesser disciples. On His way south to the capital city, He crossed Esdraelon and went through Samaria where, according to some of the other gospel accounts, the Samaritans attacked Him bitterly. As a result, John and James, "the sons of thunder," proposed that Jesus call down fire from heaven upon the unfriendly village and destroy its inhabitants. This gave Jesus occasion to remind the disciples that He had come to save men, not destroy them.

After this repulse at the Samaritan border village, Jesus changed His route. Turned eastward, He followed a road between Samaria and Galilee that led to the meadows of Bethshean, across the Jordan and ultimately to Jerusalem.

When Jesus arrived at Jerusalem, the Feast of Tabernacles, which every Jew was required to attend, was being observed. It was held across the span of two Sabbaths — the latter Sabbath being "that great day of the feast." It commemorated the tent life of Israel in the wilderness and was also a feast of thanksgiving for the harvest which had ended.

During these eight days everyone lived in booths or tabernacles made of the living branches of olive, myrtle and fir. These were raised up in the courts or patios of their houses, on rooftops and in the streets. On each morning of the seven feast days the priests went out with music and a choir of the Levites, amid the shouts of the people, to draw water from the spring of Siloam. Later the water was poured out at the time of the morning sacrifice in the temple.

When this feast was at its height, Jesus made His appearance in the temple (v. 14). Calmly taking His seat, He began to teach the crowd that soon gathered around Him. The Jewish leaders, intrigued by His regal bearing, calm dignity, and the fullness of His knowledge, said, "How can a common man like this, who has never been educated as a rabbi, understand the scriptures?" Jesus immediately revealed the source of His wisdom: "My doctrine is not mine, but his that sent me" (v. 16).

How can you know that what Jesus says is what God wants you to do? How can you know what is right? Jesus tells you how: "If any man will do his will, he shall know of the doctrine, whether it be of God, or whether I speak of myself" (v. 17). Obedience is the key that unlocks the mystery of God's will.

In Israel's history their prophet Samuel spoke as did Jesus: "Hath the Lord as great delight in burnt-offerings and sacrifices, as in obeying the voice of the Lord? Behold, to obey is better than sacrifice, and to hearken than the fat of rams" (1 Sa 15: 22). Religious observances are not enough; we must do God's will. God expects us to "do his will," and then we will "know of the doctrine."

Later on the temple porch, Jesus heard the open and hostile disparagement of His Messiahship (vv. 20-27). Standing in the dignity and serenity of His deity, He spoke these words: "Ye both know me, and ye know whence I am: and I am not come of myself, but he that sent me is true, whom ye know not. But I know him: for I am from him, and he hath sent me" (vv. 28-29).

This was it! Jesus had put Himself on record. There was no turning back. There was nothing further for which the Jews needed to wait. Jesus had made this claim of deity once before; now He had made it again. The only thing that prevented the

Jews from taking Him was the restraining hand of God, because His hour was not yet come.

The Pharisees, however, were convinced that they had to act immediately. This blasphemer had gone far enough. He had to be stopped now, for in stopping Him they would also stop the flow of disciples to His cause. So the Pharisees and the Saddu-cean chief priests issued a warrant to apprehend Him and sent temple police to arrest Him. At the sight of these police, Jesus calmly anticipated His death: "Yet a little while am I with you, and then I go unto him that sent me. Ye shall seek me, and shall not find me: and where I am, thither ye cannot come" (vv. 33-34). This would be the penalty of their unbelief and obstinacy. What a day of disappointment will be brought to all by unbelief! What a tragedy to seek Him and not find Him; to desire to go where He is and not be able to!

It was the last day, that "great day" of the feast. Jesus, as be-fore, was in the temple area on this day of great rejoicing. A huge procession of pilgrims marched with music and loud-voiced choirs through the city, commemorating the fall of Jericho, while others streamed to the brook Siloam where the priests had gone with golden vessels to draw water for the last of the libations.

As the priests carried the water to the temple, Jesus rose to say, "If any man thirst, let him come unto me, and drink. He that believeth on me, as the scripture hath said, out of his belly shall flow rivers of living water" (vv. 37-38). He was saying that the water borne by the priests was only a type and a sym-bol of the more satisfying water which He would give. If they would but believe on Him and drink, this water would become a living spring from their innermost being from which would flow peace, forgiveness, righteousness and perpetual power.

Jesus meant, adds John, that this power would result from the Holy Spirit's presence within them. When the Holy Spirit came, streams of holy and righteous influence would flow like rivers of living water to all the world.

We could all fittingly pray that the channels of our lives would be cleared out and cleaned up so that this up-springing and out-flowing water of the Spirit might come in. We could pray that, from the posture of our soul's yieldedness, this living water might be a veritable Amazon of the soul.

The incident was almost over and, as the people dispersed, Jesus was standing where He had stood to bid them drink of the living water. But out among the people were the police of the Sanhedrin who had come to arrest Him. Because the power and majesty of His discourse had held them spellbound, they dared not touch Him; they returned empty-handed to their superiors. Challenged for an explanation of their failure, they said, "Never man spake like this man." Instead of Jesus being their captive, they were His, for He has made them captive to His words. Jesus had said the last word on truth and life and, although two thousand years and billions of words have passed, "never man spake like this man" (v. 46).

20

Condemnation or Rehabilitation

8:1-11

NOT ONCE in Jesus' life did He have to face sin as a personal experience. He faced it as an expiation for mankind when He was made "to be sin for us, who knew no sin; that we might be made the righteousness of God in him" (2 Co 5:21). It was sin that Jesus met, not sins. Sin is character; sins are conduct. Sin is the cause; sins are the effect. Sin is the root; sins are the fruit.

Returning from a night spent outside the city near the Mount of Olives, Jesus had resumed His teaching in the temple, where He had moved from the arcades of the royal court into the women's court. To this place the scribes dragged a woman of the plebeian class who had been accused of immorality.* It was a clever maneuver to ensnare the hated Galilean, for they were not concerned with high-minded motives of righteousness. This was solely a case of religious opportunism, for they wanted to destroy the prestige of Jesus and damage His reputation among the people.

"Teacher," they said, "this woman has been guilty of sin. Moses charged us that such should be stoned. What is your opinion?"

This put Jesus on the horns of a dilemma. If He said, "Stone her," it would injure Him in the eyes of the people, for the law in this particular point had long been obsolete. If, on the other hand, He advised them to dismiss her, they would charge Him with slighting the law.

---

*Because some early copies of the Bible omit the story of the woman taken in adultery, it has been claimed that it does not belong to the original text. Westcott and Hort cast doubt upon its authenticity, yet they say: "The argument that has always told most in its favor in modern times is its own internal character. The story itself has justly seemed to vouch for its substantial truth." There exists no sufficient reasons for casting doubts upon the truth of this incident.

Aware of their clever dissimulation, Jesus stooped and began writing in the dust, using His finger as a quill and the flagstone of the temple floor as parchment. His readers were the scribes, the people, and the embarrassed and degraded woman.

The sole objective of the priests, as far as the sinning woman was concerned, was condemnation. It should have been rehabilitation, for they should have sought her repentance, recovery and restoration. This is the degradation of religion, for by our holier-than-thou attitudes, our selfish indignations, and our self-righteousnesses, we do more condemning than saving.

It is the first duty of the Christian to restore to useful life and service any who have erred. "Brethren, if any man be overtaken in a fault, ye which are spiritual, restore such an one in the spirit of meekness; considering thyself, lest thou also be tempted. Bear ye one another's burdens, and so fulfil the law of Christ" (Gal 6:1-2).

What did Jesus write in the dust? Perhaps it was what He was about to say, for — looking straight at the scribes and Pharisees — He said, "Let him who is without sin cast the first stone." To save the woman from death He challenged any of her accusers to cast the first stone if they were without sin. Sinlessness is the credential for accusation; its prevalence is our accuser and silencer.

Embarrassment shifts from the accused to the accusers, for Jesus blamed them for a greater sin — that of self-righteousness and hypocrisy. While He continued to write on the flagstone floor, the power of self-accusation in Jesus' presence brought such conviction that, one after another, the scribes and Pharisees moved off and melted into the crowd. And when Jesus looked up, He stood alone, except for the woman.

One of Jesus' most gracious recorded acts was His treatment of this hapless person. She had been dragged before Him, despised and degraded, without hope of living a decent life. Adding nothing to her embarrassment, Jesus said tenderly, "Woman, where are those thine accusers? Hath no man condemned thee?" (v. 10).

He was not accusatory or condemnatory, vindictive or punitive. He was not condoning her sin; He was loving her soul.

The woman uttered these words: "No man, Lord." He responded, "Neither do I condemn thee; go, and sin no more" (v. 11). When she said, "No man, Lord," she consciously confessed Him as her Lord and indicated her trust in Him for forgiveness. Her confession of Him as Lord and His absolution of her in divine forgiveness lay bare the whole purpose of Jesus' coming into the world — to save.

Forgiveness was predicated on repentance from past sin and a resolute purpose against future sin. When Jesus said, "Go, and sin no more," it meant that a new life must follow forgiveness. This woman was not forgiven as a religious convenience but as a means of restoration to live a new life.

Observe the simplicity of forgiveness. It consisted simply of the woman's confession and contrition and of Jesus' absolution, without sanctions, penalties or penances imposed upon her. It was solely of grace. In his first epistle, John wrote, "If we confess our sins, he is faithful and just to forgive us our sins, and to cleanse us from all unrighteousness" (1:9). It was confess, forgive, cleanse — that simple. But by the time of the Middle Ages these simplicities were forgotten in the corruptions that had grown up in the church. Paul Tillich wrote,

> At that time a vast penitential system was set up by men who could not believe the words of the Bible as they stand. In this system it was necessary for the priest to pronounce absolution. This was believed to give freedom from eternal punishment, but temporal punishment still had to be undergone by the sinner, either in this life or in purgatory. Catalogues were therefore made of the penances which should be performed to make up for sins. In these catalogues all the different kinds of evildoing were listed, and the corresponding things were specified which man must do to make up for the wrongs committed. For one sin a man must stay up all night and pray. For another he must make a visit to a holy place. For yet another he must go on pilgrimage for ten years; or instead, if he chose, pay a certain sum of money. This was the most dangerous part of the system. Forgiveness might be purchased by paying money.

The forgiveness of sins in the New Testament is not a form of religious barter. All one needs to do to be forgiven is to repent

— both the easiest and hardest thing a person can do. It is easy because it involves repentance only, not a set of religious prescriptions, and it is hard because we must turn to God with our whole heart and life.

Consider the generosity of God's offer of justification by faith. Old Testament legalism said a man was guilty if he broke as little as one part of the law. Medieval religion said salvation was a quantitative thing — so many good works had to be brought as an evidence of good faith to obtain salvation. But God's Word says that we may be justified by faith alone. If we have simple faith in God, He will account us as righteous in His sight on the basis of the righteousness of His Son Jesus through death.

Where did this forgiven woman go after Jesus dismissed her to a new life? We do not know but we have no doubt that she went to live a new life. Perhaps she made her way down from the temple heights to her home and her one-time lecherous companions where her first act must have been to tell them what happened and to describe Jesus in the glowing terms that only a forgiven sinner can use. We believe she did her best to undo prior acts of evil, disassociating herself from the community of evildoers where she had lived her sordid life. And then, with the power of new life, she probably did her best to make up for wasted years of sinning, for she had come home to "sin no more."

Suppose she had feared to leave the presence of Jesus because she was afraid of failure? Forgiveness is not merely the canceling of the past; it is courage for the future. It is conquering environment by character.

God's biddings are always enablings. A man whose heart had been deeply touched by the death of a friend, expressed a desire to the minister to begin the Christian life. "Just one thing makes me hesitate," he said. "I'm afraid I can't hold out. You know, where I work there are some pretty rough fellows. I don't believe there's a real Christian in the crowd." The minister reached down and lifted a flower from the vase on the table. "Do you see this flower, Arthur?" he asked. "It grew right in the mud and slime of a marsh. Yet, see how clean and spotless it is. That's because God kept it. And He can keep you, too!"

21

The Light of the World

8:12-32

JESUS USED EVENTS and objects about Him as illustrations for His teaching. On the last and great day of the Feast of Tabernacles when the priests bore water in their golden vessels from the pool of Siloam to the temple altars, Jesus said, "If any man thirst, let him come unto me and drink." In this way He pointed to Himself as the living water. Now He sat in the treasury of the temple, and around the court in which He sat stood the great candelabra. This probably was Jesus' inspiration for His present discourse when He said, "I am the light of the world."

No doubt the sun had just risen over the Mount of Olives and shone with dazzling splendor on the white houses of the city and the gold and marble of the temple. Jesus wedded the light of redemption to the light of creation and told His contemporaries that following Him meant having "the light of life."

It was not enough that men should live under the benign influence of the sun; they had to have another light — the Son of God. To have this light required following it, for he "that followeth me" will not walk in darkness. This meant that light was not an automatic benefit to all who lived. When we deliberately purpose in our hearts to follow what is revealed through Jesus Christ, we will have the daily experience of life's illumination.

Jesus was not a person circumscribed by Jewish provincialism. Rather, He claimed universalism when He said He was "the light of the *world*." As would be expected, one of the rabbinical party immediately challenged His claims, charging Him with promoting Himself and His own interests. In response Jesus identified Himself with God, saying, "I and the Father" (v. 16). This was

His outspoken claim, His right to say "I am the light of the world."

The Jews were infuriated when Jesus went past His human paternity, to God, making claims that had to be heard and obeyed. The Jews knew they had to get rid of Him. Consequently they pressed their case still further and demanded that He tell them where His Father was. They claimed to speak for God, but their position was untenable. Jesus said, "Ye neither know me, nor my Father: if ye had known me, ye should have known my Father also" (v. 19). In other words, if these Jews who were contemporaries of Jesus really knew God, they would have been able to identify Him, because Jesus came to reveal God to men through words and deeds.

These Jews were dealing with God and did not know it. Pride, sin, nationalism and even religion blinded their eyes. Today many of us are in the same condition, treating the claims of Jesus as we would those of any man when, in fact, they are the claims of God. Whatever judgment will come to us will be all the greater because we have rejected the highest of all claims — the claims of God.

The issues raised in the temple court are still alive today. Who is Jesus Christ? What are the claims of God upon us? What are we going to do with our lives? We must deal with these and other similarly classified issues on the basis of the biblical record in John. The pertinent question is, How will we as modern individuals answer the claims of God upon our lives?

What these first-century people said to Jesus is a variation of this old argument: "Show me God and I will believe Him." God's only answer is that He can be seen in His Son. He who sees Him, sees God. He who believes in Him, believes God, because They are one.

In a palace in Rome is a ceiling painted by one of the great masters. The ceiling is high and beyond the range of vision because the room is obscure and because man cannot easily look up. The owner, therefore, has placed a highly polished mirror on the floor so that those who look upon the reflected picture may study and know it. The whole history of human thought proves that man cannot find God by looking up, so in the fullness of time Christ came. He was the "Image of the invisible God" who reflected His glory, so that as we see Him, the invisible things become clearly seen!

Just as religion had obscured God in Jesus' time and just as it corrupted truth in medieval times, so today religion may keep us from taking a necessary fresh and full look at the Son of God so we may see what God is like.

For Jesus to make a claim of oneness with God was a very bold and dangerous thing to do in this stronghold of His enemies. But Jesus could do it with justification because it is recorded again, as it was prior to this, that "his hour was not yet come" (v. 20). This seems to reveal a very comforting truth: the events of life cannot damage us or lay a hand on us apart from God's will. As long as one is in God's will, life cannot be a series of disconnected accidental happenings. If we are "the called according to his purpose" then "all things" will "work together for good."

Jesus spoke again:

> I go my way, and ye shall seek me, and shall die in your sins: whither I go, ye cannot come. Then said the Jews, Will he kill himself? Because he saith, Whither I go, ye cannot come. And he said unto them, Ye are from beneath; I am from above: ye are of this world; I am not of this world. I said therefore unto you, that ye shall die in your sins: for if ye believe not that I am he, ye shall die in your sins (vv. 21-24).

Jesus was saying that the time was rapidly approaching when He would leave the people of His generation. When He was gone they would seek the Messiah in vain and look for Him without success, and would not find deliverance from approaching calamities. Instead, these people would die unforgiven and unpardoned; and the heaven to which He would go would be barred against them, for only through Him could they gain entrance.

This means that the issues of death as well as life, of heaven as well as earth, of eternity as well as time, are involved in our attitude to Jesus Christ. These issues must be settled here, in time and on earth, while we live, for they cannot be settled elsewhere.

Jesus had told His generation, "I am he" (v. 24). He is the sum of Jehovah's self-proclamation in the Old Testament and the visible incarnation of Jehovah in His Messianic role. But these willfully blinded people refused to acknowledge this and asked in reply, "Who art thou?" (v. 25). This is the question that Jesus had been answering by every word He had been saying and by every miracle He had been performing. In spite of the plainness of His words and the persuasiveness of His works, they neither understood nor believed Him (v. 27).

This was not a case of misunderstanding Jesus. Rather, it was the characteristic of all unbelief: the lack of disposition to believe. No one remains unsaved because he cannot believe; it is because he will not.

There remained one supreme evidence of the validity of Jesus' claim to be the Son of God — His death. Then they would know who He was. This is both the mystery and the glory of the kenosis or self-emptying of Jesus. "When ye have lifted up the Son of man, then shall ye know that I am he, and that I do nothing of myself; but as my Father hath taught me, I speak these things. And he that sent me is with me: the Father hath not left me alone; for I do always those things that please him" (vv. 28-29).

The problem which all men face in dealing with Jesus Christ is not an intellectual one; it is moral and spiritual. The failure of the Jews to understand the Messianic nature of Jesus' presence in their generation was not due to stupidity or ignorance. It was because of their unbelief.

It is one of the miracles of grace that in this hostile atmosphere of animosity and unbelief there were "many" who "believed on him." What does it mean to "believe" on Him? Agreement with what He says? Conformity to religious rules? Emotional fervor? None of these things satisfies the question of belief in Him. It is easy to give a superficial assent to Jesus and become religious. It is quite another thing to "follow" Him. This involves taking up a cross and continuity, for He said, "If ye continue in my word, then are ye my disciples indeed" (v. 31).

True discipleship rests ultimately in God's Word, which is both the source of life and the substance of faith. It is also the power and strength of the new life. Why does the test of discipleship lie in God's Word? Because Jesus said, "Ye shall know the truth, and the truth shall make you free" (v. 32). This is not always contextually applied or rightly used. It has no reference to political or intellectual freedom and liberty. Instead, it refers to personal spiritual freedom from the bondage of personal sin and from personal moral and spiritual limitations and enslavement. It is a reference to the Word of God implanted in the human heart and bringing emancipation and freedom from the inbred sinfulness of human nature.

The "word" and the "truth" must be the atmosphere and substance of our lives, for as long as this is true we remain free. There can be no political or intellectual freedom without spiritual freedom because "the truth" of God's Word and "the life" of God's Son are what make us free. If one would be free from sin, "the truth" will make him free. If one would be free from insecurity, "the truth" will make him free. This also applies to boredom, anxiety, death, inner conflict and material domination. "Ye shall know the truth, and the truth shall make you free."

The nature of "the truth" which makes us free is established by the context. It is the truth which is found in "my word." Limited to the revelation of Jesus as the incarnation of God, it is not a mishmash of religious expression, but "the truth" which is "my word."

22

What Does It Mean to Be Free?

8:33-59

WHAT JESUS THEN SAID was apparently a fragment of a discourse delivered in the temple on one of the following days. The immediate circumstances are not recorded, so we retrace our steps to consider what Jesus was saying to those Jews who believed on Him as the result of His discourse on "the light of the world." Jesus spoke of a new freedom — "Ye shall know the truth, and the truth shall make you free" (v. 32). He was speaking of spiritual freedom, of emancipation from a sinful life. However, they understood this as political freedom and interpreted it in terms of nationalism and liberty from human bondage.

The fierce Jewish pride of nationalism blazed forth as they challenged Jesus and said, "We be Abraham's seed, and were never in bondage to any man: how sayest thou, Ye shall be made free?" (v. 33). Although they had conveniently forgotten their bondage to Egypt, Babylon and Rome, Jesus was not referring to this kind of slavery. He was dealing with the slavery of sin.

Jesus said they were slaves to a worse tyranny than political tyranny. It was from this type of slavery that Jesus came to deliver, because all men, whether Jews or not, are sinners and must be made free before they can claim, as these Jews did, to belong to the household of God.

The sin problem has to be dealt with before any other problem, even before the political problem, because there cannot be any lasting freedom as long as there is slavery to sin. The successive civilizations which have come and gone demonstrate the temporary and fluctuating nature of society. The average age of the world's great civilizations has been estimated at two hundred years, and their mortality was not due to the lack of mental capacity, but to moral deficiency. In Gibbon's *The Decline and Fall of the Roman Empire* he based the dissolution of Rome on moral decay rather than military conquest.

The inherent weakness of all civilization and government is human nature, while the fault lying at the base of human nature is sin. Until this is dealt with, nothing will be permanent or lasting.

Sin is that element in human nature which makes it easier to break a commandment than a habit. It is the Gordian knot of life. When the Phrygians needed a king, they were instructed by the Oracle at Delphi to choose the first person they met riding on an oxcart toward the temple of Zeus. This they did. It was Gordens, a poor peasant who afterward dedicated his cart and yoke to Zeus, and tied the knot so skillfully that the oracle declared that whoever should unloose it would be ruler over all Asia. Many tried to do it, only to fail. Then came Alexander the Great and cut the knot in two with his sword. Sin is such a Gordian knot. It is the intricately tied knot that none has solved but Jesus. He cut it, not with a sword, but with a cross.

This mission of Jesus seemed to be anachronistic to the Jews, who were thinking of freedom and liberty in terms of present physical and political bondage. Jesus spoke of it spiritually. There may seem to be something anachronistic about the modern emphasis of this same message. Those who deal with outer space could very easily say that security rests in superior military power, but the needs of our generation are basically the same as any other. While we invest in systems to explore and conquer outer space, we are confronted with the greater challenge and dangers of inner space. Man has gradually come to know physical inner space. "More than twenty centuries ago the Greeks speculated that in spite of the wide diversity of matter it was all composed of minute particles which they called atoms. . . . Today, based on experiments, we know that atoms exist; we even know their sizes and shapes, although they are invisibly small." But there is also moral and spiritual inner space consisting of human nature with all its intricate parts. Herein lies the secret of human behavior. Jesus' mission was to this inner space.

Jesus told the Jews of His generation that they were only super-
ficially religious and that the problems of inner space lay un-
solved and untouched. Although the Jews claimed Abraham as
their father, Jesus said, "If ye were Abraham's children, ye would
do the works of Abraham" (v. 39).

Sin is self-deceiving. The sinner, unaware of his true identity,
is under delusions of grandeur because he considers himself to
be better than he is. This was a condition true of Jesus' contemporaries. He revealed their identity and exposed them as being
sinful and unworthy of the places of trust which they occupied.

JESUS DEALT WITH THESE SIN-DELUDED LEADERS IN TWO WAYS

HE REVEALED THEIR FALSE IDENTITY

They did not believe in the Word of God. "I know that ye
are Abraham's seed; but ye seek to kill me, because my word
hath no place in you" (v. 37). They wanted to destroy the thing
that was convicting and bothering them, for sin cannot tolerate
that which exposes it. If the Jews were without sin and if they
were the true sons of Abraham in the highest spiritual sense,
they would have believed in Jesus.

They did not do the works of God. "They answered and said
unto him, Abraham is our father. Jesus saith unto them, If ye
were Abraham's children, ye would do the works of Abraham"
(v. 39). Abraham was a man of faith and obedience who received the truth and acted upon it. He did the works of God.
If these people were truly his sons, they would do what he did.

They did not love God. "Jesus said unto them, If God were
your Father, ye would love me: for I proceeded forth and came
from God; neither came I of myself, but he sent me" (v. 42).
The failure of the Jews to love Christ was evidence of their true
nature, for if they were in Abraham's succession, love for and
recognition of the Messiah would be present.

They were not of God. "He that is of God heareth God's
words: ye therefore hear them not, because ye are not of God"
(v. 47). The Jews were advocates of God and custodians of
Scripture, yet they did not know God. Here lies a dreadful possibility for modern man. He may have inherited religious tradi-

tions and been placed in a religious environment, yet he has failed to perceive the true nature of a religious experience, the knowledge of God. Religion is no guarantee of salvation.

HE REVEALED THEIR TRUE IDENTITY

They sought to kill Jesus. "Now ye seek to kill me" (v. 40). Sin cannot abide its accuser. They eventually killed Him to silence Him, but this was their downfall because the resurrection put Jesus back into life with a confirmation and condemnation that could not be denied.

They were of their father the devil. "Ye are of your father the devil, and the lusts of your father ye will do" (v. 44). Although the Jews claimed to be the sons of God because they were the children of Abraham, they were actually the children of the devil. Jesus then laid a terrible indictment against them. True to their nature, they copied their father the devil, who from the beginning was a murderer, an enemy of truth, and a liar. Now his sons the Jews were proving their true nature by desiring to kill, by destroying the truth, and by lies. And all of this was revealed by their attitude to the Messiah.

Jesus then inserted one of the great and profound utterances of His entire career: "If a man keep my saying, he shall never see death" (v. 51). One reason for Jesus' coming was to do away with death. Likewise, the condition Jesus set forth for escaping death was to believe and keep His word. The very Jews to whom Jesus was speaking were excluding themselves from eternal life by their failure to repent and obey Him.

In what sense would a believer never die? Not in a physical sense, for all who followed Jesus ultimately died. Escaping death was a spiritual experience. Those who believed in Jesus would not die spiritually or eternally, but would share that continuing life which was in Christ. Spiritual life is a condition that will go on eternally.

23

Is Sickness Caused by Sin?

9:1-41

SAINT AUGUSTINE SAID, "To be born here and in a mortal body is to begin to be sick." Another corollary of life is of the same nature: "To begin to live is to begin to die." Both sickness and death are intimate parts of living. There will be no escape from sickness and no escape from the fact that we must deal with it when it comes.

Jesus had returned to Jerusalem and the temple where the poor and the afflicted were gathered, seeking help. Among them was a man whose blindness had not been the result of either disease or accident. It was congenital.

Followed by a number of disciples, Jesus was attracted to this blind man. John does not say that Jesus spoke to the man or that he spoke to Jesus. He simply says, "And as Jesus passed by, he saw a man which was blind."

This produced an inquiry from His disciples who had been taught that when children were born lame or blind or otherwise defective, it was because of some sin of their parents or in the sick person's life. "Who did sin . . . that he was born blind? (v. 2).

One feature of rabbinical theology was a strict order of rewards and punishments according to the merits or demerits of either good or bad deeds. Thus, if a person sinned he would be punished by some kind of physical affliction. The Jews were committed to the idea that children were punished for parental sins by various physical afflictions. The question about the blind man's parents was in keeping with their theology.

Jesus faces, one by one, the great issues and questions of life. Here was one of great significance — the problem of human suf-

116

fering. This is a specific instance of physical affliction – blindness. The disciples asked a specific question (v. 2) and Jesus gave a specific answer (v. 3).

The Answers

jesus' answer was negative

"Neither hath this man sinned, nor his parents" (v. 3). This dispelled the idea of punishment for sin on the part of the child or his parents. The Bible indicates that it is possible to inherit certain parental weaknesses which result in sickness. But no one actually inherits acquired disease – this is no more biologically possible than to inherit acquired characteristics. What can be inherited are weaknesses and a disposition to certain conditions and sicknesses. Jesus is saying that sickness as punishment is not inherited.

jesus' answer was positive

"But that the works of God should be made manifest in him" (v. 3). Did God deliberately create this man blind so He could display the power of healing? Between the disciples' question about the cause of this man's blindness and his healing, Jesus interposes a statement: "I must work the works of him that sent me, while it is day: the night cometh, when no man can work. As long as I am in the world, I am the light of the world" (vv. 4-5). Here is the reason why Jesus healed the blind man. It was not because God deliberately created him blind, so Jesus could heal him, which would have made healing the main purpose of Jesus' mission. If verses 3 and 4 are put together it is evident that in both of these statements Jesus is speaking about "the works of God." Verse 3 speaks about God's work in connection with a man, while verse 4 is about His work in relation to time.

When the disciples asked Jesus about the origin of sickness, He replied that blindness is not God's will for anyone. He said He had come to do God's work and that He had to do it while it was day – the day of His redemptive mission. The time was the time He was doing His redemptive work. Therefore, He indicated that His healing ministry would be while He was on earth redeeming men.

A secondary meaning of this statement applies to all continuing disciples of Jesus. We are to do God's work while we have the light of life, for we can no longer work when death comes. Jesus said, "As long as I am in the world, I am the light of the world" (v. 5). This does not mean that the light ceased when He left the world, because His disciples have been the light of the world from then until now.

Jesus then proceeded to heal the blind man, employing moistened clay, which we may liken to means. Nothing indicates why He used means in this instance, except perhaps to teach us that He does not always work by a rigid pattern. The essential lesson is not that He used means, because the power of healing was not invested in moistened clay but was in Himself.

We have already established one important truth, namely, that sickness, either congenital or accidental, is not related to sin. But there is another important truth. If Jesus healed in this case, does He heal in every case? The answer is no. Jesus has already indicated His diminishing activity in healing. It was something associated with His redemptive ministry while on earth. Then He indicated that He had another purpose in coming into the world: to remove the cause of sickness which is sin. This was to be His great "work" which He would do while it was "day," and this He would do on the cross.

We are not to expect a succession of authority and power flowing from Jesus which makes healing mandatory. Healing has been providential and not universal, selective and not elective.

THREE NOTEWORTHY THINGS IN THIS INCIDENT

THE CAUSE OF SUFFERING

The cause of suffering lies in the nature of a disordered world. This is not a perfect world; its imperfections are the root cause of sickness. These take us back to sin as the basic cause of all wrong, evil and sickness.

THE PLACE OF SUFFERING

Suffering is universal. Whatever its manifestations, it is without limitations of time or place. In mental illness, for instance, the records of early Massachusetts courts show that there were just as many commitments to mental hospitals, in proportion to population, in the quieter and more rural Massachusetts of the nineteenth century as in the speeded-up industrial Massachusetts of today. A study of the old-fashioned island of Bornholm off the coast of Denmark, an eighteenth-century type of society, has shown the same types of psychosis and neurosis found in our most frantic cities. Anthropologists say they have found familiar patterns of mental aberrations in every society and culture they have ever studied.

THE PURPOSE OF SUFFERING

The incident of the blind man established the fact that God did not create or permit sickness so He could display the power of healing. However, God permits it as an instrument for our development.

In Archibald Rutledge's "Beauty in the Heart" he tells of one of the purposes of suffering:

> Going up a mountain path one day, I met a mountaineer with an ax in his hand. I walked with him and asked him what he was going to cut. "I need a piece of timber to fix my wagon," he said. "I need the toughest kind of wood I can get. That kind always grows on top of the mountain, where all the storms hit the hardest."
>
> Storms rend and mar; but they strengthen, they build, and they may bring forth serene and changeless beauty. The beauty born of storms has a nobility about it. A girl's first bloom lacks significance and spiritual durability. It can represent no effort, no decision, no struggle, no strength or valor on the part of its possessor. Years later, when the girl has become a woman, if she has reacted gallantly to trouble there will come to her a beauty that has about it the air of immortality. That is because it is rooted in character.
>
> We are prone to lament that the world is not better. Yet the fact that it is full of trouble affords us our only chance to spend our hearts. A time of prosperity is a dangerous time; the soul loafs and grows fat. Times of storm and peril are the ones that show what we are made of. A storm is always a challenge; there seems to be something in the heart that rises up to meet it.

SEQUEL TO THIS HEALING

There was a sequel to the healing of this blind man which involved his neighbors, his superiors and his Lord.

HIS NEIGHBORS (vv. 8-12)

Apparently the healed man went back to that part of Jerusalem where he lived and became the center of wonder and awe. When his neighbors asked who had opened his eyes, he recounted what happened but said he did not know who had healed him. Here is a wonderful thing. Although the former blind man could not explain all that had happened or identify the source of his healing, he did enjoy the reality of his experience.

HIS SUPERIORS (vv. 13-34)

The discomfited council was at a loss as to how it could handle this difficult and delicate situation, so it turned on the man and warned him to tell the truth. He gave this classic answer: "One thing I know, that, whereas I was blind, now I see" (v. 25). Nothing is more important than reality, assurance and experience.

HIS LORD (vv. 35-41)

The beggar was able at last to identify His seeing with the Lord, in the knowledge and acquaintance of a personal experience with Jesus. Now seeing, he became the first confessor of the Lord in the new kingdom of life He had come to establish.

24

A Picture of Life

10:1-9

JESUS' VIEW OF LIFE begins with the assumption that all men exist outside of an intimate and actual life relationship with God. Into their experience must come a moment when they cross a threshold of decision and enter a new living relationship with God with new ideals, convictions and experiences. There are two inviolate conditions for entering this relationship with God: First, a person must believe and accept Jesus Christ as his personal Saviour (Jn 1:12-13; 3:16, 18; 5:24). Second, a person must believe that Jesus Christ is the Son of God (Jn 20:31).

Many modern appeals for men to become Christians fall far short of the conditions Jesus set down for discipleship. One was life — this life depicted by the sheepfold with its living sheep and their relation to a shepherd. Another was death — the death associated with the cross: "If any man will come after me, let him deny himself, and take up his cross daily, and follow me" (Lk 9:23).

Many of today's church members are not reasonable facsimiles of the original model but products of what a modern religious satirist calls the "small print" — reservations in religion which nullify the true commitments which Christians are expected to make. One is found in the words of a well-known hymn, "Take my silver and my gold, not a mite would I withhold," with this appendage in small print at the back of the mind: "Provided there is no immediate use for the gold or silver." In a real Christian commitment there are no small-print reservations; everything is in large print without compromise or contraction.

First Jesus set forth the negative — how not to be a Christian:

121

"He that entereth not by the door into the sheepfold, but climbeth up some other way, the same is a thief and a robber" (v. 1).

Jesus Establishes Two Facts

THERE IS A SHEEPFOLD BUT MAN'S NATURAL STATE IS OUTSIDE

The fact that man is not naturally within God's sheepfold dispatches the false notion that all men are by natural birth the children of God, and that all they need is a change of environment and the application of religious culture. H. G. Wells of England had high hopes that man would grow out of his barbarity and, as a cultured, considerate being, would form a brotherhood capable of worldwide expansion. He was completely disillusioned before his death, due to the degrading and devastating experiences of two world wars.

Man is outside. He cannot be left to his own devices and expect to improve; he must be brought in. The problems of society, like peace, do not solve themselves. Too many people speak as if peace were the natural state of the world, disturbed from time to time by men like Alexander, Napoleon and Hitler. But there is no peace in nature, nor is there peace in human nature. Each generation must find and establish its own peace. This is an individual matter too, for peace is a problem of the heart.

THERE IS A PRESCRIBED WAY TO GET INTO THE SHEEPFOLD

Jesus speaks of a door to the sheepfold (v. 1) and later identifies Himself as that door (v. 9). The narrative moves on as it unfolds the story of Jesus' coming into the world to gather a people for God (vv. 1-6). He spoke of Himself as the Shepherd, the people as sheep, and the fold as a new community. In this new community there are true leaders and false. The true undershepherd enters by the door; the false tries to get in some other way.

This is Jesus' estimate of the efforts of natural religion which circumvents the true and only way. He said, "All that ever came before me" as if to remind us that every major religious system except one was already in existence before His coming. All these are identified as "other ways" and lead us nowhere but into confusion, frustration and trouble.

Where there is a fold there automatically are two classes: those on the inside and those on the outside, the saved and the lost. This fact poses several questions: First, how did those who were on the outside get inside? Years of religious obscurantism have clouded the answer given by Jesus: "I am the door." A door is both an opening and an obstacle — an opening to the desiring and believing, and an obstacle to the undesirable. The way for those outside to get inside is by "the door." Jesus Christ is that door.

A door is not only an obstacle; it is an opportunity. It gives comfort, security and protection to all who are on the inside. A door is a wonderful thing, especially if it is that door which is Christ.

The other question asks, How do those inside react to their new life? The answer is threefold:

They have a new identity. Those who have come in through "the door" are now members of God's new community. They are sheep and they belong to the Shepherd.

They have a new response. They react to the voice of the Shepherd. There is a new affinity within them that responds to God, for "the Spirit itself beareth witness with our spirit, that we are the children of God" (Ro 8:16).

They have a new character and environment. Now they "go in and out and find pasture." The shepherd is the symbol of character; the pasture is the symbol of environment. Jesus dominates both. He gives us our entrance and existence, and He provides our new character and new environment.

25

More Than Enough

10:10

TODAY WE ARE at a peak in the world's scientific progress. We stand in awe before science's achievements and are surrounded on every hand by its magic. At the same time we are in peril of nuclear destruction and are witnessing the slow erosion of our culture by crime and evil. At this point of peril the Christian faith comes with its dynamic influence of truth. Jesus said, "I am come that they might have life, and that they might have it more abundantly" (v. 10). The greatest discovery that an individual caught in the vortex of this world's problems can make is the discovery that his Creator understands the needs and longings of his soul and has peace and power for him in a more abundant life.

Jesus told His disciples, "I am the good shepherd: the good shepherd giveth his life for the sheep" (v. 11). As the good Shepherd, Jesus stands in contrast to two things: first, to the thief (v. 10); second, to the hireling (v. 12). A thief comes on a mission of destruction, to steal even if he must destroy and kill whatever and whoever stands in his way.

But Jesus comes to make alive, not kill; to give, not take away; to construct, not destroy. Many times Jesus is misunderstood as a thief who has come to take away joy, pleasure, happiness, comfort and initiative. Salvation is not properly understood in this light. It is not negative, destructive or inhibiting, but constructive, positive, expansive and growing.

The life which God originally breathed into man when He made him "a living soul" was His own. In this creative process He shared His own life with us, which is precisely what the good Shepherd does in redemption: He gives "his life for the sheep."

In the beginning, God's life was imparted by creation. In the new beginning, God's life is imparted by redemption.

This higher life is not the common life of man refined by culture and education, nor is his life reformed by morality and ethics. The very best that refinement and reformation can do is to take away what is offensive.

This higher life is something regenerated. To regenerate means to begin again, which is what Jesus said to Nicodemus: "Ye must be born again."

Beyond the quest for life is the conquest of life. Jesus said that not only could we have life, but we could have it "more abundantly." Christianity is something more. More than quest, it is conquest; more than conversion, it is attainment; more than birth, it is growth; more than beginning, it is continuing.

This Christian encounter with life is not only life regenerated from what it was, but also life lifted above what it usually is. When Jesus described it as something He would give "more abundantly," He was actually saying "above the common life around us." "More abundantly" means more than enough.

The disciples at Antioch were called Christians largely because their lives were different:

> The early Christians were known because of the things they did not do. They believed in the dignity of all human life; consequently, they would not attend the amphitheater and watch people slaughtered to make a Roman holiday. They believed that their bodies were temples of the Holy Spirit, therefore they would not defile themselves in pagan immoralities. Believing in purity and decency, they refused to attend the Roman theaters and witness the obscene stage productions which were so popular in a decadent society. It was because they refused to participate in these and other sins of the day that the disciples were mocked and derided and scornfully referred to as "Christians."
>
> But the Christians were also known for what they were and for the things they did. They lived life fully and abundantly. At regular intervals they gathered together for worship and fellowship. They prayed for themselves, for each other, and for their enemies; they obeyed the exhortation to walk in the way

of love even as Jesus walked. The Christians were well-known for their patience, kindness and gentleness, even to their enemies.

The Christian is unlike the world about him because of the nature of the new birth within and the nature of the new life without. What we do is a response to what we are. This is the genius of Christianity.

DESCRIPTIONS OF THE MORE-ABUNDANT LIFE

IT IS MORE ABUNDANT IN ITS LOVE

Jesus did not love us as other men do with a philanthropic affection or even a brotherly love. He loved us with the love of God. This is the difference between *agapē* love, the love of God; and *philanthropia* love, the love of mankind; and *philadelphia* love, the love of brethren. Jesus' love is the more abundant love, *agapē*. It is the love which is more than enough.

IT IS MORE ABUNDANT IN ITS GRACE

Grace is our means of conquest as it enters every facet and aspect of life. No one has a life situation who does not already have access, in Christ, to more than enough grace to meet it.

IT IS MORE ABUNDANT IN ITS POWER

When Jesus gave the promise of the Holy Spirit He said, "Ye shall receive power, after that the Holy Ghost is come upon you" (Ac 1:8). This is the expulsive, dynamic power of a new life — more than enough.

IT IS MORE ABUNDANT IN ITS COMFORT

Comfort in its biblical context means to make strong. It is more than sympathy for sorrow; it is support for life which has to be lived in the face of disasters and disappointments. It is more than enough.

IT IS MORE ABUNDANT IN ITS HOPE

The last citadel that must be conquered before we go down to defeat is the citadel of hope. Hope is the bright star of the future, the promise of something better, the borrowed ray of tomorrow.

IT IS MORE ABUNDANT IN ITS JOY

When Jesus promised peace to His disciples He said, "Not as the world giveth, give I unto you" (Jn 14:27). This is why the Christian's sufficiency is more than enough, for it is according to Christ's measure of abundance, not the world's measure of meagerness. The world has average joy and commonplace peace, while the Christian has uncommon peace and joy because it is "the joy of the Lord" and "the peace of God, which passeth all understanding" (Phil 4:7).

Life more abundant — more than enough.

26

The Laid-down Life

10:10-29

"AND IT WAS WINTER" (v. 22). It was near the end of the Jewish calendar month of Kislev, equivalent to our December. Jesus had been in Jerusalem for about three months, ever since the Feast of Tabernacles, in His last visit before the triumphal entry. Because it was winter, the weather had been wet and rough. With the people who were attracted to the temple because of His presence, Jesus sought the shelter of the arcade running along the east side of the temple enclosure.

There were stirrings among the people, who still had doubts and unbeliefs after the weeks and months of contact with Jesus. On perhaps a wet and dreary day they began to ask Him for a direct and explicit declaration as to whether He was the Messiah: "How long dost thou make us to doubt? If thou be the Christ, tell us plainly" (v. 24). Jesus could have fabricated words with a finesse equaled by none. Yet, words by themselves were not enough; the situation demanded proof by action through miracles (v. 25).

One great barrier kept the Jews from believing in Jesus' words and works. They were not His sheep, therefore they believed not (v. 26). Although these people were Jews, to whom belonged the covenants of God, they were not automatically guaranteed the Messianic blessings. The basis of these blessings would be the new life about which Jesus had been talking.

What makes it possible for people to understand what Jesus is talking about? Jesus answers this question by bringing up the subject of sheep. He said if the ones to whom He had been speaking were His sheep they would have known what He was saying, for His sheep hear His voice and follow Him (v. 27).

This is the basis of belief. We must have a certain nature, a certain kinship to Jesus, based upon something He has given us. "And I give unto them eternal life; and they shall never perish, neither shall any man pluck them out of my hand. My Father, which gave them me, is greater than all; and no man is able to pluck them out of my Father's hand" (vv. 28-29).

The apostle Paul says something parallel to this requirement is necessary to believe:

> But as it is written, Eye hath not seen, nor ear heard, neither have entered into the heart of man, the things which God hath prepared for them that love him. But God hath revealed them unto us by his Spirit: for the Spirit searcheth all things, yea, the deep things of God. For what man knoweth the things of a man, save the spirit of man which is in him? Even so the things of God knoweth no man, but the Spirit of God. Now we have received, not the spirit of the world, but the spirit which is of God; that we might know the things that are freely given to us of God. Which things also we speak, not in the words which man's wisdom teacheth, but which the Holy Ghost teacheth; comparing spiritual things with spiritual. But the natural man receiveth not the things of the Spirit of God: for they are foolishness unto him: neither can he know them, because they are spiritually discerned. But he that is spiritual judgeth all things, yet he himself is judged of no man. For who hath known the mind of the Lord, that he may instruct him? But we have the mind of Christ" (1 Co 2:9-16).

The basis of understanding is not nationalism, rationalism or ritualism; it is the new life (v. 10).

STATEMENTS CONCERNING THIS NEW LIFE

JESUS BROUGHT LIFE

"I am come that they might have life, and that they might have it more abundantly" (v. 10). This reflects the purpose of Jesus' coming into the world — to bring life. The gateway into any kind of life is by birth. It is as true spiritually as it is physically.

Dr. Ernest White, a practicing psychiatrist of England, in his book *Christian Life and the Unconscious* says, "All life, either natural life as we see it around us on the earth or spiritual life as we discern it by faith and by its effects, is the gift of God. With all his progress in science and in skill, man has not yet succeeded in producing a living thing. Spontaneous generation is unknown to science. All life springs from preexisting life. The life peculiar to the Christian is a new creation within him."

The preexisting life from which the life of the Christian begins is Christ's life. And since the only way any kind of life can be passed on is by the process of birth, this life is received by a spiritual birth.

JESUS LAY DOWN HIS LIFE AND TOOK IT AGAIN

"Therefore doth my Father love me, because I lay down my life, that I might take it again. No man taketh it from me, but I lay it down of myself. I have power to lay it down, and I have power to take it again. This commandment have I received of my Father" (vv. 17-18).

Jesus had given proof through all manner of miracles that He was indeed the Christ. But there was something more which would establish the validity of His claim to be the Son of God. He said, "Therefore doth my Father love me, because I lay down my life, that I might take it again" (v. 17). Here are two things: first, a laying down of life; second, a taking up of life. These refer to crucifixion and resurrection, the two basic facts of the Christian faith.

The manner in which Jesus would die and live again would establish His identity beyond all successful contradiction. Up to this moment in history no one had died and lived again as He was about to do. His death was by crucifixion, the most cruel and inhuman form of execution known to man. For six hours He hung impaled upon the death instrument. With the approach of the sacred Sabbath and its great feast, when it was unlawful for bodies to hang in the agonies of death, soldiers were dispatched in order to induce death before it would normally occur in crucifixion. They were to break the legs of the three victims, thus causing death through nervous shock.

The soldiers found both of the thieves alive and, breaking

their legs with spears, killed them. But coming to the Saviour, they discovered He was already dead. Death had occurred apart from the normal effects of crucifixion, which in some cases took several days. This is what Jesus meant when He told the Jews in the temple arcade, "I lay down my life."

Each of the four gospels says that Jesus "gave up the ghost" or that He "yielded up the ghost," which indicates that He had accomplished His own death by an act of will. In this manner Jesus "lay down" His life by God's commandment: "This commandment have I received of my Father" (v. 18). While Jesus was under divine command, He was not forced or coerced to act. He obeyed freely, gladly and willingly.

The same thing happened in reverse in the resurrection when Jesus took again what He had given up in death. How could a living man voluntarily choose to die and how could a dead man voluntarily choose to live? Some men have willed to die and have accomplished their death at a certain time, but how could one in the embrace of death consciously determine to live?

In Jesus' experience of death He willed in the unconscious part of His being to live again, and conscious, breathing life throbbed through His body. He slipped from the graveclothes without disturbing their bodily contour and, being possessed with new physical characteristics which released Him from the limiting effects of gravitation and locomotion, He burst from the tomb and appeared in succession to the soldiers, Mary, Peter and the disciples in numerous places.

JESUS GIVES ETERNAL LIFE

"And I give unto them eternal life; and they shall never perish, neither shall any man pluck them out of my hand. My Father, which gave them me, is greater than all; and no man is able to pluck them out of my Father's hand" (vv. 28-29). This result is achieved when the life which Jesus laid down and took up again is imparted to men in a new birth. The physical life to which we are born is transitory, ephemeral and evanescent; the spiritual life to which we are born again is permanent and perpetual.

A question is asked and answered in this third statement: Can a man who has eternal life ever lose it? This question is argued perennially by theological disputants. On one side Calvinists contend that one so born cannot lose it; on the other side Arminians say that one so born can lose it. According to Dr. Ernest White, Jesus seems to say that "a person who has been born again into God's spiritual family can never cease to be by nature the child of God."

To remember the two aspects of salvation is to see how this fact is true. Salvation is a work of grace on both the conscious and unconscious levels of life. On the unconscious level it is irrevocable, never to be repented of, rescinded or lost. On the conscious level the manifestations of salvation are subject to human weaknesses and therefore it may fluctuate and undulate.

It is also possible to have a psychological conversion without a spiritual new birth, to profess conversion without any vital change taking place in the life of the convert, to assume the name of Christian without any real change of personality. But he to whom eternal life has been imparted by the Holy Spirit can never perish.

THREE REASONS FOR THIS PERMANENCY OF LIFE

THE WORD OF GOD

"And I give unto them eternal life; and they shall never perish" (v. 28).

THE WORK OF CHRIST

The work of regeneration is irrevocable. It cannot be undone and done over again. The work of Christ is finished and final. Those who were saved by Christ's work on the cross are kept saved by Christ's work at the throne. "Wherefore he is able also to save them to the uttermost [clear to the end] that come unto God by him" (Heb 7:25).

THE POSITION OF THE BELIEVER

The believer is in Christ; he is part of a divine and eternal building; he is a member of Christ's body. He may falter in his condition, but he is faultless in his position. He may sin in his condition, but he is sinless in his position. He may stumble in his condition, but he is secure in his position.

27

Jesus' Oneness with God

10:30-42

JOHN'S DECLARED PURPOSE for writing his gospel is to set forth Jesus as the divine Son of God. Coupled with this is life through faith. "But these are written, that ye might believe that Jesus is the Christ, the Son of God; and that believing ye might have life through his name" (20:31). Faith and life are cause and effect. Faith is belief in Jesus' divine nature, while life is the effect of this kind of faith which results in eternal life.

The opening statement of the gospel sets its theme and tempo: "In the beginning was the Word, and the Word was with God, and the Word was God." Jesus had earlier established the fact of His deity. Now, on His last visit to Jerusalem before the triumphal entry, it is established again in a most convincing way. The Jews had demanded an answer, "If thou be the Christ, tell us plainly" (v. 24). Jesus had answered plainly, "I and my Father are one" (v. 30).

The fanatical crowd in the temple arcade then scattered in search of stones with which to kill Him. In the face of this threat Jesus stood undismayed and countered with these words: "Many good works have I shewed you from my Father; for which of those works do ye stone me?" (v. 32). They answered, "For a good work we stone thee not; but for blasphemy; and because that thou, being a man, makest thyself God" (v. 33).

Instead of retraction in the face of threats, Jesus gave a defense of His claims to deity based upon His works: "If I do not the works of my Father, believe me not. But if I do, though ye believe not me, believe the works: that ye may know, and believe, that the Father is in me, and I in him" (vv. 37-38).

The deity of Jesus Christ does not mean a state of character or a condition of life in which He acted in a godlike manner. Rather, it means that He was God in essence. John tells us what it means when He said, "And the Word was made flesh, and dwelt among us" (1:14). Jesus as God came down to be man; He did not as man rise up to act as God.

SEVEN REASONS WHICH SUBSTANTIATE FAITH IN JESUS' ONENESS WITH GOD

THE CLAIMS OF CHRIST

Other men have had deity claimed for them, but Jesus claimed deity for and by Himself.

He claimed it in His preexistence. "And now, O Father, glorify thou me with thine own self with the glory which I had with thee before the world was" (17:5).

He claimed it in His words. "I and my Father are one" (10:30).

He claimed it in His works. "If I do not the works of my Father, believe me not. But if I do, though ye believe not me, believe the works: that ye may know, and believe, that the Father is in me, and I in him" (10:37-38).

Because of these claims of deity the Jews sought to kill Jesus.

THE STATEMENT OF THE BIBLE

The Bible is documentary evidence which recognizes the uniquely divine nature of Jesus.

He is expressly called God. "In the beginning was the Word, and the Word was with God, and the Word was God" (Jn 1:1).

He possesses the attributes of God. Among these are self-existence, immutability, truth, love, holiness, omnipresence, omniscience and omnipotence.

He has the works of God ascribed to Him. These include the creation of the world, the upholding of the created system, and the raising of the dead.

He receives the honor and worship of God. He is called God, and divine honor is paid Him such as only God would receive in both prayers and worship (Heb 1:6).

He is named on an equality with God. This is found in the

baptism and benediction formulas, as well as in instances in which eternal life is said to be dependent equally upon Christ and upon God (Mt 28:19; 2 Co 13:14).

He is given the names of God. He is called Emmanuel (Mt 1:23); the Word (Jn 1:1); Lord (Jn 20:28); our great God (Titus 2:13).

THE EVIDENCE OF REASON

One evidence of reason is based upon the deduction that either Christ is God or else three things are not true:

Christ is not true. His claims of deity are either true or deliberately false. If they are true, then He must be what He claimed to be — divine. If they are not true, He was an imposter and fraud, a fact which disqualifies Him to be the Saviour of the world.

The Bible is not true. Colossians 2:9 says, "For in him [Jesus] dwelleth all the fulness of the Godhead bodily." If Christ is not divine, this statement is false; if it is false, the Bible is unworthy of our confidence.

The Bible, which is God's written Word, and Jesus Christ, who is God's incarnate Word, stand or fall together. If Christ is not God's Son, the Bible is not God's Word.

The Trinity is not true. Jesus Christ is the Son of God by nature, thus linking Him to God the Father and God the Holy Spirit. This completes what we call the Trinity and what the Bible calls the Godhead. Every convert to Christianity is baptized in a trinitarian formula which is false if Jesus Christ is not God.

THE WITNESS OF HISTORY

The divine nature of Jesus Christ is supported and proved by what He did and how He lived. He dared to say, "Believe me that I am in the Father, and the Father in me: or else believe me for the very works' sake" (14:11). This witness is reported in such numerous instances that it stands without successful refutation.

THE CONFESSION OF HIS DISCIPLES

When Jesus asked His disciples who they thought He was, Peter responded, "Thou art the Christ, the Son of the living God"

(Mt 16:16). Current opinion saw in Him just another prophet; but because of their intimate association in His daily life, the disciples said He was God.

THE ADMISSION OF HIS ENEMIES

In the wilderness temptation when Jesus met Satan in spiritual combat, Satan was not deceived as to the identity of his antagonist. Three times he challenged Him with the appellation, "If thou be the Son of God." Satan was not paying tribute to a superior man, but giving recognition to the supreme Son of God.

In other instances, "Unclean spirits, when they saw him, fell down before him, and cried, saying, Thou art the Son of God" (Mk 3:11). The centurion who observed the events surrounding His crucifixion came up with this conclusive judgment: "Truly this man was the Son of God."

THE EXISTENCE OF THE CHURCH

After Peter's confession that Jesus was God, Jesus said, "Upon this rock [His deity] I will build my church." Following His crucifixion and resurrection, the disciples preached His deity as the cornerstone of the church.

Here was a truth so important in the eyes of Christ's enemies that He had to die for it, and so important in the eyes of His friends that they had to proclaim it, even if they died for it.

Nothing is expendable about this great truth. It matters greatly whether one believes or disbelieves it, for there cannot be a true and authentic Christian faith apart from such a belief. A minimum Christian faith must include the deity of Christ. Anything less is not Christian.

There can be no true Christian salvation apart from such belief, because belief or disbelief at this point not merely involves a difference of opinion but the difference between being lost and saved, life and death.

28

Lord over Death

11:1-21

DEATH IS ONE of the reigning sovereigns of this world, but its reign is temporary, for it is doomed to cease in the ultimate lordship of Christ who will destroy death as man's last and greatest enemy.

In order to escape the murderous intentions of His enemies, Jesus had retired from Jerusalem to Perea, a quiet and unobtrusive place. But this quiet retreat was soon broken by an urgent message from friends at Bethany in whose home Jesus had spent many happy hours. The message from two sisters, Mary and Martha, said, "Lord, . . . he whom thou lovest is sick" (v. 3).

The matter seemed to demand immediate attention. Jesus had healed hundreds whom He had never known; surely He would hurry and heal someone He greatly loved. However, "when Jesus heard that, he said, This sickness is not unto death, but for the glory of God, that the Son of God might be glorified thereby" (v. 4).

This is an example of what we call unanswered prayer. It involves a delay in Jesus' response to the sisters' appeal for help as well as a result contrary to their expectation. Lazarus was sick and his sisters had appealed to a source of hitherto unfailing help. But Jesus' response was not immediate; He deliberately delayed two days, and during that time the sick man died. Why this delay? Why the unanswered prayer?

Jesus was not an ordinary healer at work. He had oneness with the Father. For this reason He saw things in a different light than either the sisters of Lazarus or His disciples. To raise the dead would be a revelation of the glory of God and a clear evidence of His deity. This was the unseen reason for His delay in going to Bethany.

This delay was not what it appeared to be. It was not due to indifference or lack of ability to help. Although it left Jesus open to suspicion and left His friends disappointed, it was for a far greater work than the immediate healing of Lazarus would have been. The ultimate results achieved were far greater than if Jesus had done the obvious. This is likewise true in our Christian experience. What we consider unanswered prayer and denied requests can often have an unseen purpose which results in greater good. Spurgeon said, "The spade of trouble digs the reservoir of comfort deeper, and makes more room for consolation."

So-called unanswered prayer is not unheard prayer, for all prayer is heard, even as the message of Mary and Martha was received by Jesus and given His immediate attention. Furthermore, unanswered prayer is not unheeded petition. Jesus heeded the message of Lazarus' sisters and was greatly moved by the plight of His friend, but He had something better in mind for him.

All prayer is answered, for what appears to be unanswered prayer is responded to just as any other prayer. The only difference is that the things God does are channeled in another direction, resulting in the accomplishment of God's will while temporarily disappointing us.

The purpose of God was so much higher than Mary and Martha's original request that Jesus could say later on, "I am glad for your sakes that I was not there, to the intent ye may believe" (v. 15). The important thing is to learn to "believe." There may be delay, but there is no denial in unanswered prayer as long as prayer conforms to God's will.

There is another aspect of this incident which we do not always take into account. The sisters were so urgent in their appeal because to men there is finality in death, but with God this finality does not exist. Jesus held the mastery of death. Because He was "the life" He did not view death as men did. He simply understood death differently, for a little later He said, "Our friend Lazarus sleepeth" (v. 11). After a two-day interval Jesus went to "awake him out of sleep."

What Jesus did in Lazarus' sleep of death will be accomplished for us by the resurrection in the case of physical death. But we are mistaken if we assume there is a soul sleep in death. Most of the so-called soul-sleeping passages are taken from the Old Testament where, by the very nature of a progressive revelation, we have only a partial understanding of the nature of death. Not until we get to the New Testament do we see the true nature of death and the resurrection.

In the New Testament, death becomes conscious life in the presence of a conscious Lord in the midst of an environment of conscious living. To be "absent from the body" is equal to being "present with the Lord" (2 Co 5:8). This is the equivalent of conscious life. Paul's experience with death consisted of a consciousness that enabled him to comprehend the beauty and magnificence of the place he was permitted to see (2 Co 12).

With these things settled, Jesus set out for Bethany, where He arrived four days after Lazarus died. Those four days had been sad ones in the little household. The bereft sisters had fasted all day after their brother died. A few hours after death, the body of their beloved brother had then been borne to the grave. At the mouth of the grave, which was a cave, the bearers chanted the sublime ninetieth psalm. Then the body was put in the sepulcher, the grave was closed, and the funeral party departed for the mourners' home.

In their desolate home the saddened and bereft sisters rent their clothes and cast dust upon their heads in further demonstrations of mourning.

On the fourth day of the seven-day mourning period, Jesus arrived. When He came the whole situation was altered; mourning ceased, desolation disappeared, and a new concept of life and death developed. At first Martha, who had gone out to meet Jesus, was resentful about her brother's death. Assuming that Jesus had ignored their urgent request, she greeted Him with these reproachful words: "Lord, if thou hadst been here, my brother had not died" (v. 21).

Here is the constantly present hypothetical *if*. How often we use it in life! We can respond to life with the questioning *if*, or we can respond with the affirmative *is*. When Jesus experienced Satan's temptation, the satanic thrust was, "If thou be the Son of God," while the Saviour's parry was, "It is written."

We must learn to meet death before it meets us. The preparation for death lies in our preparation for life — the preparation of faith. We must learn that if death is an end it is also a beginning. Death is the end of life, but the beginning of a new life. It is a transition from one to another.

Jesus raised Lazarus from the dead to demonstrate that He was master of death as well as life, and that faith in Him meant the mastery of both. If we learn how to live we will have learned how to die. To do both demands the presence and power of Jesus.

We who live now must take death into account, for someday we will face it in the death of our loved ones as well as in our own experience. Here we have God's answer: the undying life of Jesus — eternal life.

29

Life from Death

11:21-57

PERHAPS by imagining that we are in a familiar cemetery beside the freshly filled grave of a loved one, with a friend who has the power to work miracles standing beside us, we can feel the drama of Lazarus' resurrection. It had been our hope that our friend, for whom we had sent, would have prevented our loved one's death, but he came too late. After an appropriate silence, our friend steps closer to the grave, speaks our loved one's name, and a thrilling thing happens — a resurrection! What a joyful reunion there is in that cemetery.

The prelude to Lazarus' resurrection began early on the fourth day after his death. Hearing that Jesus was approaching Bethany, Martha had left her home where the mourning ritual was being held. She intercepted Him on the outskirts of the village, where she voiced her bitter disappointment: "Lord, if thou hadst been here, my brother had not died" (v. 21). But Martha could summon a reserve faith, for she added, "But I know, that even now, whatsoever thou wilt ask of God, God will give it thee" (v. 22).

Jesus confirmed Martha's faith by saying, "Thy brother shall rise again" (v. 23). But Martha understood this in the indefinite terms of a resurrection day a long time hence, which gave scant comfort to her broken heart. But her misunderstanding was the occasion for Jesus to give that wonderful assurance which has given hope to millions of the dying and their bereaved: "I am the resurrection, and the life," He said, "he that believeth in me, though he were dead, yet shall he live: and whosoever liveth and believeth in me shall never die. Believest thou this?" (vv. 25-26).

The resurrection is a Person, not a day. In saying, "I am the resurrection," Jesus brings a concept which revolutionizes our thinking about death and salvation. Its solution is in a Person and its hope is now.

This is the boldest among all the "I ams" claimed by Jesus, for it holds out hope for man's greatest sorrow — the sorrow of death. Jesus distinguished between the dead who shall live again, and the living who shall never die. First, there are the dead who will live again. Whoever believes in Jesus Christ, though he die, will continue to live in heaven. Second, there are the living who will never die. Those who believe in Him may die in the sense of physical death, but eternal life is not subject to physical death. We can expect to experience the process of death if the Lord tarries, but the effects of such death cannot touch eternal life because "whosoever liveth and believeth in me shall never die."

This includes only those who believe, for Jesus said, "He that believeth in me" (v. 25) and "whosoever liveth and believeth in me" (v. 26). The promise is to believers.

Jesus immediately asked for an affirmation: "Believest thou this?" And Martha affirmed her belief: "Yea, Lord: I believe" (v. 27).

Why are faith and belief required? First, faith is necessary because of the nature of salvation which deals with two creations — an old and a new. By reason of the old we are all dying creatures; everyone who lives must die. But now we have a new creation with the purpose of supplying eternal life to counteract the dying life of the first creation. The basis of this new life is faith. Second, faith is required because we are dealing with Jesus Christ, the Son of God, and the only way to embrace Him is by an act of faith.

This was Martha's great confession which entitled her to all the benefits and blessings which flow from salvation, not the least of which would involve the life of her brother Lazarus.

Each individual should pause and ask, What about my confession? What has my response been to Jesus' "Believest thou this?" A confession involves faith and decision, both of which are related to Jesus Christ.

IT HAD CHANGED THE CONCEPT OF DEATH

Death was no longer final. It was no longer something to be feared. It had become an experience which immediately led into life. Death was something very personal, involving the restoration of loved ones and heaven in all its most intimate family aspects.

IT HAD CHANGED THE CONCEPT OF LIFE

Here were reason and incentive for living. Life had continuity and therefore purpose. It did not end in a blind alley but was a highway leading to the new heavens and earth. Halford E. Luccock wrote:

> *The New York Times* published a very interesting and sad news dispatch from Lincoln, England.
>
> A young woman climbed out on the three-inch stone ledge of the central tower of the cathedral at Lincoln, and while a crowd 240 feet below watched, she jumped to her death. For an hour she stood in that perilous position, while Canon Theodore Milford of the cathedral and three policemen pleaded with her to climb back to safety.
>
> Now, in addition to the tragedy, there is in this scene a very pertinent question which each of us might well consider. Suppose that you were out on the ledge of the cathedral with that distracted girl and were trying to persuade her to go on living, what would you have said?
>
> "What are to you the supreme incentives to living?" It is a question to which all Christians ought to have an answer. For that, in essence, is what the Church with its Gospel is trying to do, to persuade people to live bravely, effectively.
>
> Probably no one could have done anything to prevent the suicide. There was evidently severe mental derangement. But it does pose a vital question.
>
> Life has meaning in that relationship to God which it acquires in no other way. That has been a great incentive to multitudes. William James, the great philosopher, describing a time when he was in the grip of deep despair said, "Fear was so invasive and powerful that if I had not clung to scripture texts like 'the eternal God is my refuge,' etc., and 'Come unto

me all ye that labor and are heavy laden,' etc., and 'I am the resurrection and the life,' I think I should have grown really insane."

Another incentive is the remembrance of the service one may render to others. That has kept many people going along a hard way, the realization that they counted in others lives.

There is also the incentive that "the game is not over." This day may be black. But God is still God, and tomorrow will bring a new situation if we are faithful.

By this time Mary, followed by all the family's mourning friends, had joined Jesus and Martha on the outskirts of Bethany. There was uncontrolled weeping.

The tearful sorrow of a Christian is a legitimate expression of his emotional nature. While differing from other sorrow in that it is sorrow which has hope, it is the normal expression of the temporary parting of a loved one or friend. Paul says, "Ye sorrow not, even as others who have no hope" (1 Th 4:13). Ours is the sorrow of an intelligent hope, the sorrow of an abiding faith and an eternal love.

On two occasions Jesus was observed weeping, both times over man's greatest sources of trouble. Once, over life, when He wept over the city of Jerusalem with its unrepentant and unresponsive inhabitants. Once, over death, when He wept at the grave of Lazarus, although He knew that here was reversible death.

The mourners arrived at the grave which, like most graves in Palestine, was a recess cut in the side of a natural cave and closed by a huge stone fitted into a slot or inclined groove down which it had been rolled into place. On this recess lay Lazarus, four days dead, swathed from head to foot in white linen wrappings.

When Jesus ordered the stone removed, Martha shrank from the consequences of exhumation, pleading that her brother had been interred for four days. Of course she greatly erred, for whatever Jesus would do would have none of the evidences or consequences of death about it. It would be a resurrection to life, as Jesus said, for "the glory of God." So they took away the stone.

Notice the simplicity of the miracle — no breast-beating, no incantations, no clamoring or shouting. In fact, the prayer of the miracle was a silent one, spoken to His Father within His own breast. And then, "Father, I thank thee that thou hast heard me" (v. 41). That was all there was to it. "And when he thus had spoken, he cried with a loud voice, Lazarus, come forth" (v. 43), and immediately Lazarus stood out in the sunlight, blinded by the brightness of the sun.

When one views death in its Christian context he cannot rightly say that it is a tragedy. It is no tragedy to be with Christ, to go to heaven, and to live forever.

Jesus used two simple words which describe the nature of a believer's death and resurrection. He said, "Come," which brought Lazarus into life and out of the confines of the grave. That is what resurrection will do to all who believe. He said, "Go," which brought Lazarus into mobility and released him from the limitations of the graveclothes. That is what resurrection will do; it will take from us the hampering limitations of a body which is unsuited for the new life to which it will introduce us.

When do you think Lazarus prepared for death? His preparation came in the midst of life when Jesus frequently visited with him and his sisters in their home. Out of this intimacy he distilled and crystallized a faith that prepared him for death's unexpected visit.

30

After Death, What?

12:1-11

FROM THE TIME Jesus raised Lazarus from the dead His own death was only a question of time and opportunity. His enemies had determined to put Him to death because the incontestable fact of the resurrection of Lazarus had made Him dangerous to their power and position (11:47-54). Knowing this, Jesus retired with His disciples to Ephraim, where He experienced some of the most notable events of His life during the few remaining weeks before His death.

Jesus taught most of His parables at Ephraim. Here He cured a woman on the Sabbath, blessed little children, and told the rich young ruler what he had to do to have eternal life. And while passing through Jericho, He met Zacchaeus, the commissioner of customs, and changed the course of his life.

Six days before the Passover Jesus arrived at Bethany where He stayed in the house of His friends, Lazarus, Mary and Martha. These friends represent three patterns: Lazarus, the witness; Martha, the worker; and Mary, the worshiper.

LAZARUS — THE WITNESS

Lazarus was witness to the life-giving power of Christ, which made his position almost as dangerous as that of Jesus. Since many Jews were becoming believers because of Lazarus, the chief priests concluded that he must die also.

The most prominent New Testament word for witness means martyr. The one overshadowing credential for discipleship was taking up the cross, for Jesus had said, "If any man will come after me, let him deny himself, and take up his cross daily, and follow me" (Lk 9:23).

146

The nature of all witnessing is inherent in the Lazarus situation. Every Christian's existence is due to spiritual resurrection. Having been dead in a sinful nature, the saving power of God raises him to new life in Christ. He is as Lazarus was: a witness to God's resurrecting power.

A witness is a person with something to say because of what has happened to him in his encounter with Jesus and the new life. When the day comes that the church becomes a society of witnesses to the new life in Christ, it will mark the beginning of the church's greatest influence in the world.

Perhaps our present-day religious preoccupations would not begin to measure up to the magnificent living and dying of the early Christians. A young woman who had moved into a new community was a devoted member of her church and wanted an identification worthy of her faith. She said, "I went to see the minister and talked to the president of the Women's Society. I told them of my interests and experiences. I hoped they'd let me teach, or be on a program committee, or take part in a study group. Do you know what they have asked me to do? Be chairman of knitting for the bazaar." We must move beyond the simple preoccupations of our religious life into the maelstrom of human life where we can vocalize and demonstrate our faith as witnesses to Jesus' saving power.

Jesus told His disciples that they were to let their light shine "before men," to be as cities set on hills with their light extending over great areas. Few man-made things are as beautiful as a brightly illuminated city on a hill. Flying over the city of Denver at the height of 35,000 feet, one can see its tens of thousands of lights against a fresh mantle of snow — a beautiful sight indeed. It is enough to inspire candlestick witnessing. We glibly talk about loving the Lord with "all our heart," but not until we love Him with all our time, all our money, all our life, and all our influence can we truly profess a love with all our heart.

The simplest form of witnessing may lie in a sincere invitation to church:

> A group of businessmen were talking about the most significant questions they had ever asked. One after another recalled the question which had changed their lives: "Which school

shall I attend?" "Will you marry me?" "Which stock should I buy?" At last a bank president, a man of high standing in the community, told his story. "The most important question I ever asked," he said, "had nothing to do with money." He related the day long before when the village drunk, shunned by society and a burden to his family entered the bank with a request for a loan. "In the course of our conversation I simply asked, 'Why don't you come to church, Frank?' He was surprised and confused, but the following Sunday he attended church with me. The whole congregation was amazed to see him there and even more so when he became a believer and a new man in Christ. From then on he lived and at last died a faithful disciple. I've asked many questions, but none equals those simple words, "Why don't you come to church, Frank?"

MARTHA — THE WORKER

In recording Jesus' visit to Bethany, John says, "Martha served." The fact of Martha's service is worthy of emulation, for the state of the church is one of almost constant unemployment. It is crying for workers — people who are willing to dig in and not merely stand aside and watch the parade go by or sit in the stands as a spectator to the game.

The normal posture of the church is as a militant force for righteousness in a world of predatory evil. Too often it is like soldiers who are AWOL or on permanent furlough, or like ships in permanent dry dock.

Two great words are in the vocabulary of the Christian faith — *faith* and *works* — go together as naturally as horse and carriage, bread and butter, salt and pepper, peaches and cream, and love and marriage. They had better not be parted, for their affinity to each other belongs to the nature of their being. You cannot have faith without works.

An old Scotsman was operating a small rowboat for transporting passengers across one of the little lakes in Scotland. One day a passenger noticed that he had carved on one oar the word "Faith" and on the other oar the word "Works." Curiosity led him to ask the meaning of this. The old man said, "I will show you." He dropped one oar and plied the other called "Works," and they just went around in circles. Then he dropped that oar and began to ply the one called "Faith," and the little boat went around in circles again — the other way. Then the old man picked up both "Faith" and "Works" and, plying both oars together, sped swiftly over the water, explaining to his passenger, "You see, that is the way it is in life as well as in the boat."

We extol the more idealistic part that Mary played in her worship and adoration of Jesus. We should not do less, but we cannot long survive without the necessary part of Martha the worker. Christianity is to be displayed and dispensed by more ways than singing hymns and saying prayers. There is the worker aspect and the service side to Christianity. Get out your yellowed cookbook, clean up the stove, wipe off the dinnerware, polish the tarnished silver service, brighten up the door mat, hang out the old welcome sign, and bid others come in for some old-fashioned Christian hospitality. Let this grace lead you into a new and useful service for Christ.

MARY — THE WORSHIPER

One of our most mistaken notions about worship is the idea that we worship in order to get something from God. The fact is that when we truly worship we give something to God, as Mary did when she broke the alabaster box of aromatic ointment and anointed Jesus' feet.

In appeals to stimulate church attendance we stress what we will get out of worship, such as peace of mind, happiness, forgiveness and respectability. But this is the wrong approach, for it is what we give to God that constitutes an act of worship.

We can neither witness nor work effectively until we have worshiped. Where are the people who are doing the witnessing and the work of the church? They are invariably worshiping.

The anointing of Jesus at the supper at Bethany pointed up His impending death. Worship is a preparation for both our life and death. If we knew when we were to die it would undoubtedly make a difference in our church attendance. But we do know that we have to live, and this should matter too.

31

Life's Finest Hour

12:12-50

MOST PEOPLE are born into this world to live; not so the Son of God. We die because we must; He died because He chose to. His death was the object and main feature of His life. It was His life's "finest hour."

Jesus' life was occupied with many things. One description says, "He went about doing good." Another speaks of "the wonderful things that He did." John concludes his gospel by saying, "Many other signs truly did Jesus" (20:30). These things, however, were not an end in themselves.

Half of John's gospel is occupied with events relating to the death of Jesus. The most important thing in Christ's life was neither His teaching nor miracles, but His death and resurrection.

Jesus had arrived at His finest hour. He described it in these words: "The hour is come, that the Son of man should be glorified" (v. 23). This hour was in reality the whole week which stretched from what became our Sunday to the next Sunday. It was Tuesday of that week. On the first Sunday Jesus had entered the city of Jerusalem to the acclaim of the multitude who said, "Hosanna: blessed is the King of Israel that cometh in the name of the Lord" (v. 13). To this acclaim He proceeded on His way to the temple over garment-spread streets.

While this entry was the cause of acclamation from the people, it was also the cause of consternation among their leaders, who viewed with great concern the rising popularity of the man they considered dangerous to their power and position. Their comment was, "Behold, the world is gone after him" (v. 19).

Among the pilgrims who came to the feast in Jerusalem were many foreign proselytes. Some were Greeks who had heard much of Jesus and were anxious to meet Him. They appealed to Philip, saying, "Sir, we would see Jesus" (v. 21). Philip repeated their request to Andrew, and the two of them went to Jesus. Up to this moment what Jesus did was related entirely to the Jews. Now the worldwide aspects of His redemptive ministry were becoming apparent. But Jesus answered His disciples, "The hour is come, that the Son of man should be glorified. . . . Except a corn of wheat fall into the ground and die, it abideth alone: but if it die, it bringeth forth much fruit." Jesus had come as the Saviour of the world, but until His death on the cross He was not yet their sacrifice for sin.

There is something poignant in the appeal of these Greek pilgrims — "Sir, we would see Jesus." Was it curiosity of Jesus' looks that made them want to see Him? Was it curiosity of His dress and manners? Probably not. It must have stemmed from an inner longing which they wanted satisfied. No doubt they felt the urge to know God, although they came from a nation of many gods. It was the hunger for life they wanted satisfied. This is the real reason for anyone wanting to see Jesus: the satisfaction of human longings, the fulfillment of human hopes, the realization of human desires.

The desire of the Greeks is a characteristic of human nature. We are made for God, and only God can satisfy the basic demands of our natures. Jesus said, "Man doth not live by bread only, but by every word that proceedeth out of the mouth of God."

How did these foreigners know about Jesus? Undoubtedly they were in the crowd that saw Jesus come into the city a few days previous. Luccock writes,

> Did you ever see a person looking at a photograph of a group of which he was a member? He searches eagerly to find his own picture. One concern dominates him: "How did I come out?" We are all inevitably interested in what concerns us. Here is a similar game you may try with another picture. It may prove to be a disturbing, but a rewarding thing. The picture is the large painting by Robert Haydon of Christ entering Jerusalem. This is how it is described in Hewlett's life of Keats, *Adonais* —

Christ's Entry in Jerusalem, now in St. Mary's Seminary, Norwood, Ohio, shows Christ riding on an ass, and closely surrounded by a throng of people. In imitation of Old Masters, Haydon put in figures of modern historical personages, and also of living persons. Voltaire, at this time the hero of the liberal free-thinkers, and the devil of the orthodox, was put in as a smiling scoffer; Sir Isaac Newton as a believer; Hazlitt as a detached observer; Wordsworth as a devout man; and Keats, a bright amazed face in the background.

Take it from there! Think of Christ in our world and His cause in the world. Then think of yourself and your actions and attitudes. How would you find yourself in that picture? Would you be a "smiling scoffer" or a "detached observer"? Would there be any "bright amazement" in your face? We are in the crowd which watches Christ coming into our world. What would be the truest painting of ourselves in that picture?

What did Jesus do to satisfy the curiosity of these men? He told them of His impending death:

The hour is come, that the Son of man should be glorified. Verily, verily, I say unto you, Except a corn of wheat fall into the ground and die, it abideth alone: but if it die, it bringeth forth much fruit. He that loveth his life shall lose it; and he that hateth his life in this world shall keep it unto life eternal. If any man serve me, let him follow me; and where I am, there shall also my servant be: if any man serve me, him will my Father honour (vv. 23-26).

This was to be Jesus' finest hour — when He would meet and satisfy the deepest desires of the human heart, consisting of peace with God, forgiveness of sin, purpose for life, life after death, and the knowledge of God. Jesus said, "My life is like a seed that must fall into the ground and die in order to bring forth a harvest. My life remains limited and bound up in itself as long as I live, but when I die this life of mine will pass on to others and multiply itself throughout the world." Then He revealed one of the greatest secrets of life: "He that loveth his life shall lose it; and he that hateth his life in this world shall keep it unto life eternal" (v. 25). Luccock says,

There is a striking narrative in de Harsanyi's novel of the life of Galileo, entitled *The Star Gazer*. Young Galileo became so depressed and discouraged in his early life that he decided to drown himself. He went down to the banks of the Tiber river, and paused a moment before throwing himself in. He got to thinking of his lifeless body floating in the river. But from that morbid thought his quick mind went on to raise the question, would the body float, and if so, why? The next step was to think of the law of specific gravity, and how it could be measured. The idea took such possession of his mind that suicide was forgotten, and he rushed home to begin the experiments which resulted in the invention of the hydrostatic scales. He was saved by an idea! The negative thinking which was dragging him down was replaced by a stronger positive thought which set him free from despair. It is a picture of the way in which the ideas of Christianity have a saving power. Here are some saving ideas of the Christian gospel: the reality of a God of love, the power that comes into life when Christ is given an entrance, the forgetting of self in serving the needs of others.

The heart of the Christian gospel is the cross. Jesus had just spoken of this. You cannot have life without death, a crown without a cross, gain without loss. We cannot go up except we go down.

Whatever men hate about Christianity is centered in the cross. Even non-Christians think well of Jesus; it is the cross they hate. Paul said, "For many walk, of whom I have told you often, and now tell you even weeping, that they are the enemies of the cross of Christ" (Phil 3:18). It is one thing to preach Christ, and another to preach the cross of Christ. One can extol Jesus as a great teacher, example and healer, but it is the cross that provides salvation.

Twice in Jesus' career God spoke concerning His Son. Once, at the beginning of Jesus' ministry at the Jordan, God said, "This is my beloved Son: hear him" (Mk 9:7). Now at the conclusion, God spoke concerning the cross. After Jesus said, "Father, glorify thy name," a voice from heaven said, "I have both glorified it, and will glorify it again" (Jn 12:28). God has spoken; this is the divine way.

One of the great tragedies of human experience is recorded in verse 37: "Though he had done so many miracles before them, yet they believed not on him." With all the advantages of proximity, of sight and sound, of observation and conversation, these people "believed not on him."

Jesus went on to say to the people that when they believed on Him they were also believing on God: "He that believeth on me, believeth not on me, but on him that sent me. And he that seeth me seeth him that sent me" (vv. 44-45). The consequences of faith are life, forgiveness and heaven.

The alternative to faith is unbelief. The alternative to life is death. The alternative to salvation is judgment. The person who rejects Christ rejects God. "I am come a light into the world, that whosoever believeth on me should not abide in darkness. And if any man hear my words, and believe not, I judge him not: for I came not to judge the world, but to save the world. He that rejecteth me, and receiveth not my words, hath one that judgeth him: the word that I have spoken, the same shall judge him in the last day" (vv. 46-48).

What Jesus said is that each person judges himself. When we reject His witness and salvation, we do not need to be charged with a bill of particulars. We have our own judgment, and it is in our own heart. We will and have been judged by our own conscience. More than this, the final judgment will be rendered against us on the basis of our self-judgment and Jesus' word.

Jesus preached judgment as well as salvation and proclaimed law as well as love. He mentioned the consequences of unbelief as well as the blessings of faith.

The important thing at the moment is our attitude to these things. What have we done with our privileges? What is our relationship to God? Where are we going when we die? We are the only ones who can answer these questions.

32

The Secret of Happiness

13:1-17

THURSDAY MORNING of the last week was spent in preparation for the Passover, with its Paschal supper which would be held that evening in commemoration of the departure of the Israelites from Egypt. When all was ready Jesus took His place on the cushions on which the guests reclined at meals.

But before the Paschal supper was served, Jesus arose and girded Himself with the linen cloth of a slave and prepared to wash His disciples' feet. He began with Peter, who misunderstood the intentions of Jesus and shrank from allowing His Master to humble Himself to such a degree. He did not realize the meaning of this symbolic act. When Jesus told him that if He did not wash his feet he would have no part in Him, Peter then wanted not only his feet washed, but his whole body. At this point the real significance of the feet-washing act is evident, for Jesus told Peter it was not necessary for him to have the whole bath (v. 10). This had already been done according to Jewish custom before the meal. He who then had the whole bath needed only to have his feet cleansed, for on his way to the feast, street dust would have made him unclean.

The spiritual application shows the difference between regeneration and sanctification. Regeneration is comparable to the bath which cleansed the whole body, while sanctification is comparable to the washing of the feet which takes care of our walk, for as we engage in the ordinary contacts of life we accumulate defilement and need this washing. In the believer's life, regeneration is a once-for-all act of God which cleanses and purifies the whole person. When he is contaminated by the defilements of daily life, he does not need the total spiritual bath of regeneration, only the washing of sanctification — cleansing from life's daily defilements.

There is no evidence of any feet-washing practice within the church before the fourth century, showing that the practice itself did not immediately follow the apostolic experience in the upper room. Like the ancient practice of the "holy kiss," feet-washing had a practical meaning in local customs which are now outmoded. But the spiritual implication is still valid. The most significant teaching of this incident lies in the fact that if we have been regenerated, we stand in daily need of the sanctifying grace of God to be kept clean from the daily defilement of an earthly walk.

The focus of the whole event in the upper room is then placed on the disciples by Jesus: "If ye know these things, happy are ye if ye do them" (v. 17). Our happiness rests on how well we do what Jesus teaches. One great pedagogic principle is that we learn by doing. *Do* is an action verb and Jesus places its responsibility upon us by saying that our well-being rests on our doing: "Happy are ye if ye do them." The instruction given by Jesus is centered in two focuses — to know and to do. We must know, and what we know we must do.

Most people have all the knowledge they need for the right kind of life, but they need to put that knowledge into practice. It is much like the farmer who said, when he was urged to attend a meeting on better farming methods, "I already know more about farming than I can put into practice." Most of us know more about the Christian life than we put into practice.

Currently the American public is spending one hundred million dollars on mood pills which promise a new pleasure world of relaxation, freedom from worry, and assurance of regular sleep. But it is quite impossible to put on happiness like a garment, or swallow it through a pill. Happiness does not come from the state of relaxation but rather from action — "Happy are ye if ye do them."

The secret of happiness is in knowing that we live by the law of expenditure. We find the greatest joy, not in getting, but in expressing what we are. There are tides in the ocean of life, and what comes in depends on what goes out. The currents flow inward only where there is an outlet. Empty your lungs and breathe. Run, climb, work and laugh; the more you give out, the more you shall receive. Be exhausted, and you shall be fed. It is a higher joy to teach than to be taught. It is good to get justice, but better to do it; fun to have things but more fun to make them. The happy man is he who lives the life of love, not for the honors it may bring, but for the life itself.

The beginning of the Christian life is becoming someone new, whereas the goal of this life is becoming someone better. Most problems of faith will be found not to be doctrinal, but to be concerned with the problems involved in the everyday struggle to become someone better.

If one thing is more certain than another, it is that the Christian church needs to marshal all its resources of grace so that its people will become these better persons. Let us put action into our faith and we will get somewhere in our lives.

The Christian life is a fine balance between knowing and doing. It is not something you believe and tuck away for six days of the week and then give a religious airing. It is action.

We have tried to persuade people that they will be happy if they will go to church. But happiness comes only by putting into action what has come to our knowledge through a worship experience. Jesus is telling us what He found true in His own experience. He had said to His disciples at the well of Sychar, "I have meat to eat that ye know not of. . . . My meat is to do the will of him that sent me, and to finish his work" (Jn 4:32-34). He had found a greater satisfaction in spiritual experience. He really was saying, "I'd rather do this than eat."

The book of James is an action book full of activity, movement, adventure and exploration. Its great instruction is: "But be ye doers of the word, and not hearers only" (Ja 1:22). This doing is personal, not corporate, for it belongs to the individual, not the community.

Our technological revolution has put the awesome computer at our disposal. Even the text of the Bible is now submitted to automation. The new Revised Standard Version concordance of the Bible was produced with the help of Univac. By means of tapes fed to the computer it has produced a new concordance, sorting alphabetically and in Genesis-to-Revelation order the 800,000 words of the Bible's sixty-six books, with contexts. But while automation may come to the Bible in this way, its teaching and principles cannot be automated; this is left for individual action. One will never know the Bible as a living book without living it. These are days for doing Christians, not dozing Christians. Sleep is not for this thrilling hour of history. This is time for doing, for adventure, for action.

When we know and do not do, we are neglecting our responsibility; but when we do and do not know, we are acting with zeal that lacks knowledge. When we know, we are like a thermometer registering the temperature. When we do we are like a thermostat, doing something about it. If we put the "know" and the "do" together we will have a thrilling adventure on the highest level of life.

KNOWS AND DOS

THE "KNOW" AND THE "DO" OF SALVATION

Paul said, "I know whom I have believed" (2 Ti 1:12). Put the "do" with this "know" and then "work out your own salvation with fear and trembling" (Phil 2:12).

THE "KNOW" AND THE "DO" OF PRAYER

John said, "And this is the confidence that we have in him, that, if we ask any thing according to his will, he heareth us; and if we know that he hear us, whatsoever we ask, we know that we have the petitions that we desired of him" (1 Jn 5:14-15).

THE "KNOW" AND THE "DO" OF CONSECRATION

Paul said, "What? Know ye not that your body is the temple of the Holy Ghost which is in you, which ye have of God, and ye are not your own? For ye are bought with a price" (1 Co 6:19-20). A purpose and meaning for life can only be established in our relationship with God, a relationship which can only have significance by a life of "knowing" and "doing."

33

"This Do in Remembrance"

13:18-30

IT WAS THE NIGHT BEFORE Jesus' crucifixion. Earlier in the day He had given instructions to two of His disciples to prepare the Passover. Upon entering the city of Jerusalem from Bethany, they would meet a man bearing an earthen jar of water. They were to follow him to his house and say, "The Teacher told us to ask you where we would find the room in which He intended to eat the Passover with His disciples." This man would show them his guest chamber on the upper floor, provided with couches, and would have the supper prepared.

According to prearrangement, the disciples assembled at the appointed hour. Before the Passover was served, Jesus rose and, putting on the slave's apron, washed His disciples' feet. Following this act of humility, the events of the upper room unfold in all their significant proportions.

Two suppers were served on this night: the first, or Paschal supper, and the second, or Lord's Supper. The Paschal supper was the end of an old era; the Lord's Supper was the beginning of a new era. The Paschal supper was under the old covenant; the Lord's Supper is under the new covenant. The Paschal supper was a memorial of the Passover when the death angel passed over Egypt and the firstborn were killed or saved; the Lord's Supper is a memorial of the death of Christ as Saviour of the world. Both of the suppers are related to death: the Paschal supper to the death of a lamb to save the firstborn, and the Lord's Supper to the death of the Son of God to save the world. The Paschal supper was done away with by the death of Christ; the Lord's Supper was begun as a memorial to the death of Christ. The Paschal supper was observed with the use of a lamb

159

roasted over coals and was a sign that death had already taken place; the Lord's Supper was observed by the use of bread and wine. The bread was a memorial of Christ's body, and the wine a memorial of Christ's blood, both of which were a part of His act of redemption on the cross.

The formula of the Lord's Supper is described in Matthew's account: "As they were eating, Jesus took bread, and blessed it, and brake it, and gave it to the disciples, and said, Take, eat; this is my body. And he took the cup, and gave thanks, and gave it to them, saying, Drink ye all of it; for this is my blood of the new testament, which is shed for many for the remission of sins" (26:26-28). What did Jesus mean by these words? Theology expresses many opinions. The Roman Catholics hold the view of transubstantiation in which the wafer, or host, becomes the corporeal flesh and the molecular body of Christ when the priestly celebrant of the Mass says, "Hoc est corpus meum." The Lutherans believe in consubstantiation, in which the bread does not actually change into the fleshly substance of the body of Jesus, but the real presence of Jesus comes alongside, or with the bread, so that Jesus is present in the supper. The Episcopalians speak of "the Real Presence," by which they mean that Jesus is personally and bodily present in the Eucharist. This constitutes a sacrament through which God communicates either saving or special grace by the observance of the supper. To the opposite extreme are such groups as the Quakers and the Salvation Army, who neither observe the Lord's Supper nor practice baptism because they believe both are superceded by the spiritual experience of believers who do not need physical rites of any kind.

The bread used at the Lord's Supper was said by Jesus to be "my body." Upon numerous occasions Jesus had cause to say similar things. He said, "I am the light of the world, I am the water of life, I am the bread of life, and I am the door." In these instances these were figures of speech which took physical things to set forth a spiritual truth. When He said, "I am the door," Jesus did not mean a door of wood, giving ingress or egress to or from a room, but that He was the door of life, giving access to God.

The bread and wine of the communion table remain what they were when placed upon it — just bread and wine, nothing more and nothing less. They do not need to be anything more than bread and wine. The disciples were to hold Jesus "in remembrance," not in participation. They were to commune, not consume.

The significance of the Lord's Supper lies in its spiritual representation, for the elements are representative of the things which brought salvation into being. When we partake of them we are not eating Christ's body or drinking His blood; we are partaking of the spiritual properties of Christ's nature in order to nourish our spiritual being. God does not use physical things to nourish spiritual beings. If the bread dipped in wine becomes the body and blood of Jesus, it is the wrong use of a spiritual intention.

Furthermore, this is not a sacrifice; it is a supper. The sacrificial part of salvation is finished, and there is no further need to reconstruct a body or reproduce a viscous fluid for sacrificial purposes. The communion of the Lord's Supper is celebrated at a table, not upon an altar. It is the remembrance of a past act, not the reconstruction of a present sacrifice. Those who preside at this table are not priests but witnesses.

When the Lord's Supper is linked with baptism we see both of them as spiritual ordinances to be observed as symbolic acts that call attention to the nature of our salvation. In baptism the element is water. Some use this water to pour over the head of the person being baptized, while others use it to sprinkle over the head. Still others totally immerse the body.

In the use of water, a symbol of death or the grave, we never say that it is actual death or a literal grave. It is only representative of death into which, in the case of immersion, the body is laid in burial and out of which it is raised in resurrection, with the further scriptural obligation to "walk in newness of life."

To carry out the significance of both ordinances of the Lord's Supper and baptism, we do not need to say that the bread is the physical body of Jesus, that the wine is the viscous fluid of His bloodstream, or that the water is physical death and a grave.

The Lord's Supper is unlike baptism in that baptism symbolizes the beginning of the new life within the soul of the believer,

whereas the Lord's Supper symbolizes the continuous sustaining
of that new life through the power of the living Christ. As baptism symbolizes the incorporation of the believer into Christ, the
Lord's Supper symbolizes the incorporation of Christ into the believer.

It is wrong to assume that a miracle occurs and the bread is
literally changed into Christ's body every time a celebrant of the
mass blesses it. This is because the bread that was used for the
first Lord's Supper in the upper room was the same bread that
was used for the Paschal supper that preceded it; the same is
also true of the wine. Four cups of wine were successively used
in connection with the Paschal meal, and it was the fourth and
final Paschal cup that became the wine of the Lord's Supper.
Why should not the bread and wine of the Paschal supper, which
had been used figuratively, symbolically and memorially for almost two thousand years, not continue to be used in the same
sense in the Lord's Supper? The disciples were accustomed to
the memorial nature of both suppers. One had been a memorial,
and nothing more, for centuries before. The other would be a
memorial, and nothing more, for centuries to come.

The purpose of this memorial supper was to have a physical
means by which to hold in view the redemptive work of Christ.
It was also a common gathering place for the fellowship of believers throughout all ages and in all places.

The Lord's Supper is a

> feast of remembrance — "This do in remembrance of me."
> feast of representation — "This is my body."
> feast of appropriation — "Take eat."
> feast of witness — "Ye do show forth the Lord's death till
> he come."
> feast of communion — "a communion of the body and blood
> of Christ."

THE LORD'S SUPPER IN TERMS OF DIRECTIONS

IT LOOKS BACKWARD TO THE CROSS

"Ye do shew forth the Lord's death" (1 Co 11:26). In looking
backward to the cross this supper recognizes the finished nature

of Christ's death. There He exclaimed, "It is finished." By this token we recognize that if the cross finished redemption, it also finished the priestly system, all sacrifices, all works of satisfaction, and all human efforts of self-salvation.

While this supper looks backward it leads forward, since the strength of our forward progress is in the backward look that gives us our spiritual stamina and stability. At the table of the Lord's Supper we stand beside the cross.

IT LOOKS UPWARD TO HEAVEN

"This do in remembrance of me" (1 Co 11:24). The Lord's Supper brings the remembrance of Jesus in heaven performing His high-priestly ministry: "This man, after he had offered . . . sat down on the right hand of God" (Heb 10:12). We understand this not as a physical act, but as a spiritual position symbolizing completeness, finality and authority.

IT LOOKS INWARD TO THE SOUL

"Let a man examine himself" (1 Co 11:28). The table of the Lord's Supper is a place both for spiritual and moral cleansing, but also for spiritual protection, self-introspection and examination.

IT LOOKS OUTWARD TO THE COMMUNITY OF BELIEVERS

"For we being many are one bread, and one body" (1 Co 10:17). This supper not only renews our fellowship with Christ; it establishes fellowship with believers — here and everywhere — who gather in similar observance.

David A. MacLennan, who was a well-known dean of theology, used to say that he scarcely believed that the devil is terrified when he sees a Presbyterian forefinger, or a Lutheran middle finger, or an Episcopalian thumb, or a Methodist or Baptist third finger pointed at him. It is when those fingers and thumb were doubled up in one compelling fist that his satanic majesty began to take notice.

IT LOOKS FORWARD TO CHRIST'S RETURN

"Ye do shew the Lord's death till he come" (1 Co 11:26). The table of the Lord's Supper is security against the common frustrations and disappointments encountered in the affairs of this world. It is the church's answer to the world's inability to compose its mounting nuclear problems. Here is both continuity and destiny. Our future is foreshadowed in the multicolored "northern lights" surrounding the Lord's Supper.

34

Quo Vadis?

13:31-38

THE INSTITUTION of the Lord's Supper at the end of the Passover meal was the farewell occasion when Jesus bade good-bye to His disciples in the quiet and tender intimacy of the upper room. This was to indicate the exact nature of the Redeemer's death, for when, at the Lord's Supper, He said, "This cup is the new covenant in my blood" (1 Co 11:25, margin), His disciples understood that Jesus must die. It was a new covenant and therefore different from the Old Testament rites. It was to be in the Saviour's blood and therefore would require His death.

A sad and sinister event transpired at this memorable feast. It was the identification of Judas as the betrayer, and his final and complete separation from the twelve by leaving the room to go about his traitorous business.

When Judas went out it was described in these words: "And it was night" (v. 30). How deep and wide is the contrast between the fate of Judas and that, for instance, of John. One went out into the night, the other into the light. One went to the company of the crucifiers, the other to the company of Jesus. Judas, and no one else, was responsible for his fate and we must all decide our own fate. We must all make up our minds with whom our lot of life is to be cast — with the Son of God as our Saviour, or with His enemies. The difference is determined by an act of faith by which we determine our destiny.

It was custom among the Jews to mingle songs of praise to God with their feasts. Because of this the little company in the upper room had already sung the first two of the six psalms which formed the great hallelujah of the Passover (Ps 113, 118). Then came the other psalms and, finally at the close, the final words

of Psalm 118, "O give thanks unto the Lord; for he is good: for
his mercy endureth for ever." With this song all was over, and
Jesus said, "Now is the Son of man glorified, and God is glorified
in him" (v. 31). And turning to His disciples, He gave them a
final intimation of the ordeal that awaited Him: "Little children,
yet a little while I am with you. Ye shall seek me: and as I
said unto the Jews, Whither I go, ye cannot come; so now I say
to you" (v. 33).

Where was Jesus going that His disciples could not come?
Surely no place in Jerusalem, for they knew every part of that
ancient city. Surely no part of Palestine, and no part of the
world. He was speaking of an experience and not a place. The
experience was death and He had to die alone, for only He
could die the death of redemption. This is where He would go
and they could not come.

Jesus then put a new dimension to that death of love. He said,
"A new commandment I give unto you, That ye love one another; as I have loved you, that ye also love one another. By
this shall all men know that ye are my disciples, if ye have love
one to another" (vv. 34-35). It does not say that loving one another is a condition of salvation. Rather, it says that love is a
proof that we possess salvation and are Christ's disciples.

We have used all manner of tests: reciting creeds, wearing
clothes, observing rites, performing deeds and a multitude of religious exercises. But Jesus indicates that the final and conclusive
test of true discipleship is the measure of our Christian love.
Tertullian, one of the early church Fathers, said that the remark
most commonly made by the pagans about the early Christians
was "See how these Christians love one another."

When Christendom is equated with Christianity, the result is
embarrassing. Armin C. Oldsen relates that during World War I
a cartoon pictured the so-called Christian nations of Europe and
America engaged in a death struggle in an arena. The Japanese,
Chinese and African people were viewing the bloody spectacle
with bewilderment, and a grinning Japanese was saying, "How
these Christians love one another." The problem is that so few
are truly Christian.

Jesus' statement tells us that the most important aspect of Christianity is in the personal relations of Christians. Here is the greatest apologetic for Christianity. We have been restricting the defense of our faith to the terminology of words which have divided rather than united us. They divide us at the Lord's table, where we become separated by definitions; in our understanding of Scripture, where we are separated by interpretations; and in our public relations, where we are separated by conduct. Something is basically wrong with anyone's faith if there is not love enough to embrace the whole community of Christians. Love is described as the greatest thing in the world. Why then should it be the least of our virtues?

Jesus Was Going to the Cross

One of the most intriguing questions of all the Bible is asked by Peter of Jesus, "Lord, whither goest thou?" (v. 36). Having risen from supper, there was no mistaking the direction in which Jesus was going. He was bound for the cross. This is indicated by His answer to Peter's question: "Whither I go, thou canst not follow me now; but thou shalt follow me afterwards. Peter said unto him, Lord, why cannot I follow thee now? I will lay down my life for thy sake. Jesus answered him, Wilt thou lay down thy life for my sake? Verily, verily, I say unto thee, The cock shall not crow, till thou hast denied me thrice" (vv. 36-38). Jesus was going where Peter could not come — to the cross.

Peter would die, as would most of the disciples, a martyr's death; but this was not the nature of Jesus' death. It would be the Redeemer's death, not a martyr's death. Jesus went to the cross without deviations or detours. This was settled at the temptation in the wilderness where Satan offered Him the crown of universal dominion without the cross of universal redemption. Jesus settled this forever and marched forthrightly to the cross.

Jesus Was Going to the World

Jesus went to the world by way of the cross. The cross rather than the sword proved to be the most effective way to win the world. Alexander the Great, who died at the approximate age of Jesus, proved this; for his work did not endure. He had conquered the world, but death overtook him before he could consolidate his vision of a universal commonwealth. He died in Babylon surrounded by all its ancient glory, but today not a trace remains of Alexander's brief passage. He used a sword, Jesus a Cross. Alexander made history, Jesus changed it.

How will Jesus go to the world? A story tells of Jesus' return to heaven after His ascension. He talked with the angel Gabriel about His work on earth, and Gabriel asked what provision He had made for the spread of the gospel to the world. Jesus said, "I told it to Peter, James and John and a number of other faithful disciples. The plan is that they shall tell it to their generation, and that generation to the next generation, and so on until the end." Gabriel asked, "But suppose the disciples fail to tell it to their generation, or suppose some other generation should fail, what other plan have you?" Jesus replied, "I have no other plan." Jesus' way to go to the world is through the lips and lives of His disciples. If they fail, He does not go.

Jesus Was Going to the Human Heart

Jesus' ultimate intention and the purpose of redemption were that He would find His place in the hearts of men. Here the problems of the world will be settled, for here the world will be changed and made better, not on the battlefields, in the laboratories, in the classrooms, in the libraries, or even in the parliaments.

Today's two most desired goals of scientific research are the creation of life and the preservation of life. In an article on scientific achievements in surgery, a writer said, "Man may strain even farther into space, even deeper into the heart of the atom, but in the operating room all the results of the most improbable reaches of research, all the immense accumulation of medical knowledge are drawn upon in a determined drive toward the most awesome goal of all: the preservation of one human life." Is this indeed the most awesome goal of all? Does it not seem strange that we are spending so many millions in our efforts to create life when our greatest problem is to care for and correct the life we already have?

Jesus knew where He had to go if He would complete His redemptive mission. The most notable journey He ever took was His journey to the hearts of men, and He was bound there by way of the cross.

Rachel Saint, writing from the jungle home of the Auca tribe in Ecuador, rejoiced in the effects of the gospel on these primitive people. Uncle Gikita, the oldest man of the group and the leader of the team that killed the missionaries in 1956, said recently, "I used to be hateful, but now my heart is healed." He gives every evidence that the once-bitter fountain is now sending forth sweet water. It was to such a heart that Jesus went when Peter asked him, "Whither goest thou?"

It is to all hearts that Jesus would go for "God so loved the world, that he gave his only begotten Son, that whosoever believeth in him should not perish, but have everlasting life."

35

Heaven — How to Get There

14:1-6

IT IS FAR MORE IMPORTANT to know how to get to heaven than to know what heaven is like. Yet, most of our concern and inquiry is about the place. We can be sure of one thing: heaven as a place will be wonderful and beautiful. Jesus describes it as "my Father's house," Paul calls it a "King's garden" (paradise), and John names it the "new Jerusalem."

When we think of getting to heaven it implies a place, and this implies a location. Where is heaven located? We instinctively say "up," but this direction is only relative and does not indicate a specific location. Yet heaven as a place must have a location.

Most of our thinking about heaven has been dictated by our emotions, for we think of it in terms of a place of blessed reunion with departed loved ones. But considered objectively we must conceive of heaven not so much in terms of so many square miles of territory but as a new creation with all its vast and varied implications. The New Testament speaks of a new heaven and earth: "And I saw a new heaven and a new earth: for the first heaven and the first earth were passed away" (Rev 21:1). This would indicate the end of an old order and the beginning of a new, which is described in 2 Peter 3:10-13. Far from being the end of the world, it is the beginning of a new system whose governing and qualifying distinction is found in the words "wherein dwelleth righteousness."

What is in view is not only a new heaven but a new earth. This means a new creation which is the heart of the idea of heaven. As there will be a new people by regeneration, so there will be a new place for these people.

If heaven poses a problem of place, another problem arises when we think of God. He is described in the Bible in terms of personality, which means a person, and a person implies a body. While the human person is identified with a physical body, this is not true of God, who is identified as a "Spirit." But that Spirit which is God is neither ghost, sprite, nor apparition. Spirit when related to the new creation indicates reality. For instance, when we will be related to the new creation we will have spiritual bodies. But a spiritual body is not a body which is spirit but a body suited to the uses of the spirit in an environment as substantial as our physical environment.

Outer space, if that is where heaven is located, is a different place from space. The spacemen who are preparing for an extensive invasion of outer space can only do so by protecting their bodies from the absence of atmospheric pressure and the lack of vital oxygen. But the Christian is not going to invade outer space with his present body. The Bible speaks of a new body (1 Co 15:35-44; 48-58) which will have locomotion, a new form of nutrition, and will be recognized in terms of its earthly relationships.

When all the descriptive parts are put together, there is a place called heaven, embracing a new heaven and earth. There will be new bodies capable of sustained life throughout the vast reaches of the new creation. This means a vast new world of experience which, at present, we are not even capable of imagining.

In an age when man stands poised on the edge of outer space in the foreseeable future, the Christian can look beyond these prospects to a permanent abode with God. He will not be hampered and limited by spacesuits or spaceships, but will have a body which is perfectly suited to his new environment.

The question of heaven and how to get there involves two things — direction and dynamics.

DIRECTION

Heaven is a place, for Jesus said, "I go to prepare a place." It is not simply a state of mind or a condition of life. The heavenly life is not going to be less than our earthly life, which is not a state of mind. It is in a body, and that body is in a place.

All the directions concerning heaven and how to get there are spiritual because getting to heaven is a spiritual problem, not a physical one. It is related to the spirit, not to the body, for "flesh and blood cannot inherit the kingdom of God." Before we can get to heaven, there must be a change from a physical body to a spiritual body for "this corruptible must put on incorruption, and this mortal must put on immortality" (1 Co 15:53).

In our world, getting to New York from Los Angeles is principally a problem of dynamics in transporting a body by some means of transportation. But getting to heaven, while also a problem of dynamics, is more particularly a problem of direction, for it involves a spiritual body; hence the spiritual conditions involved.

A great many questions are involved when thinking about the future. Three important statements appear in this textual vicinity:

Peter asks in John 13:37, "Lord, why cannot I follow thee now?"

Jesus answers in John 14:1-4, "Let not your heart be troubled: ye believe in God, believe also in me. In my Father's house are many mansions: if it were not so, I would have told you. I go to prepare a place for you. And if I go and prepare a place for you, I will come again, and receive you unto myself; that where I am, there ye may be also."

Thomas asks in John 14:5, "Lord, we know not whither thou goest; and how can we know the way?"

Jesus answers in John 14:6, "I am the way, the truth, and the life: no man cometh unto the Father, but by me."

Philip says in John 14:8, "Lord, shew us the Father, and it sufficeth us."

Jesus responds in 14:9, "Have I been so long time with you, and yet hast thou not known me, Philip? He that hath seen me hath seen the Father."

When Jesus said, "And whither I go ye know, and the way ye know," two things are involved:

WHERE — "WHITHER I GO YE KNOW"

This refers to the place which Jesus had described as His Father's house, a place of mansions or resting places. This is where He was going — to a place. But this location of heaven is only the nerve center of the new creation from which the whole expanse of the new world is operated. It is to that extent God's residence, but it is not the total extent of the new heavens and earth.

THE WAY — "THE WAY YE KNOW"

The way to heaven, as already noted, is spiritual and not physical. Thomas asked the second question of these three statements: "Lord, we know not whither thou goest; and how can we know the way?" Jesus answered, "I am the way, the truth, and the life."

Jesus makes no reference to Thomas' statement, "We know not whither thou goest." He says nothing about where He is going or where heaven is, but He does talk about how to get there when He says, "I am the way." Jesus is the way to heaven. We do not get to heaven by being good, saying prayers, balancing the budget of morality by having sufficient credits to offset the debits, by going to church, by paying our debts, or because we are baptized or catechized. Nothing of this sort is involved in the directions or conditions of entrance into heaven.

Involved in Jesus' reply are three things related to the person of Jesus, the Redeemer and Saviour of the world:

1. *Following* — "*I am the way.*" We walk or follow in the same direction Jesus is going. He repeatedly called upon men to "follow" Him. This is both principle and direction, both a way *to* life and a way *of* life.

2. *Believing* — "*I am the truth.*" You can do just two things with truth: reject it or accept it. Faith in Jesus Christ as a personal Saviour is made the paramount condition of salvation, and salvation is the paramount condition of getting to heaven. What does it mean to believe and have faith? It means to have faith in the Bible as the Word of God, and in Jesus Christ as the Son of God. It means to have faith in His directions for life, His work as the Redeemer, and in His death upon the cross. If we are to

believe the Bible, a saving faith is something exclusive and not inclusive. It centers in Christ and excludes all others.

3. *Living* — *"I am the Life."* In one of His earlier announcements Jesus said, "I am come that they might have life" (Jn 10: 10). This was His greatest and most important contribution to man. Life can come in only one way: by creation and procreation. Creation is origin, and procreation is birth. Jesus said to Nicodemus, "Marvel not that I said unto thee, Ye must be born again" (Jn 3:7).

All three — following, believing and living — are tied together. They are related to a single experience, salvation, that becomes the direction of life and the way to heaven.

Dynamics

Direction as we have considered it means two things: (1) a line or course in which anyone is moving, or toward which anything is pointed; and (2) the principles and conditions by which we gain our objective. The word *dynamics* means the energy or power to get to our objective, which in this case is heaven.

A law of dynamics, which is so important in this day of preparation for and movement into outer space, involves the motion of bodies and the power by which these bodies are propelled. The same law in its spiritual sense is connected with getting to heaven. Many people are pointed in the right direction and have good and proper ideals, but power is as necessary as purpose.

If the directions involved in getting to heaven are spiritual, it is also true that the energy and power to get there are spiritual. A person does not get to heaven just because he wants to, any more than he can get to cities like New York and Paris by desire alone. Getting there involves dynamics.

In this life, dynamics are always associated with the proper vehicle because getting anywhere on this earth requires the proper vehicle and is not achieved in a disembodied state or desire. Getting to heaven requires the proper vehicle too. While it is true that it partially involves a disembodied relationship, such as that described in 2 Corinthians 5, yet the final state is in a spiritual body. The real power involved in these dynamics is the power of a new life.

John Wesley once told of a dream in which he stood at the gates of hell. He asked the gatekeeper if there were Catholics there. "Many" was the answer. "And Presbyterians?" "Many" was again the answer. "And Methodists?" "Many." Later he stood before the gates of heaven, where he asked the same questions. "There are no Catholics, no Presbyterians, no Methodists here" was the answer. "Only Christians."

Since heaven is a place for Christians, it is because the Christian's life is of such a nature that it has the right direction and the proper dynamics. Therefore there is great importance in having our lives pointed in the right direction and equipped with sufficient energy to go that way.

In the Louisiana hurricane-flood disaster some years ago, the National Civil Defense Administrator estimated that at least five hundred victims perished needlessly. "Not a single life need to have been lost," he said, "if people had only heeded the warnings and the weather bureau and moved to places of refuge. Instead, those who were drowned or crushed to death by the hurricane winds and the wall of water which swept twenty-five miles inland, refused to leave their homes." Here catastrophe could have been averted if people had only followed directions. The same is true where salvation and heaven are involved. Safety lies in following directions; missing the way is a needless tragedy.

36

Seeing God

14:7-11

ONE OF THE GREAT unsatisfied curiosities of the human mind is what God looks like. No one has been able to accurately satisfy this curiosity with an authentic description, so we are left to such statements as Jesus made to Philip: "He that hath seen me hath seen the Father" (v. 9). This is not a contradiction of an earlier statement to the Samaritan woman, "God is a Spirit" (4:24). Christ is the human manifestation of the divine, and the physical incarnation of the Spirit. God said to Moses, "Thou canst not see my face: for there shall no man see me, and live" (Ex 33:20).

What is being described in the gospel of John relates to a personal crisis which will sooner or later come to all men — the crisis of seeing God. Men have an unsatisfied hunger to see God, even if that seeing is not by physical sight. This seeing is not by the eyes, but by the soul.

The circumstances of this personal crisis are found in the events of the Lord's Supper which had just been concluded. Jesus and His disciples were still gathered in the upper room. Jesus, who had been speaking about the untroubled heart, had disclosed that for earth He can provide peace of heart, and for heaven He can provide the way. In verse 7 He said to Thomas, "If ye had known me, ye should have known my Father also: and from henceforth ye know him, and have seen him." Here the question, How can I see God? is answered by a personal encounter with Jesus Christ. If any person is to see or know God, he must do so through this experience.

Man's encounter with God is limited to Jesus Christ. When this becomes obvious, men and women are not going to say that the way to God is any way you choose to take. It is limited to one way.

Jesus said to Philip, "*If* ye had known me, ye should have known my Father also: and from henceforth ye know him, and have seen him" (v. 7). Two things will happen when we have this encounter: First, we will know God; and second, we will see God. Philip then asks a question: "Lord, shew us the Father, and it sufficeth [will satisfy] us" (v. 8). Jesus' reply was to point to Himself and say, "Have I been so long time with you, and yet hast thou not known me, Philip? He that hath seen me hath seen the Father" (v. 9).

Notice two things: First, the result of seeing Jesus is seeing God. No one has actually seen God in the sense of optical vision, although there have been theophanies, and there was an Incarnation as well as a Transfiguration. There was also Moses' experience, but whatever man saw of God was relative, never direct or absolute.

Seeing God cannot be direct and immediate, hence the incarnation by which we behold the glory of God. John said, "The Word [Jesus] was made flesh, and dwelt among us, (and we beheld his glory, the glory as of the only begotten of the Father,) full of grace and truth" (1:14). In this incarnate form, Jesus made it possible for the human to see the divine. It is like the electric transformer which takes high-voltage electricity and steps it down to low-voltage electricity so we can use it. Man would be destroyed by high-voltage current, just as man "cannot see God and live."

Second, the result of seeing God is satisfaction. "Shew us the Father, and it sufficeth us." The meaning of life is essentially an experience, the experience of seeing God. Out of this sight come satisfaction and the ultimate answer to the problem of being. Perhaps this can be illustrated by the life of Sally:

> She was three years old when she came to Nursery School. Her father had left her mother shortly before she was born. Her mother had taught school to support the two of them. At Nursery School Sally (for that was not her name) insisted on doing a peculiar thing. She would locate every available con-

tainer — jars, lids, saucers, bowls, even ashtrays — and fill them with water. The psychologist in charge of Nursery School noticed that Sally became very anxious if she could not fill each container to the very top. She *had* to fill it completely full. What was Sally trying to say in her ritual of filling the containers? The psychologist interpreted Sally as saying she was empty and needed to have herself filled.

Through the months that followed the psychologist and her staff became to Sally her means of being fulfilled. In play, on walks, under the shade tree, in the Nursery School Kitchen they communicated their fulness to her. No matter how many times she came to one of them for reassurance, they responded appropriately to her need. Sometimes it was a kind hand on her shoulder; other times, a member of the staff listened as the little girl poured out her heart. Gradually she became less anxious as she filled her containers. Then she stopped filling them at all. She turned enthusiastically to cooking. She liked best to make cupcakes. These she would take to members of the staff for their approval. They not only tasted them; they helped her to become a very excellent little cook. And all the while Sally was becoming fulfilled. She began to trust herself as others trusted her. She gained self-respect because others respected her. Her emptiness began to be filled as members of the staff imparted their love to her. She even began to venture a little love on her own.

Like Sally, most of us are living unfulfilled lives, trying to fill ourselves with things when only God can satisfy. Every Sunday as our churches fill with worshipers, the people of America are offered the basic ingredients out of which they may find life's meaning. But, for a mess of pottage, they sell on Monday the birthright of Sunday. Failing to recognize the value of their worship experience, they are like the antique dealer in Bethlehem to whom a dusty Arab nomad offered several of the original Dead Sea Scrolls for fifty-six dollars. He turned the Arab away, saying the antiquities were of no value.

How does one get the experience which gives life a meaning? It is by faith, which is something more than a pious attitude. Faith is both an act of affirmation that believes and an act of will that accepts God's way of life to be our way. Jesus once said, "If any man will do his will, he shall know of the doctrine, whether it be of God, or whether I speak of myself" (Jn 7:17). This makes faith an act of doing.

The trouble with most men is that they want faith on their own terms. They want to believe what they want to believe and do what they want to do in their own time. But the terms and time are God's, not ours. These people are like an old hunter who often lost his way in the woods. Finally he purchased a pocket compass and was instructed in its use, but shortly he lost his way again. When a search party found him and asked why he did not travel by compass, he said the compass had failed him. He wanted to travel north and so he tried to set the needle in that direction. But, he said, "It wasn't any use, for the ornery thing would shake, shake, shake back and forth and would always point southeast." This is the problem of the self-willed; they want God to direct them in the way they intend to travel. When God's will points in a different direction, they say God's Word is wrong. You cannot tamper with the compass and not get lost.

The basis of any faith which produces a meaning for life is God, but God as an item of faith does not stand alone. Jesus said, "Ye believe in God, believe also in me." If the basis of faith is God, then the basis of faith in God is Jesus Christ. But what is the basis of faith in Christ? The answer is found in these words: "Believest thou not that I am in the Father, and the Father in me? The words that I speak unto you I speak not of myself: but the Father that dwelleth in me, he doeth the works. Believe me that I am in the Father, and the Father in me: or else believe me for the very works' sake" (vv. 10-11).

We are asked to believe in God on the basis of Jesus Christ, and we are asked to believe in Jesus on the basis of two things: first, His words; and second, His works. The proof of Jesus' deity lies in the fact that God speaks through Him and works through Him. This, said Jesus, constitutes union with and likeness to God, and is indisputable and observable proof of His deity.

First we are asked to believe *what Jesus says*. We are asked to believe in these things because they are what God is saying. But if men are not dialectically minded and cannot sort out truth from error, then they are asked to believe *what Jesus does*.

What Jesus does is what God is doing through Him; it is proof that what He says is God's Word. We do not need to believe merely because Jesus says so, for we have the proof of His divine words in His divine works.

How many words of Jesus do we have to believe in order to believe in God? How many works of Jesus do we have to observe in order to substantiate our faith in Him? Those that are recorded are sufficient to substantiate any man's faith. Nothing more is necessary. Nor is it necessary to have any new works today. No one needs to perform any modern miracle to prove that God is God. What has been done is enough; what is written is sufficient.

37

Answers Unlimited

14:12-26

JESUS' LAST WORDS to His disciples hold three great promises: first, the promise of a new power; second, the promise of a new prayer; and third, the promise of a new presence. The disciples would need these in order to make Christianity the force and power which God intended it to be in the world.

THE NEW POWER — THE PROMISE OF GREATER WORKS

Jesus had established His claims to the loyalty of His disciples on the basis of His likeness to and oneness with the Father. He had said, "He that hath seen me hath seen the Father" (v. 9), which is likeness. He also said, "Believe me that I am in the Father, and the Father in me: or else believe me for the very works' sake" (v. 11), which is oneness. The first claim is based on *who He is* and the second on *what He does.*

On the basis of this likeness and oneness Jesus makes His promise of "greater works": "Verily, verily, I say unto you, He that believeth on me, the works that I do shall he do also; and greater works than these shall he do; because I go unto my Father" (v. 12). Three focal points are in this promise:

THE FAITH — "HE THAT BELIEVETH ON ME"

Faith is the condition on which any promise is to be realized as well as the basis of Christianity's accomplishments. What is faith? It is not what the psychologists call a philosophy of faith, which is "faith in the ability of ourselves and others to improve and grow; faith in the desire and capacity of human beings to work out problems cooperatively; faith in spiritual and moral values, in the essential decency of mankind. This faith

will carry us through stresses that might otherwise shatter us."
This is not the kind of faith Jesus was talking about, for it
amounts to nothing more than human confidence. Jesus identifies
faith as something related to Himself: "He that believeth on *me*."
The demand of faith upon anyone who expects to claim any divine promise is a commitment of life, heart and mind.

THE PERFORMANCE — "GREATER WORKS THAN THESE SHALL HE DO"

Did Jesus mean greater in kind, greater in comparison, greater
in time or greater in extent? Surely He could not mean greater
in kind, for how could man surpass God? At the end of the gospels and into the book of Acts, the apostles are seen doing works
similar to Jesus' miracles, but never greater. It is not a question
of simply doing physical miracles, as if the apostles were to succeed Jesus as a miracle worker; nor is it greater in comparison,
for, as Meyer says, "A measuring of miracles of this kind by their
magnitude is foreign to the New Testament."

It is greater in the broader sense of an expanded Christianity,
in the diffusion of the gospel, in the conquest of Judaism and
paganism, and in the triumph of the disciples over evil forces.
What Paul did in Asia in the transforming of human lives and
in the world-subduing effects of the gospel are these "greater
works." A transformed life is a greater miracle than the healing
of a leper, or the raising of a dead man. The bestowment of eternal life is greater than the postponement of death by a miracle
of healing.

The things recorded in Acts are greater than what happened
in the gospels because, as Jesus said, "I go unto my Father," and,
following the ascension and the coming of the Holy Spirit, we
witness the multiplying of His power in the lives of the disciples.
The disciples multiplied from twelve to one hundred and twenty,
while the area of their influence was expanded from Jerusalem
to "the uttermost parts of the earth." There was a reduction in
the number of miracles performed, but there was a corresponding increase in the power of God in the lives of His people.

Christian apologetics moved from the arena of physical miracles into the area of the transformed lives of believers. The divine nature of the gospel, the transforming power of the Word
of God, and the presence of God in human affairs — these are

what we ought to be able to prove to the satisfaction of modern inquirers and skeptics. We ought to be God's best advertisement. To this extent, God's cause is in our hands.

THE REASON — "BECAUSE I GO UNTO MY FATHER"

This in no sense implies that "greater works" would come in a vacuum resulting from the absence of Jesus, for God does not work in vacuums. Jesus' absence would result in the presence of the Holy Spirit, which would result in power distributed to the disciples. In His death Jesus gave way to the coming of one like unto Himself through whom the disciples were multiplied. This meant "greater works" because they were greater in extent and in frequency. In the light of this great promise, what are we doing today to fulfill the prospect of "greater works"? Is the fruit of our lives commensurate with the promises of God?

There are three classes of people: those who *make* things happen, those who *watch* things happen, and the overwhelming majority who have *no idea* of what is happening. The first is by far the smallest class. Yet, in any church there is this smaller group of activists who pray, envision, give, work, and witness to get things done for God. On the fringe of this activity are the watchers, and out beyond them, the unconscious ones.

There are two ways to go through this world: one is to stop thinking, and the other is to stop and think. Perhaps if we stopped to think we could see some application to our lives of the principle in these "greater works."

THE NEW PRAYER — THE PROMISE OF UNLIMITED ANSWERS

"And whatsoever ye shall ask in my name, that will I do, that the Father may be glorified in the Son. If ye shall ask any thing in my name, I will do it" (vv. 13-14). Unlimited answers are promised in these words. The prayer for these answers is clearly defined by two things:

THE CONDITION OF UNLIMITED ANSWERS — "IN MY NAME"

The most important consideration in prayer is the condition of prayer. The believer's relationship to God is one of grace: his salvation is by grace, his position before God is of grace, the provisions of his Christian life are based upon grace, and his credits before God are based upon the merits of Jesus. Therefore, the basis of purposeful prayer rests in the merits and righteousness of Christ; hence, praying in His name is a recognition of these facts of grace.

If I go to the bank and present a check in my name without adequate deposits, it is rejected. But if I go to that bank in the name of one whose deposits are adequate, the check is honored. Likewise, prayers presented in our name are unsupported by the credits of grace and have no acceptance. But, when presented in the name of Christ, they bear the integrity of His righteousness and grace. This is the meaning of Paul's statement, "He hath made us accepted in the beloved" (Eph 1:6).

THE REASON FOR UNLIMITED ANSWERS — "THAT THE FATHER MAY BE GLORIFIED IN THE SON"

The reason for unlimited answers does not lie in *when* we pray nor in *how* we pray, for Jesus said we would not be heard because of multiplied words in "much speaking." The reason does not lie in *where* we pray, for answers will not come because of preadvertised prayers in the synagogue and the streets. Rather, the reason for unlimited answers lies in *why* we pray. We assume our needs are the reason for answered prayer, but Jesus gave us one reason — *the glory of God.*

There are some practical directives that this reason will take, such as the good of the one praying. Henry Ward Beecher told of a woman who prayed for patience and God sent her a poor cook. We pray for virtues as if they could be packaged and handed to us ready for use. "The best answers to prayer may be the vision and strength to meet a circumstance or assume a responsibility." God puts us in situations where, by His help, we can develop the specific virtues for which we pray. Prayer is not presenting God with a bill of goods; it is learning lessons in His school of life under the master Teacher. It is not an exercise in asking; it is an experience of spiritual growth.

The promise of unlimited answers rests upon the fact that the petition of the one who prays in the name of Jesus is in harmony with God's will and that he is seeking God's glory alone. Thus, any apparent denial of any request under these prayer circumstances is, in fact, the fulfillment of prayer.

"And I will pray the Father, and he shall give you another Comforter, that he may abide with you for ever; even the Spirit of truth; whom the world cannot receive, because it seeth him not, neither knoweth him: but ye know him; for he dwelleth with you, and shall be in you" (vv. 16-17). Henry Pickering wrote:

> The word "Comforter" is an inadequate rendering of the original. The impossibility of conveying the full meaning of any one single word, doubtless led to the adoption, in various versions, of the original untranslated term "Paraclete" (r.v.). The original word implies also the office of a Helper, a Strengthener, a Monitor, a Guide, and also of an Advocate. In I John 2:1, the same word is applied to Christ, and is translated "Advocate."

The Comforter was to be like Christ. This promise meant the *likeness of personality* because the Holy Spirit is a person. This promise meant the *likeness of association* because the Holy Spirit is a member of the Godhead or Trinity and His presence would reproduce the presence of Jesus, as God, in our midst. This promise meant the *likeness of performance* because the Holy Spirit would do for us what Jesus would have done had He continued His presence on earth. This would be, among other things, the reproduction of power. This promise meant the *likeness of Christ's presence*. "I will not leave you comfortless [orphans]: I will come to you" (v. 18). Paul S. Minear wrote:

> Early Christians did not speak so much of a person going to church, but more often thought of the church as being present with each person at his place of daily employment. To the degree that his work represented the Spirit's call and the Spirit's response, to that extent the Church was actively fulfilling its mission through him. In his chores were embodied its repentance and forgiveness, its struggle with temptation, its victory. In his inward thoughts and outward activities were manifested

its faith, its prayers, its hopes. His faithfulness in love helped to
knit the Body together. Thus early Christians located the fron-
tier of God's war along the line of human associations and de-
cisions encountered in their day-to-day living.

The Holy Spirit is described as "the Spirit of truth" (v. 17).
This is amplified in verse 26: "He shall teach you all things,
and bring all things to your remembrance, whatsoever I have
said unto you." This is a reference to the function of inspiration
which has created that body of truth called the Bible. It is God's
Word because it is God who said it. This is also an indirect reference to another kind of inspiration — the inspiration of fellowship in another body, the body of believers, in which blessings
are mediated to us by the Holy Spirit.

38

Life and Love

14:19-31

THE DEPARTING SAVIOUR'S ANXIETY for the disciples extends itself in concern, not merely for their physical well-being, but for their spiritual triumph. They are to be His representatives among men, contending with the powers of evil and experiencing intense tribulation; for these things they must be prepared.

Two things distinguish Jesus' disciples from other men: life and love. The assumption that all men are the children of God is a monstrous theological misconception which puts the church off base in its attitude to the world. To conclude that all men are God's children is to infer that we are entitled to divine privileges and blessings merely on the basis of being human beings. This view takes no account of the entrance of sin, which alienated God from man and brought man into a state of perpetual rebellion. It ignores the need for personal repentance and regeneration before man can be in a position to receive the divine blessings. It equates the gospel with a list of social objectives, as if these were the ultimate goals of society and not the fruit of personal transformation.

The disciples were a new breed of men, the first citizens of the kingdom of God. They had nothing in common with either the Roman or Jewish world. Before leaving the upper room, Jesus would say of these men, "They are not of the world, even as I am not of the world." They were not to be sent out to make the world better, but different. The gospel they were to carry was one of personal regeneration and not social reformation. For these reasons Jesus and great concern for their well-being and survival in a hostile world.

Unseen but Seen

"Yet a little while, and the world seeth me no more; but ye see me: because I live, ye shall live also. At that day ye shall know that I am in my Father, and ye in me, and I in you" (vv. 19-20). It will not be long, Jesus was saying, before He would leave. Then He would be unseen to the world, but seen to His disciples. The world would no longer see Him because death, resurrection and ascension would take Him out of the realm of physical perception. The disciples, on the other hand, would see Him for the reason Jesus gave: "Because I live, ye shall live also." The disciples would share in the life of Jesus and would have the spiritual perceptions that would enable them to maintain this spiritual relationship which the world can never enjoy.

Jesus mentioned a time when the disciples would know beyond any doubt His true and divine nature: "At that day ye shall know that I am in the Father, and ye in me, and I in you." Was He referring to the day of resurrection, the day of Pentecost, or the day when He will come back again? It is a combination of all three. The *day of resurrection* would bring Jesus alive from the dead, restore Him to their presence, and make them partakers of Jesus' deathless life. The *day of Pentecost* would bring the Holy Spirit by whom they would behold Christ both corporeally and spiritually. The *day of His appearing* will reveal the heavenly glory of Christ and remove all doubts concerning the union of Jesus with the Father, and the union of the disciples to the Lord.

Loving and Doing

He that hath my commandments, and keepeth them, he it is that loveth me: and he that loveth me shall be loved of my Father, and I will love him, and will manifest myself to him. Judas saith unto him, not Iscariot, Lord, how is it that thou wilt manifest thyself unto us, and not unto the world? Jesus answered and said unto him, If a man love me, he will keep my words: and my Father will love him, and we will come unto him, and make our abode with him. He that loveth me not keepeth not my sayings: and the word which ye hear is not mine, but the Father's which sent me (vv. 21-24).

Until the day of the final and complete revelation of Jesus there will be a test of discipleship which will distinguish the true from the false. This will be the test of loving and doing, for those who love God will do what He says. It is also the reason why Christ manifests Himself to certain men rather than to all men. He said, "I will love him, and will manifest myself to him." This is another evidence of the separation that exists between the disciples and the world — to one Jesus manifests Himself; to another He does not.

At this point Judas Thaddaeus injects a question. Failing to understand what Jesus had said about manifesting Himself only to individual believers and not to all men, he still expected a Messianic appearance of Jesus that would establish Israel as the dominant nation.

In answer, Jesus spoke further about loving and doing. Not all men have the capacity of receiving a manifestation of God, He said. The world is not morally capable of receiving a manifestation of Christ and maintaining communion with Him.

Jesus said, "If a man love me, he will keep my words: and my Father will love him, and we will come unto him, and make our abode with him" (v. 23). There are conditions and restrictions for this abiding of God with man. God is not in all men as a divine spark which we fan into flame. He is only in those who love Him and, loving Him, keep His commandments. Both love and life are the distinguishing characteristics of those in whom God dwells.

The devotional value of this fact of God's abode in us is incalculable. Who can wholly comprehend the miracle of God in human affairs? Who can estimate the honor of God in making His dwelling in us? Who can compute the value of the blessings which accrue to us because God makes His home with us? It is not possible to compute the value but, thank God, it is possible to enjoy the experience.

Divine Light

"These things have I spoken unto you, being yet present with you. But the Comforter, which is the Holy Ghost, whom the Father will send in my name, he shall teach you all things, and bring all things to your remembrance, whatsoever I have said unto you" (vv. 25-26). Evidently there was a brief interval of time at this point while Jesus considered all the things He had said to His disciples, with the feeling that much would not be understood or even remembered. They would need divine enlightenment, and He reminded His disciples again of the one who would be sent in His stead, the Holy Spirit.

THREE NOTABLE THINGS

To whom the Holy Spirit is sent. The Holy Spirit is sent to the disciples, not the world. Jesus had said, "Whom the world cannot receive." Those who do not have the Saviour cannot have the Spirit.

How the Holy Spirit is sent. He is described as the one "whom the Father will send *in my name*," and as the one "whom I will send unto you *from the Father*" (15:26). This is called the procession of the Holy Spirit. The Holy Spirit is sent in the name of Jesus because, as Redeemer, Jesus comprises the total sphere of redemption within which the Holy Spirit operates. The Holy Spirit mediates all the blessings of salvation to us because He comes in the name of Jesus.

Why the Holy Spirit is sent. "He shall teach you all things, and bring all things to your remembrance, whatsoever I have said unto you." There is both an immediate and an ultimate meaning in these words. The immediate meaning is to the disciples, to whom Jesus had spoken many things which they did not fully understand. The Holy Spirit would instruct them in every point of divine truth. The ultimate meaning carries the thought of inspiration. The Holy Spirit would bring to the disciples' remembrance those facts which He deemed worthy of inclusion in God's written revelation.

Peace Without Fear

"Peace I leave with you, my peace I give unto you: not as the world giveth, give I unto you. Let not your heart be troubled, neither let it be afraid" (v. 27). This is Jesus' farewell greeting.

Luther said: "These are last words, as of one who is about to go away and says good-night or gives his blessing." This is like a divine benediction, blessing the recipient with conditions and protections that will surround him in the absence of the blesser. It is like a legacy, bestowing one's treasure upon an heir. It is the legacy of an untroubled heart which is priceless to its possessor.

The specific commodity bequeathed by Jesus is peace: the peace of reconciliation to God, of eternal life and salvation, of forgiveness with all the debt of sin paid and all the stain of sin removed, of fellowship with God, and of security against life's changing fortunes.

In all these ways it was a peace which the world could not give — "Not as the world giveth, give I unto you." The world could give treasure, pleasure, honor and fame, but not peace. What the world gives is temporary. What Jesus gives is permanent — peace and prosperity with true and unfailing happiness.

While this is peace without fear, it is not peace without cost for it was made "through the blood of his cross" and cost Jesus His life. Peace on every battlefield is at the price of the blood of man, while peace on the battlefield of the human heart is at the price of the blood of the son of man.

GOING AWAY AND COMING AGAIN

Ye have heard how I said unto you, I go away, and come again unto you. If ye loved me, ye would rejoice, because I said, I go unto the Father: for my Father is greater than I. And now I have told you before it come to pass, that, when it is come to pass, ye might believe. Hereafter I will not talk much with you: for the prince of this world cometh, and hath nothing in me. But that the world may know that I love the Father; and as the Father gave me commandment, even so I do. Arise, let us go hence (vv. 28-31).

Jesus gently rebuked His disciples for holding an unhappy view of His departure. Being human, they looked on its dark and forbidding side, but Jesus bid them look upon its bright and triumphant side. There was nothing frivolous in Jesus' rebuke because He was looking at the providential and overruling fact that God reigns. The reasons Jesus gave His disciples to rejoice in His going away were two fold:

HE WAS GOING AWAY TO HIS FATHER

The Father, Jesus said, is "greater than I." This is not a reference to inequality in the Godhead, but to Jesus' submission to the Father. Now He was returning to His Father to enjoy the glories which He had suspended by His own self-surrender. Because of this gain, His disciples should have rejoiced in His going away.

HE IS GOING AWAY TO COME AGAIN

"And if I go and prepare a place for you, I will come again." Jesus had yet to fulfill the Messianic hopes of His nation, which would be fulfilled when He came again. But He could not come again without first going, for by leaving He would accomplish all the purposes which God had for man's redemption, including atonement, justification, resurrection, ascension, and a high-priestly ministry. These were the reasons why the disciples should have rejoiced.

39

Abiding and Abounding

15:1-11

WHEN JESUS ANNOUNCED His departure in His impending death, the whole company of disciples in the upper room arose and prepared to leave the room. But Jesus continued speaking to them: "I am the true vine, and my Father is the husbandman [nurseryman or vine-dresser]." Jesus described Himself as the spiritual counterpart of this vine, pointing out the vital spiritual union between Himself and believers.

SEVERAL ELEMENTS IN THE FIGURE

THE VINE

The vine refers to Christ as the parent spiritual organism.

THE HUSBANDMAN

The husbandman refers to God who sent Christ to establish this union of believers with Him.

THE BRANCHES

The branches are believers as distinguished from lip-service Christians who do not possess a vital union of life with Christ.

THE PRUNING

The pruning is cleansing or purification which comes through the Word (v. 3).

THE FRUIT

The fruit is production as the result of union with the vine and its pruning.

THE PROCESS

The process is by abiding or maintaining a vital spiritual relationship with one's environment, which is Christ.

What Jesus says in verse 2 poses a problem. Even as there are fruitful and unfruitful branches, in all vines and trees so there are those in the spiritual world who give evidence of faith by their fruit and those who do not.

THE DIVINE VINE-DRESSER DEALS WITH THE VINE

FRUITLESS BRANCHES ARE REMOVED

"Every branch in me that beareth not fruit he taketh away" (v. 2). These fruitless branches are synthetic Christians, the lip-service Christians who the horticulturist would call suckers or nonproducers. They are "taken away." This is not the true believer but the apparent or simulated believer being severed from the parent vine.

FRUITFUL BRANCHES ARE PRUNED

"Every branch that beareth fruit [or is capable of bearing fruit], he purgeth [cleanses] it, that it may bring forth more fruit" (v. 2). These are the believers who are joined to the parent vine and are capable of extensive fruit-bearing. They are purged or cleansed through the working of divine grace by the Word of God: "Now ye are clean through the word which I have spoken unto you" (v. 3).

Jesus now introduces the idea of abiding that there may be abounding: "Abide in me, and I in you. As the branch cannot bear fruit of itself, except it abide in the vine; no more can ye, except ye abide in me" (v. 4). He links abiding with cleansing through His Word. If the cleansed disciples abide in this spiritual state, they will abound in spiritual production.

Abiding. Abiding means spiritual continuity. It is staying on, not in a static sense, but in growth and grace. Paul said to the Colossians, "As ye have therefore received Christ Jesus as Lord, so *walk* ye in him" (2:6). Abiding is faithful persistence in our fellowship with Christ.

1. The spheres of abiding.

a. Abide in Christ. This has a double sense: First, we are to abide in His person — "abide in me." This is our relationship to Christ *in living* and refers to the branch's relationship to the vine in order that it may draw vital life and strength from this union. It does not refer to any person's deliberate attempt to sever himself from the vine, but rather to any condition that may cause us to lose the free flow of Christ's life and strength to us as branches. Second, we are to abide in His presence — "and I in you." This is our relationship to Christ *in fellowship* which had just been illustrated in the Lord's Supper. A growing vine illustrates the need for continued spiritual fellowship.

There is something very intimate in a branch's relationship to its parent vine. It is the intimacy of feeling, interest, activity, friendship and comradeship. This is the kind of intimacy in which we must abide if we are to abound.

b. Abide in faith. This is the relationship of *trust*: "If ye abide in me, and my words abide in you" (v. 7). It is the thought of uninterrupted faith. Many people can summon faith for emergencies, and trust God when the going is difficult. But this means a state of continuous trust, not merely in the time of trouble.

c. Abide in prayer. This indicates the relationship of *intercession* and carries the thought of continuance rather than the employment of prayer as an escape hatch. It is a way of life suggested by Paul's words, "Praying always with all prayer and supplication" (Eph 6:18).

d. Abide in the Word. This is the relationship of *obedience*. "If ye keep my commandments, ye shall abide in my love" (v. 10). We abide in Him through *obedience* to His Word and *adherence* to His Word. A leading Protestant minister stood before a collegiate audience at Columbia University and for a text used 2 Timothy 1:5, "When I call to remembrance the unfeigned faith that is in thee, which dwelt first in thy grandmother Lois." For a few minutes he cited the great strides taken in the way of material progress which in some respects have placed us in a world ahead of our forefathers. And then he turned to his audience and said, "We may go far, but if we lose the faith of our grandmothers, we lose everything; if we lack this, we are lost!" We must abide in His Word.

e. Abide in love. "As the Father hath loved me, so have I loved you: continue ye in my love" (v. 9). As the uniting bond of fellowship between Jesus and the Father is love, so it will be between Jesus and His disciples. This is the highest level of Christian fellowship, and also the highest expression of Christian faith, without which we are like "sounding brass and tinkling cymbal."

2. The results of abiding.

a. The negative results. "If a man abide not in me, he is cast forth as a branch, and is withered; and men gather them, and cast them into the fire, and they are burned" (v. 6). Here is the horticultural process of pruning unproductive branches. In the case of branches which do not produce fruit, they are cut off by the vine-dresser and are cast into the fire for burning. The illustration specifically uses the words "cast forth as a branch" in the sense of usefulness and production. Because of the lack of abiding, believers "as branches" can be cast away in periods of fruitlessness.

b. The positive results. "If ye abide in me, and my words abide in you, ye shall ask what ye will, and it shall be done unto you" (v. 7). Here is the result of a wonderful fruitfulness that is summed up in three progressive stages — "fruit" in verse 2; "more fruit" in verse 2; "much fruit" in verse 5.

Abounding. If we abide we will:

1. Abound in joy. "These things have I spoken unto you, that my joy might remain in you, and that your joy might be full" (v. 11). This is expansive joy — something that is "full," not meager or small. It has the fullness of abundance which overflows.

2. Abound in fruit. "Ye have not chosen me, but I have chosen you, and ordained you, that ye should go and bring forth fruit, and that your fruit should remain: that whatsoever ye shall ask of the Father in my name, he may give it you" (v. 16). What is this fruit? In a vine it is grapes, in a sheep it is wool, and in a mine it is gold. But in a Christian it is all the things that flow from a believer's relationship with the Lord. Out of this relationship come the experiences of influence, witnessing, goodness, good works, generosity and kindness.

This is to be distinguished from the fruit of the Spirit detailed in Galatians 5. There it is the *fruit of personality;* here it is the *fruit of production.* This fruit is one of Christianity's answers to the meaning of life.

The Japanese grow forest trees in flowerpots. Some of these miniature trees are a hundred years old, and are only two or three feet in height. The gardener, instead of fertilizing the trees and trying to get them to grow large, takes pains to keep them little. From the time the seeds are first planted, they are starved and stunted. When the tender buds appear they are nipped off and the tree remains a dwarf.

Our troubles are largely due to doing the same thing with our lives. We do not allow our souls to grow because we rob ourselves of spiritual nourishment and shut the power of God's Word out of our hearts. We are dwarf Christians when we might be strong giant Christians.

3. Abound in answered prayer. "If ye abide in me, and my words abide in you, ye shall ask what ye will, and it shall be done unto you" (v. 7). Prayer imposes its own conditions. It says "if." When the condition of this abiding is met, the abounding will be: "Ye shall ask what ye will, and it shall be done unto you." In Matthew 9:29 Jesus said to His disciples, "You shall have what your faith expects." The only limit of our accomplishments is the extent of our faith. If we are abiding we are abounding; and if we are not abounding, it is because we are not abiding.

40

Love — The World's Greatest Force

15:12-27

CONSIDERING that man has not at any previous time commanded such awesome power and that a single nuclear bomb has more destructive power than all the bombs dropped in World War II, it almost seems anachronistic to speak of love as the greatest force in today's world.

Think then how anachronistic it seemed for Jesus to say, "Greater love hath no man than this, that a man lay down his life for his friends" (v. 13). But it was no more so in His time with Roman power than in our time with atomic power. In this kind of world, or any kind of world, how can you say that love is the greatest force? The reason is because *Jesus said it*. Another reason is that *history proves it*. Look what happened to the world in which Jesus said this. Rome is gone, the Roman Empire vanished, but Jesus' kingdom stands. If history proves anything, it proves that physical, materialistic, secular force can never ultimately win.

Jesus' answer to life was love. Each of us has a measured amount of living to do. You cannot run away from life no matter how old you are, how much of a failure you have been, or how frustrated you are. The answer to life's problems, issues, difficulties and frustrations is love.

Love is the basic ingredient of the gospel. We should love people instead of criticizing them, arguing with them, and coercing them. Of all the things Jesus mentioned in the upper room, love is the greatest.

NOTABLE THINGS

THE COMMANDMENT TO LOVE

"This is my commandment, That ye love one another, as I have loved you" (v. 12). Love is the result of a whole new set of motives. What motivates the Christian is not a set of laws, but a new condition of life. Love was henceforth to be the standard of behavior, the inner source of action that would motivate all human relationships.

THE INCENTIVE TO LOVE

"Greater love hath no man than this, that a man lay down his life for his friends" (v. 13). The incentive to love is the example of Jesus. As He loved, so we must love. He said, "Love one another, as I have loved you" (v. 12).

Jesus, prepared to show the highest form of love in the sacrifice of Himself, said, "Greater love hath no man than this, that a man lay down his life for his friends." There can be no greater love between man and man than the sacrifice of life itself. Jesus provides the highest example as our incentive to love.

THE COMMUNITY OF LOVE

Ye are my friends, if ye do whatsoever I command you. Henceforth I call you not servants; for the servant knoweth not what his lord doeth: but I have called you friends; for all things that I have heard of my Father I have made known unto you. Ye have not chosen me, but I have chosen you, and ordained you, that ye should go and bring forth fruit, and that your fruit should remain: that whatsoever ye shall ask of the Father in my name, he may give it you. These things I command you, that ye love one another" (vv. 14-17).

The community in which this new commandment operates is that of the friends of Jesus, the new society of the kingdom of God. Jesus names four things concerning this society of friends:

The condition of friendship. "Ye are my friends, if ye do whatsoever I command you" (v. 14). Friendship is conditional. We are Jesus' friends if we do His commandments. The true nature of His friends is not determined by a legalistic formula, but rather by an inner standard of life which governs our responses to the ideals of Jesus' teachings. Those who respect and heed what He says are His friends. They are without denominational distinction, social caste or prestige of position. To be among them is within reach of every person. The simple qualification is, "if ye do whatsoever I command you."

The privilege of friendship. "Henceforth I call you not servants; for the servant knoweth not what his lord doeth: but I have called you friends; for all things that I have heard of my Father I have made known unto you" (v. 15). The servant indicated here is in fact a slave. Slaves execute commands without knowing or questioning their purpose, while friends have the dignity of confidants who enter into the plans and purposes of their Master. Jesus had taken His disciples into the inner circle of friendship where He had disclosed "all things" that He had heard from His Father. This would not have happened to mere servants who are the blind instruments of a master's will.

The purpose of friendship. "Ye have not chosen me, but I have chosen you, and ordained you, that ye should go and bring forth fruit, and that your fruit should remain: that whatsoever ye shall ask of the Father in my name, he may give it you" (v. 16). We do not choose Jesus; He chooses us. The element of human choice is here, but prior choice is God's in divine election. We have not been chosen to belong to a fellowship of love for the satisfaction this would bring us. Instead, we are chosen to act as disciples whose lives bring forth fruit.

1. The result of this relationship will be twofold:

a. It will be fruit that remains. Fruit that "remains" is the fruit of service within the kingdom of God which continues while all else disappears.

b. It will be prayers that will be answered. Faith exercised in prayer has the basis of reality because it seeks the will of God above the demands of the flesh.

The obligation of friendship, "These things I command you, that ye love one another" (v. 17). This is the call to mutual love — not philanthropic love which engages in superficial acts of generosity, but the kind of love which comes from association with Jesus.

> If the world hate you, ye know that it hated me before it hated you. If ye were of the world, the world would love his own: but because ye are not of the world, but I have chosen you out of the world, therefore the world hateth you. Remember the word that I said unto you, The servant is not greater than his lord. If they have persecuted me, they will also persecute you; if they have kept my saying, they will keep yours also. But all these things will they do unto you for my name's sake, because they know not him that sent me. If I had not come and spoken unto them, they had not had sin: but now they have no cloke for their sin. He that hateth me hateth my Father also. If I had not done among them the works which none other man did, they had not had sin: but now they have both seen and hated both me and my Father. But this cometh to pass, that the word might be fulfilled that is written in their law, They hated me without a cause. But when the Comforter is come, whom I will send unto you from the Father, even the Spirit of truth, which proceedeth from the Father, he shall testify of me: and ye also shall bear witness, because ye have been with me from the beginning (vv. 18-27).

The spiritual and social climate for the citizens of the new society is love, a marked contrast to the outside world of hatred and animosity. The disciples would soon find themselves in the midst of the hostility and hatred of that world. As it hated Him, so it would hate them. The road on which they had embarked would lead to Rome and its coliseum where the city would be lighted with the blazing, oil-soaked bodies of Christians serving as torches for Nero. The floor of that coliseum would be drenched with the blood of thousands.

No matter how intense the opposition or bitter the hatred, love would not be destroyed. These Christians displayed a love which made them impervious to successful attack. They had something for which they were willing to die. Years ago an Englishman told of going twice to an English college to plead for recruits for the mission field. The first time he asked for a man to go out to India. He told of the beautiful cities, social advantages, and an adequate salary. Not a man responded. Several

years later he went to the same school and stood in the same
room and asked for a volunteer to go to Africa to take the place
of a man who had died at his post. He told of the oppressive
heat, tragic loneliness, deadly malaria, and sleeping sickness, and
of the five graves of the men who had gone there. Then he
asked if there was a man willing to go and carry on. "Perhaps,"
he said, "you will not come back." Ten young men rose to their
feet and offered to go. "If you wish to kindle the religious zeal
of youth, give them something they can die for."

To be filled with love is to be possessed of the greatest force in
the world. We love people, not because of what they are, but
because of what they can become. Love wins when everything
else fails.

41

The Promise of a Helper

16:1-15

THE MINISTRY OF THE HOLY SPIRIT is understood if one realizes the circumstances under which He was promised and given. The promise was given in this upper room to insure the disciples of help in meeting the emergencies which were bound to arise when Jesus would no longer be with them. This portion of the chapter is better understood by recognizing its three component parts.

THE NEED OF THE DISCIPLES

These things have I spoken unto you, that ye should not be offended. They shall put you out of the synagogues: yea, the time cometh, that whosoever killeth you will think that he doeth God service. And these things will they do unto you, because they have not known the Father, nor me. But these things have I told you, that when the time shall come, ye may remember that I told you of them. And these things I said not unto you at the beginning, because I was with you. But now I go my way to him that sent me; and none of you asketh me, Whither goest thou? But because I have said these things unto you, sorrow hath filled your heart (vv. 1-6).

Observe the promise of the Holy Spirit in the context of a specific need in the lives of the disciples:

IT WAS THE NEED OF THEIR ENVIRONMENT

The disciples were surrounded by a hostile, alien and inhospitable world in which Jesus had indicated they would suffer offense when He left them. The word "offended" here means "stumbling." When no longer supported by the presence of Jesus, the disciples would stumble and perhaps fall. Against this possibility Jesus made provision in the coming of the Spirit.

Jesus pinpointed what the disciples would suffer by suggesting that the Jews would put them out of the synagogues, but they not only faced excommunication but death. The gift of the Spirit was not a promise of exemption from persecution, for His coming would not mean protection from the peril of opposition and oppression. Instead, He would come as a Sustainer for the believer in His adversity.

IT WAS THE NEED OF THEIR PERSONALITIES

Thoroughly cast down and discouraged, the disciples stood silent and unresponsive in the presence of their Leader; they were overwhelmed with their impending circumstances. Jesus was going to the one who sent Him, yet the disciples, concerned with their own predicament, did not say a word to Him about His going away.

This is a common human tendency. We miss much because of our attitude of being overconcerned with our own plight. Strength must come from the divine provisions which God has arranged for us. In this case it is the Holy Spirit taking the place of the absent Christ.

If we will magnify Christ and keep Him constantly in view we will find a new source of strength to meet our discouragements. The disciples failed to remember that when Christ returned to the Father He would be in a place of intercession from which to help them. They also failed to assess the advantage they would have from the presence of the Holy Spirit whom Jesus had promised. There was no reason for discouragement, depression or fear. Their advantages would be greater than their disadvantages.

THE PROMISE OF THE HOLY SPIRIT

"Nevertheless I tell you the truth; It is expedient for you that I go away: for if I go not away, the Comforter will not come unto you; but if I depart, I will send him unto you" (v. 7). Previous to this, Jesus had said, "I will pray the Father, and he shall give you another Comforter, that he may abide with you for ever" (14:16). The words "another Comforter" imply that the Holy Spirit would be similar in kind to the Person He would replace.

SIMILAR IN PERSONALITY

The Holy Spirit is a person, even as Jesus is a person, with faculties of personality similar to Jesus. The only dissimilarity is in the fact that the Holy Spirit does not have a body. For this reason we are called upon to "present" our bodies (Ro 12:1) as habitations for the Holy Spirit (1 Co 3:16).

SIMILAR IN DEITY

The Holy Spirit is a divine person — as divine as Christ was divine. He is as much God as Jesus, and as much a part of the Godhead.

The word "Comforter" to identify the Holy Spirit is not used in the usual sense of a sympathizer, but rather in the sense of an activator. We use it for the time of death and sorrow; God uses it for life and action.

"Comforter" is translated from the Greek word *paraclete.* Its nearest English equivalent is *advocate. Paraclete* is compounded of two words, "para," meaning alongside, and *"calein,"* meaning to call. The Holy Spirit is therefore called alongside the disciple to defend, support, advise, assist and help him. He is not our advocate with God, for Jesus is that, but He is Christ's Advocate with us. He represents Christ to us; He interprets and reveals Christ to us; He administers the means of grace to us; He administrates Christ's affairs on earth.

THE NATURE OF THE HOLY SPIRIT'S HELP

And when he is come, he will reprove the world of sin, and of righteousness, and of judgment: of sin, because they believe not on me; of righteousness, because I go to my Father, and ye see me no more; of judgment, because the prince of this world is judged. I have yet many things to say unto you, but ye cannot bear them now. Howbeit when he, the Spirit of truth, is come, he will guide you into all truth: for he shall not speak of himself; but whatsoever he shall hear, that shall he speak: and he will shew you things to come. He shall glorify me: for he shall receive of mine, and shall shew it unto you. All things that the Father hath are mine: therefore said I, that he shall take of mine, and shall shew it unto you (vv. 8-15).

The Holy Spirit is to be to the believer all that Christ was while present with the disciples. They would need advice, strength, encouragement and support, which Jesus indicated the Holy Spirit would provide. They would be thrust into an alien and inhospitable environment where the Spirit would enable them and all successive believers to maintain a strong, fruitful and victorious existence in the face of every kind of opposition.

THE HOLY SPIRIT IS TO HELP TWO CLASSES OF PEOPLE

The non-Christian. "And when he is come, he will reprove the world of sin, and of righteousness, and of judgment: of sin, because they believe not on me; of righteousness, because I go to my Father, and ye see me no more; of judgment, because the prince of this world is judged" (vv. 8-11).

The Holy Spirit would not only be Christ's Advocate to the Christian, He would also be Christ's Representative to the non-Christian, for whom He performs a threefold ministry: reproving them of sin, righteousness and judgment. This ministry of reproof or conviction is theologically known as effectual calling. No sinner can volitionally determine to be saved at his own convenience; he must be called. This calling is in terms of conviction or reproof and is related to sin, righteousness and judgment.

1. "of sin" (v. 9). "Of sin, because they believe not on me." This is the great and ultimate sin, the sin for which judgment will come. Other sins make us sinful, but this sin makes us sinners. Other sins make us unrighteous, but this sin makes us unbelievers. Other sins may be against law, but this sin is against love. Other sins may be against man, but this sin is against God.

2. "of righteousness" (v. 10). Rejection of Jesus Christ is a rejection of the only source of salvation. This sin not only reveals our unrighteousness, but Christ's righteousness, which must become ours or else we have no hope of salvation. His righteousness is made ours through the Spirit's conviction of our sin, and faith's appropriation of God's provision for us in Jesus Christ. Through this faith God enables sinners to become partakers of the righteousness of God. "For he hath made him to be sin for us, who knew no sin; that we might be made the righteousness of God in him" (2 Co 5:21).

3. "of judgment" (v. 11). Having convinced the sinner of his sin of unbelief, the Holy Spirit convinces him finally of judgment. This judgment is twofold: First, Satan has already been judged by Christ's death on the cross, for "the prince of this world is judged." Because of this judgment everyone who exercises faith in Jesus Christ is removed from the dominion of Satan and will not come into judgment at the final day. Second, those who reject the Spirit's conviction of sin are now actually judged and condemned: "He that believeth on him is not condemned: but he that believeth not is condemned already, because he hath not believed in the name of the only begotten Son of God" (Jn 3:18). We are already judged and condemned if we reject the Spirit's witness.

The Christian.

> I have yet many things to say unto you, but ye cannot bear them now. Howbeit when he, the Spirit of truth, is come, he will guide you into all truth: for he shall not speak of himself; but whatsoever he shall hear, that shall he speak: and he will shew you things to come. He shall glorify me: for he shall receive of mine, and shall shew it unto you. All things that the Father hath are mine: therefore said I, that he shall take of mine, and shall shew it unto you (vv. 12-15).

The need of the Holy Spirit is indicated in the disciples' incapacity to comprehend the "many things" Jesus had yet to say to them. This is akin to John's last word: "And there are also many other things which Jesus did, the which, if they should be written every one, I suppose that even the world itself could not contain the books that should be written" (Jn 21:25).

Because of the Saviour's yearning to reveal more, and the disciples' present incapacity to understand, the Holy Spirit would come as their Teacher.

ELEMENTS OF THE GUIDANCE OR TEACHING

The Holy Spirit shall not speak of Himself (v. 13). His ministry is Christ-centered. This restraint of the Holy Spirit not to speak of Himself is a characteristic which extends to the believer, for being filled with the Spirit will be found in our speaking of Christ and not the Spirit.

Some years ago a large steam engine made of glass was on display throughout the nation. When it was operating, the moving pistons and the valves could be seen, but no one could see what made them go because steam is invisible when it is hot enough to be a continuous elastic vapor. We perceive the presence of the Holy Spirit, not by His manifestations concerning Himself, but by the effect He produces within individual believers.

The Holy Spirit shall speak of things future (v. 13). "He will show you things to come." This would come in the finished New Testament and in the prophetic gift possessed by some of the apostles.

The Holy Spirit shall glorify Christ (v. 14). This glorification of Christ would not come by inventing new doctrines not already inherent in Jesus' person and work, but by enlightening the believer so he could perceive the already existing excellence of Jesus. The glorification of Jesus is the expansion and spreading of the things He has taught His disciples — the things the Holy Spirit has come to help us understand.

He shall teach only Christ's doctrine (v. 15). This is the divine safeguard against heresy, for whoever is guided by the Holy Spirit will be led into "all truth." It is when men listen to voices other than the Spirit that they become involved in error, because heresies and schisms are human inventions spawned in the minds of misguided religious men.

The promise of Jesus is fulfilled in the historical fact of Pentecost. The Holy Spirit is here. As believers we are "baptized into one body" which is the church and are commanded to be "filled with the Spirit." The practical result of this coming to the church and this filling of the believer is summed up by George A. Buttrick in these six things:

    a. A transforming experience of the living Christ.
    b. A passion to pass this experience on to others.
    c. An indissoluble fellowship with other believers.
    d. A love for men.
    e. A sense of security independent of ourselves.
    f. A sense of peace which is not dependent on our environment.

42

A Little While

16:16-33

THE PROBLEMS which Christians face have their solutions. Some are solved by time, others by prayer, still others will be solved by the second coming of Jesus. These elements of solution are found in this concluding portion of the last discourse in the upper room.

SORROWS FOR A LITTLE WHILE

A little while, and ye shall not see me: and again, a little while, and ye shall see me, because I go to the Father. Then said some of his disciples among themselves, What is this that he saith unto us, A little while, and ye shall not see me: and again, a little while, and ye shall see me: and, Because I go to the Father? They said therefore, What is this that he saith, A little while? We cannot tell what he saith. Now Jesus knew that they were desirous to ask him, and said unto them, Do ye enquire among yourselves of what I said, A little while, and ye shall not see me: and again, a little while, and ye shall see me? Verily, verily, I say unto you, That ye shall weep and lament, but the world shall rejoice: and ye shall be sorrowful, but your sorrow shall be turned into joy. A woman when she is in travail hath sorrow, because her hour is come: but as soon as she is delivered of the child, she remembereth no more the anguish, for joy that a man is born into the world. And ye now therefore have sorrow: but I will see you again, and your heart shall rejoice, and your joy no man taketh from you (vv. 16-22).

Many things in life yield to the passage of time because they are of a transitory nature. They also yield to greater wisdom acquired through experience in time. But time itself is swift, and soon our sorrows disappear and we find ourselves in new and happier situations.

Jesus said, "A little while, and ye shall not see me: and again, a little while, and ye shall see me, because I go to the Father." The disciples were disturbed by His words because they could not understand the seeming contradiction of "a little while, and ye shall not see me" and "a little while, and ye shall see me." Also, they were perplexed by what He said about going "to the Father." This prompted their query, "What is this that he saith unto us, A little while, and ye shall not see me: and again, a little while, and ye shall see me: and, Because I go to my Father? They said therefore, What is this that he saith, A little while? We cannot tell what he saith" (vv. 17-18).

There are two ways to understand this contradictory statement of Jesus:

THE PERSONAL UNDERSTANDING

"Verily, verily, I say unto you, That ye shall weep and lament, but the world shall rejoice: and ye shall be sorrowful, but your sorrow shall be turned into joy. A woman when she is in travail hath sorrow, because her hour is come: but as soon as she is delivered of the child, she remembereth no more the anguish, for joy that a man is born into the world" (vv. 20-21).

Jesus' meaning is self-evident. While He was with them, they would enjoy the security of His presence, but when He died they would be in great trouble. But their sorrow would be turned to joy as suddenly as that of the mother who bears a son. When her child is born she forgets the pain because of the birth of her child. The disciples would sorrow at His death, but this sorrow would turn into gladness upon Jesus' return to them.

The emphasis of the solution to the disciples' problem is on the words "a little while." Their sorrow would yield to the passage of time, for time would give them a new set of circumstances. They would have to face adversity simply because they were Jesus' disciples, and also because of the absence of Jesus, upon whose presence they had come to depend.

We also have to face adversity, but for us it is not primarily a question of what kind, but *how*. Someone visited a friend stricken with an incurable disease. "How sad it is for you," remarked the visitor. "Suffering does color life so." "Yes," was the reply, "but I intend to choose the color." One way to change the face of adversity is to give it the color we want it to have by the manner in which we handle it.

The element of time enters into the solution of sorrow in another way. The Bible says, "As thy days, so shall thy strength be" (Deu 33:25). "Bridges are built to accommodate certain loads with allowances for excess stress," says Dr. Emerson S. Colaw. "However, if all the load that is to pass over the bridge during its lifetime comes at the same time, the bridge will collapse. Likewise, God has engineered us to live one day at a time. If we exceed our load limit and burden ourselves with all the problems of yesterday, today and tomorrow, we will break under the strain too."

Any condition of sorrow is for "a little while." For those who bear the cross, it is only a little while because afterward will be the crown. Paul speaks of it in these words:

> The Spirit itself beareth witness with our spirit, that we are the children of God: and if children, then heirs; heirs of God, and joint-heirs with Christ; if so be that we suffer with him, that we may be also glorified together. For I reckon that the sufferings of this present time are not worthy to be compared with the glory which shall be revealed in us. For the earnest expectation of the creature waiteth for the manifestation of the sons of God. For the creature was made subject to vanity, not willingly, but by reason of him who hath subjected the same in hope. Because the creature itself also shall be delivered from the bondage of corruption into the glorious liberty of the children of God. For we know that the whole creation groaneth and travaileth in pain together until now. And not only they, but ourselves also, which have the firstfruits of the Spirit, even we ourselves groan within ourselves, waiting for the adoption, to wit, the redemption of our body (Ro 8:16-23).

Time enters once more into the solution of many of our problems because, at best, the longest journey is only a little while. Burton Hillis tells this story:

"It's only a little farther," my father used to say when I was a little boy, winded and leg-weary, out on the long Sunday afternoon walks we used to take together. So I would brace up and struggle on a little longer, looking for the first familiar land marks that would indicate we were back in our own neighborhood. One day I asked him how far a little farther really was. "It's farther than you can see but not as far as you can go," he replied. His words were a help to me then, and on many another journey since that long ago day.

THE HISTORICAL UNDERSTANDING

"And ye now therefore have sorrow: but I will see you again, and your heart shall rejoice, and your joy no man taketh from you" (v. 22). The heart of this answer is in the words "I will see you again." In verse 16 Jesus had said, "A little while, and ye shall not see me: and again, a little while and ye shall see me." What did He mean by this double "little while"? In what sense would they not see Him and then later see Him?

Jesus could have referred to one of three things — the resurrection, the second coming, or the coming of the Holy Spirit. He probably meant His resurrection, although this is not the general theological view, for this would restore Him personally, visibly and physically to the disciples. It is the most likely immediate sense in which we can understand His promise, "I will see you again." But by linking the resurrection to the second coming, we have both the immediate and the ultimate meanings, with the intermediate ministry of the Holy Spirit with its sustaining effect on the believer's life. In this sense all three of the possible meanings are involved. The disciples would feel sorrow at Jesus' death, but joy at His resurrection. They would have sorrow at His ascension, but joy at His second coming. But for the intervening years of His tarrying, there would be joy in the presence of the Holy Spirit.

ASKING IN JESUS' NAME (VV. 23-31)

And in that day ye shall ask me nothing. Verily, verily, I say unto you, Whatsoever ye shall ask the Father in my name,

he will give it you. Hitherto have ye asked nothing in my
name: ask, and ye shall receive, that your joy may be full.
These things have I spoken unto you in proverbs: but the time
cometh, when I shall no more speak unto you in proverbs, but
I shall shew you plainly of the Father. At that day ye shall ask
in my name: and I say not unto you, that I will pray the Father
for you: for the Father himself loveth you, because ye have
loved me, and have believed that I came out from God. I came
forth from the Father, and am come into the world: again, I
leave the world, and go to the Father. His disciples said unto
him, Lo, now speakest thou plainly, and speakest no proverb.
Now are we sure that thou knowest all things, and needest not
that any man should ask thee: by this we believe that thou
camest forth from God. Jesus answered them, Do ye now believe? (vv. 23-31).

This introduces the solution of prayer into the problems of the
Christian. Jesus was saying that a new day was coming. This
day would follow Jesus' death when the Holy Spirit would come
to answer the disciples' questions and they would have no need
to question Jesus. Although He would return to them through the
resurrection, His return would be temporary, but the Holy Spirit
would be with them always.

Up to this time the disciples had asked nothing in the name
of Jesus because He was present. But now that He was going
away, their prayers would be offered in His name. Jesus was
saying, "From this time, ask in my name, and you will receive
what you ask, that your joy may be complete."

Here is the believer's new posture in prayer: He is to pray in
the name of Jesus and through the Holy Spirit. Because of the
Spirit's enlightenment he will pray in the will of God, and Jesus
says, "Whatsoever ye shall ask the Father in my name, he will
give it you." Asking in Jesus' name is asking in the virtue of
His name, for His name has value in prayer. Our names represent that which is weak, bankrupt and unimportant, but Jesus'
name stands for righteousness, power and authority.

All these assurances are related to previous promises of Jesus
regarding praying: "If ye abide in me, and my words abide in
you, ye shall ask what ye will, and it shall be done unto you"

(Jn 15:7). "Ye have not chosen me, but I have chosen you, and ordained you, that ye should go and bring forth fruit, and that your fruit should remain: that whatsoever ye shall ask of the Father in my name, he may give it you" (Jn 15:16). They are related to both Jesus' going and the Holy Spirit's coming. Because Jesus would no longer be among them, they were to use His name in prayer. Because the Holy Spirit would soon be among them, He would take the place of Jesus and be their Advocate in prayer. Therefore prayer would be another solution to the disciples' problems.

Jesus strengthened His appeal to the disciples to take advantage of the Spirit's presence in His absence. They were to use His name in prayer in the assurance that while the Holy Spirit is with the believer it will not be necessary for Him to plead with the Father for them because their prayers have already been offered in His name. Jesus said our prayers will be heard because they are offered in His name, and because the Father loves those who love Jesus (vv. 26-27). Jesus is described as the one "who also maketh intercession for us" (Ro 8:34). He is man's Intercessor with God, as the Holy Spirit is God's Intercessor with man. Together they effect a complementary intercession and perform a necessary spiritual function for the believer.

Jesus' Ultimate Triumph (vv. 32-33)

"Behold, the hour cometh, yea, is now come, that ye shall be scattered, every man to his own, and shall leave me alone: and yet I am not alone, because the Father is with me. These things I have spoken unto you, that in me ye might have peace. In the world ye shall have tribulation: but be of good cheer; I have overcome the world" (vv. 32-33).

Jesus had just asked a very pertinent question: "Do ye now believe?" (v. 31). For the coming ordeal an unwavering faith would be vital. The question is, would they stand firm? Jesus had given them the assurances of security in both the ministries of Himself and the Holy Spirit which would secure them if they truly believed and accepted them. Did they? This was the great question.

Then came the final assurance of victory and peace: "In the world ye shall have tribulation: but be of good cheer; I have overcome the world" (v. 33). Jesus demonstrated in Calvary His conquest over the evil spiritual forces which are the cause of world disorder. Satan is a defeated foe, for John has already said, "The prince of this world is judged" (v. 11). Victory is ultimately on the side of the Christian because it is already an accomplished fact in Calvary. There remains only the execution of the coming government of God over the forces of evil, man and nature, which will be accomplished at Jesus' second coming.

Jesus ended His farewell discourse with a note of triumph. He went forth from the upper room a Victor, not the vanquished. Because of this we can live and labor confidently because we are on the Victor's side.

43

The Prayer of Prayers — For Himself

17:1-5

IT WAS LATE AT NIGHT when Jesus ended His farewell discourse. It was concluded with the words of triumph which indicate the ultimate victory which will come through Christ: "In the world ye shall have tribulation: but be of good cheer; I have overcome the world." This discourse was the last of three which Jesus had delivered in the upper room. One was His message on the untroubled heart (chap. 14), another was His message on the vine and the branches (chap. 15), and the last was His message on the coming of the Holy Spirit (chap. 16).

Just as Jesus was about to go out into the night, He prayed a prayer, largely for His disciples, which can be called The Lord's Prayer in distinction to that one which is a part of the Sermon on the Mount, which is rightly identified as "the disciples' prayer."

In Jesus' last discourse, the message concerned the Holy Spirit who would be the disciples' Paraclete to take His place at their side. Then there was introduced the element of prayer as a companion to the presence of the Holy Spirit. These are important parts of the divine provision for the believer. In the Holy Spirit we have God's approach to man, while in prayer we have man's approach to God. The Holy Spirit would provide communion, and prayer would provide communication.

Until then, the disciples had no need to pray. Jesus had already said to them, "Hitherto have ye asked nothing in my name" (Jn 16:24), which meant two things: First, they had not needed to pray because Jesus was still with them; second, they had not needed to pray in Jesus' name because Jesus had not died.

The prayer is of two parts: The first is a prayer by Jesus for

Himself (vv. 1-5). The second is for His *disciples* (vv. 6-26). In the second part, Jesus prayed for His immediately present disciples (vv. 6-19), and then for all future disciples (vv. 20-26).

JESUS PRAYS FOR HIMSELF

These words spake Jesus, and lifted up his eyes to heaven, and said, Father, the hour is come; glorify thy Son, that thy Son also may glorify thee: as thou hast given him power over all flesh, that he should give eternal life to as many as thou hast given him. And this is life eternal, that they might know thee the only true God, and Jesus Christ, whom thou hast sent. I have glorified thee on the earth. I have finished the work which thou gavest me to do. And now, O Father, glorify thou me with thine own self with the glory which I had with thee before the world was" (vv. 1-5).

An analysis of Jesus' prayer yields some helpful hints about prayer in general:

PRAYER USES WORDS

"These words spake Jesus" (v. 1). These words were not for the understanding of God, who knows our thoughts and understands our desires. Words are for the understanding and participation of man. There is a fellowship in prayer, and when believers gather they do not always sit in silent contemplation. Fellowship in prayer means sharing desires by the spoken word.

Another great passage on prayer which links prayer to the Holy Spirit says He "maketh intercession for us with groanings which cannot be uttered" (Ro 8:26), or "with sighings as no language can shape into words" (Way trans.). The mode of communication between the Members of the Godhead is probably different from ours, that is, perhaps it is not by the use of words such as we speak. But our praying usually involves the spoken word. If man by electronics can throw a coded expression into the vastness of space and hear it again, then it is not impossible that the spiritual world can provide a means of communication between God and man.

PRAYER HAS DIRECTION

". . . and lifted up his eyes to heaven" (v. 1). This does not refer to the physical heavens, since a spinning globe like ours has changing directions. It refers to the spiritual heavens, the locale of God. This is a reminder that prayer is not a physical communication and does not depend on physical media. We have spiritual natures which are more important and vital in this communication than our physical natures.

Prayer is not a psychological exercise confined to the person's mind and to be engaged in for the improvement of the mind by a form of impersonal religious exercise. Nor is it a social exercise to be used as a means of improving group morale or helping human relations.

Prayer is the employment of words directed to our "Father" who is the Lord God Almighty. It is an approach to His divine person for the purpose of adoration and worship. It is an appeal for His blessing and help, not a means of religious begging. Prayer is not a tin cup in the hands of a religious mendicant seeking divine favors.

Prayer thinks of God before it considers anything else. It is sent in the direction of heaven and establishes communion before it considers and communicates the needs of earth.

PRAYER HAS PURPOSE

"The hour is come; glorify thy Son, that thy Son also may glorify thee" (v. 1). In this hour Jesus prepares Himself for His high-priestly act of atoning sacrifice. This is not an hour of sixty minutes, but that period of His passion in which Jesus would die and rise again in order to perform His great mediatorial work of redemption. In this hour both the Son and the Father would be glorified.

In trying to glorify Jesus by *His life*, men speak of His flawless character and charitable works. They try to glorify Him by *His words*, speaking of the message which Jesus left, and they try to glorify Him by *His works*, pointing to the long list of benevolent deeds as proof of Jesus' superlative character. But Jesus did not live merely to do great things and say good things; He lived to die. This was His "hour."

PRAYER HAS RESPONSE

"As thou hast given . . ." (v. 2). God responds to prayer by giving. Jesus said to His disciples, "Ask, and it shall be given you; seek, and ye shall find; knock, and it shall be opened unto you: for every one that asketh receiveth; and he that seeketh findeth; and to him that knocketh it shall be opened" (Mt 7: 7-8).

PRAYER HAS PRINCIPLE

". . . that he should give eternal life" (v. 2). All true prayer is born out of the eternal life produced by "the hour" of Jesus' sacrificial death and resurrection. This life is the beginning of redeemed man's communion and fellowship with God. In this light, prayer is not a natural means of access to God that comes automatically with physical life. Rather, it is a spiritual means of access that comes with the new life that is born out of the death and resurrection of Jesus and realized by us through faith.

The secret of this principle of prayer is found in the complete sayings of Jesus about eternal life: "As thou hast given him power over all flesh, that he should give eternal life to as many as thou hast given him. And this is life eternal, that they might know thee the only true God, and Jesus Christ, whom thou hast sent" (vv. 2-3).

Prayer is not only related to an eternal God, but is a communication with God based upon the possession of eternal life. Jesus does not define, explain or illustrate eternal life. He only tells us how to obtain it.

Jesus emphasized that the important thing is how to get eternal life: "And this is life eternal, that they might *know* thee . . . and Jesus Christ whom thou hast sent." Eternal life comes through knowledge — not knowledge acquired by learning the facts of God, but the knowledge of the experience of God. This experience is only realized through Christ, who was sent by God in order that we might be able to know Him.

Here in the heart of the greatest prayer in the Bible is one of the greatest evangelistic texts of the entire Word of God. The message on prayer now becomes a message on salvation.

Salvation is a matter of life. This life is eternal life. No person has this life by natural birth. It must be obtained by a new birth, *already* suggested by Jesus to Nicodemus when He said, "Verily, verily, I say unto thee, Except a man be born again, he cannot see the kingdom of God" (Jn 3:3).

"God has no grandchildren." He has children, but they cannot beget His grandchildren by natural generation. We may inherit national citizenship but not citizenship in the kingdom of God.

Life is a matter of knowledge. This is not the knowledge which knows that one plus one equals two. Rather, it is the knowledge of experience, for salvation comes from the experience of a divine-human confrontation. "And this is life eternal, that they might know thee the only true God." Jesus Christ came into the world to make this experience possible.

Knowledge is a matter of faith. Why should the requirement be faith? Because it is the only equitable basis upon which to base the experience of salvation. If it was *birth,* some people would have an unmerited advantage; if it was *wisdom,* some people would have greater capacities; if it was *works,* some people would be able to perform more nobly. But since it is faith, all men are leveled to one common and universal basis of salvation. It is required of all because it is just for all.

The question at this point is: How does one believe to have eternal life in order to be saved?

First, faith is an attitude to God. It believes in *divine sovereignty* in setting up the requirements of salvation, in *divine revelation* in setting forth the facts of salvation, and in Jesus Christ as the Son of God involving His incarnation, virtuous life, vicarious death and victorious resurrection. These salvation facts are necessary for a saving act of faith.

Second, faith is an act of the sinner. It is an *act of repentance* in which we express genuine sorrow for sin and a willingness to turn away from sinful acts. It is an *act of commital* in which we sincerely surrender our lives to the dominion of God and receive Christ's lordship over life, and it is an *act of confession* in which we put ourself on record before the world as a Christian. We confess the new direction, new motives and new ideals of our life and demonstrate them by a new life.

Third, faith is a way of life for the saved one. This kind of faith is not the faith of facts about God, but the faith of a new force, energy and power by which life is lived. It is the faith of direction in which we are now going, of association in the new company of people with whom we move, and of new principles to guide and activate our lives.

44

The Prayer of Prayers — For Others

17:6-26

THE CONTEXT of Jesus' prayer of prayers is as significant as its content. For Jesus, the context of the prayer was His "hour"; for the disciples it was their "hour." Jesus' hour was His death; the disciples' hour was their life. Jesus had a cross and we have one; His took Him to death, and ours takes us to life. Prayer is not a form of religious exchange for the procurement of the material- istic foibles of life. It is a preparation for life in all its grandest dimensions.

Jesus was careful to set forth the terms of this preparation in this prayer for His disciples. His concern was that they, fur- nished with eternal life, might fulfill their mission in life. The necessity for His prayer rested in the cross which the disciples had to carry into the world.

Some of our modern preaching about discipleship is a travesty on the cross. Radio evangelists have been known to offer pre- miums, from decorated tablecloths to ball-point pens, for "ac- cepting Jesus." What a far cry this is from the cross which Jesus promised to all who followed Him. Great danger lies in the cur- rent popularity of religion, because often we miss the meaning of the cross by the easy manner in which we are urged to em- brace Christ.

When large sums of money were being given away on TV quiz programs, a young Nigerian was a contestant, with the Bible as his category. Each week his phenomenal answers took him higher and higher, until he was considered a marvel in Biblical knowledge. Then it was discovered he was living in a multiple- wife situation, and his claim to be a medical student was fraudulent. He knew all about the Bible, but he did not know what the Bible was all about.

Those who bear the cross will not be facile pretenders with fluid and glib answers to biblical knowledge, for the cross is a great divider, a sieve that separates the wheat from the chaff. If living by dying is the criteria of Christianity, the pretender wants none of it.

Who are those for whose enrichment, blessing and security this prayer is offered? Their identity is found in verses 6-10:

> I have manifested thy name unto the men which thou gavest me out of the world: thine they were, and thou gavest them me; and they have kept thy word. Now they have known that all things whatsoever thou hast given me are of thee. For I have given unto them the words which thou gavest me; and they have received them, and have known surely that I came out from thee, and they have believed that thou didst send me. I pray for them: I pray not for the world, but for them which thou hast given me; for they are thine. And all mine are thine, and thine are mine; and I am glorified in them.

First, they are those who are separate from the world, given unto Jesus by the Father. The distinguishing phrase in verse 6 is "thou gavest them me." The process of being given to Jesus and thus being a child of God is described by Paul as follows: "For whom he did foreknow, he also did predestinate to be conformed to the image of his Son, that he might be the firstborn among many brethren. Moreover whom he did predestinate, them he also called: and whom he called, them he also justified: and whom he justified, them he also glorified" (Ro 8:29-30).

Second, they are those who are distinguished from the world because "they have kept thy word" (v. 6). After distinguishing between the disciple and the nondisciple, Jesus said, "I pray for them [the disciples]: I pray not for the world, but for them which thou hast given me; for they are thine" (v. 9). This does not mean that Jesus will never pray for the children of this world, because He died for it. But this prayer is concerned with the constancy of discipleship. Only in the sense of this purpose does Jesus *not* pray for the world.

Jesus Prays for Others

Observe the nature of Jesus' prayer for those *who are* His disciples (vv. 6-19) and those *who will yet become* His disciples (vv. 20-26).

THEIR UNITY

"And now I am no more in the world, but these are in the world, and I come to thee. Holy Father, keep through thine own name those whom thou hast given me, that they may be one, as we are" (v. 11).

This statement is often referred to as the divine desire for an ecumenical church. But it has a deeper meaning, for it speaks of a oneness which already exists among those who are truly His. This oneness would be continually prayed for by the interceding Christ. It arises from within, and from out of the conditions which Jesus has already pointed to as defining His disciples. The first is the *divine work of grace* and the second is the *divine word of God* (v. 6).

THEIR SECURITY

"While I was with them in the world, I kept them in thy name: those that thou gavest me I have kept, and none of them is lost, but the son of perdition; that the scripture might be fulfilled" (v. 12). True believers shall inevitably experience glorification, which means that "none of them is lost." The sole exception is Judas, who is described as "the son of perdition." In conformity to the purpose of this intercessory prayer, Meyer says Jesus prays "that God *keep* them in His name, in order that they, in virtue of one common faith and confession resting on the name of God, may be one (in the spiritual fellowship, of like mind and love)."

THEIR TRANQUILLITY

"And now come I to thee; and these things I speak in the world, that they might have my joy fulfilled in themselves" (v. 13). The tranquillity of life in the believer is a birthright secured by Jesus' intercession. The "joy" mentioned is not the emotional effervescence of a good feeling which is fluctuating and undulating; it is "my joy" — the quality of life which is the guarantee of tranquillity. It does not come from chemical tranquilizers, but from the inner peace of Christ within our hearts.

THEIR PROTECTION

"I have given them thy word; and the world hath hated them, because they are not of the world, even as I am not of the world. I pray not that thou shouldest take them out of the world, but that thou shouldest keep them from the evil. They are not of the world, even as I am not of the world" (vv. 14-16).

The disciple is in the midst of the dangers of the world's alien environment. It is alien because physically it is managed by a curse, resulting in all manner of physical perils. Also, it is alien because "the world hath hated them," and because the Christian is of such nature that he does not belong to the world. He may be *in* it, but he does not need to be *of* it.

The safety and protection of the believer in this alien environment are not achieved by taking him "out of the world," by either putting cloister walls around him or socially and physically isolating him from it. The Christian has spiritual insulation rather than social or physical isolation, and by means of this insulation Jesus proposes to "keep them from the evil."

THEIR SANCTIFICATION

"Sanctify them through thy truth: thy word is truth" (v. 17). "And for their sakes I sanctify myself, that they also might be sanctified through the truth" (v. 19). When Jesus prayed this prayer, sanctification came through the observance of physical ordinances and sacrifices, but a new era was about to dawn when this sanctification would come "through the truth." The passage and operation of the Word of God in our spiritual natures achieve cleansing, purification and preparation.

This sanctification is not automatic. Jesus was sanctified through His self-consecration in death, and we will be sanctified through our self-consecration by the Word of God. As we voluntarily read, study and apply God's Word to our lives, the sanctifying process is in progress.

THEIR MISSION

"As thou hast sent me into the world, even so have I also

sent them into the world" (v. 18). We are in the world in the place of Jesus. Our mission is identified with His mission, our work is His work, our objectives are His objectives, and our life is linked with His life. He was sent in a redemptive service, therefore we are sent in a redemptive service. The meaning of life for us is determined by the purposes of God in Christ. It is "as" and "so." His life is the *pattern;* ours is the *product.*

THEIR POSTERITY

"Neither pray I for these alone, but for them also which shall believe on me through their word; that they all may be one; as thou, Father, art in me, and I in thee, that they also may be one in us; that the world may believe that thou hast sent me. And the glory which thou gavest me I have given them; that they may be one, even as we are one" (vv. 20-22).

Jesus' prayer extends beyond His concern for His immediate disciples to all future believers. He prays for oneness. His prayer is very significant and is of two petitions:

The Oneness of All Disciples. "That they all may be one." Here is the oneness of all believers. This is almost universally claimed as a structural, organic union into one ecumenical body of all Christians, both Protestant and Catholic, from both Eastern and Western branches of the church. But Jesus is teaching ethical oneness, not organic oneness, as Meyer says, "that all . . . may be one (ethically, in likeness of disposition, of love, of endeavour, etc. on the ground of faith)" (cf. Eph 4:3).

The likeness of Father and Son. "As thou, Father, art in me, and I in thee." This is the basis of the ethical oneness. The great prototype of the ethical unity of all believers, desired by Jesus, "must correspond as to its original type," Meyer says, "to the reciprocal of all believers in fellowship with the Father and the Son, however, it shall serve to the unbelieving world as an actual proof and ground of conviction that Christ, the grand central point and support of this unity, is none other than the sent of God."

Ethical unity of all believers refers to the "body" concept of the church (1 Co 12:13-27) in which the functions of the body are directed by the Head, which is Christ. Since Christ is "the grand central point and support of this unity," He must be the rallying point of all ecumenicity. He cannot be less than the one who prayed "that they may be one, as we are." This equality with God means deity, and any rallying point for an ecumenical church must be no less than Christ, the Son of God who was sent by God.

THEIR IDENTIFICATION

"I in them, and thou in me, that they may be made perfect in one; and that the world may know that thou hast sent me, and hast loved them, as thou hast loved me" (v. 23). The ethical oneness of all believers would constitute a strong reason for the world to believe that Jesus was sent by God and would be a compelling credential of His claims. Just as love among believers would be a proof of their true discipleship (Jn 13:35), so oneness would be a proof of His true Messiahship.

THEIR DESTINY

Father, I will that they also, whom thou hast given me, be with me where I am; that they may behold my glory, which thou hast given me: for thou lovedst me before the foundation of the world. O righteous Father, the world hath not known thee: but I have known thee, and these have known that thou hast sent me. And I have declared unto them thy name, and will declare it: that the love wherewith thou hast loved me may be in them, and I in them (vv. 24-26).

The destiny of all believers is to share the eternal glory which Christ had in His preexistence and will have again in His exaltation. He said to the disciples that they were to "be with me where I am." Exalted to this heavenly glory at His ascension, He will be revealed in this heavenly glory at His second coming. The disciples would share in this coming glory at the time of the consummation spoken of by Paul when he said, "And if children, then heirs; heirs of God, and joint-heirs with Christ; if so be that we suffer with him, that we may be also glorified together" (Ro 8:17).

The prayer was finished. Its effects and its answer are revealed in the subsequent history of the church. It is the fulfill-

ment of the expectation of Jesus' prayer that nothing could
separate them from the love of God. It is the realization that
all believers can overcome a hostile world. It is reenacted in the
heroic lives of fishermen, peasants and slaves possessing the
characteristics of Jesus Christ. It is expressed in the words of
Paul:

> Who shall separate us from the love of Christ? Shall tribula-
> tion, or distress, or persecution, or famine, or nakedness, or peril,
> or sword? . . . Nay, in all these things we are more than con-
> querors through him that loved us. For I am persuaded, that
> neither death, nor life, nor angels, nor principalities, nor pow-
> ers, nor things present, nor things to come, nor height, nor
> depth, nor any other creature, shall be able to separate us from
> the love of God, which is in Christ Jesus our Lord (Ro 8:
> 35-39).

The secret of this continuing life of personal triumph in the
disciples, and their ultimate destiny, "to be with me where I
am," is found in the last words of the prayer, "I in them." It is
"Christ in you" which is "the hope of glory." Herein lies the
secret of perseverance, triumph and victorious living. The end
product of such loftly purposes and principles is the Christian
standing in the likeness of Jesus Christ.

45

The Arrest of Jesus

18:1-14

LATE ON THURSDAY NIGHT Jesus ended the last of His three discourses and finished His high-priestly prayer in the upper room. After a hymn sung, in the words of Psalm 118, it was all over, and Jesus left with His disciples for Gethsemane.

Jesus moved from prayer to passion as He crossed the brook Cedron with His little band of disciples. He moved from the sphere of benevolence in which He fed, healed, comforted and helped, to the sphere of expiation in which He offered Himself as a sacrifice for sin. Crossing the Cedron was the dividing line of His career. Behind Him lay life, notably the three years of His public ministry in which He went about doing good. Ahead of Him lay death with all the shame, humiliation and suffering it would produce.

THE MEANING OF GETHSEMANE TO JESUS

Gethsemane was the place of preparation for death. Even Jesus needed this preparation, for He was not forced to die. He had recently said to His disciples, "No man taketh it [my life] from me, but I lay it down of myself. I have power to lay it down, and I have power to take it again" (Jn 10:18). Death was to be a willing and voluntary act.

Jesus had the power of choice, and He also had the choice of the use of power. Would He use His divine power to resist death? Hitherto He had restrained Himself from using His supernatural power on His own behalf. He had used it repeatedly for others: to heal, feed, deliver from peril, and raise from the dead. Not once had He used this power for His own advantage, to make life easier or more comfortable.

In Gethsemane He would weigh the reasonings of man against
the counsels of God. Why should He be made an offering for
sin when He had never sinned? Why should He be repaid for
infinite love and goodness with ignominy and shame? Why?
Gethsemane would echo and reecho with these and a multitude
of other questions, but their answers would be locked in the
divine counsels, unknown to us. What we do know is that Jesus
surrendered the advantage of His divine power and subjected
Himself to death.

Jesus and His disciples, except for Judas, crossed over the narrow bridge on the road which leads over the Mount of Olives to
Bethany. The path wound among stone-walled orchards and
gardens, near which lay an olive orchard called Gethsemane.

Jesus' Gethsemane experience shows us two things about our
own lives. When the soul is overwhelmed it seeks God. On the
other hand, we do not want to be too far removed from human
sympathy and help, for we need both the divine and the human.

Three of the disciples went with Jesus into the depths of the
garden where He said to them, "My soul is exceeding sorrowful, even unto death: tarry ye here, and watch" (Mt 26:38).
Then He went on the distance of a stone's throw to be alone
with God. The pent-up sorrow which had been growing through
the past days burst forth into an agony of soul no human had
ever experienced. He was treading the valley of the shadow,
beginning to feel the weight of the world's sin and beginning to
see the outline of a cross. Did He have to bear that cross alone?
Did He have to drink the cup of death to its dregs? Was redemption possible only at the awful price about to be exacted?
Could this hour not pass? These and many others were the
questions Jesus wrestled with in His hour of soul agony in Gethsemane.

So vivid is the memory of the gospel writers that thirty, forty,
and, in one instance, sixty years, afterward they describe in detail the agony that came upon the Son of God. He first kneeled,
then fell on His face on the ground, and prayed with strong
crying and a flood of tears until His sweat became like great
drops of blood. He cried out, "O my Father, if it be possible, let
this cup pass from me: nevertheless not as I will, but as thou

wilt" (Mt 26:39). Here is the climax of Gethsemane — Jesus' recognition of and submission to God's will. It was not to be a subservient and apathetic submission, but an active participation in God's redemptive plan.

Jesus experienced what we must all come to understand: that perfect peace of soul can only be found in submission to the divine will. The human constitution is so arranged that it must be subject to something higher than itself. Since nothing can be higher than the will of God, and nothing greater than the lordship of Christ, we must all come into submission and surrender to find perfect peace.

The Man on His face in Gethsemane would soon be the Man on the cross at Calvary, as He would later be the Man in the tomb. Then life would burst from the tomb and Jesus Christ would be the invincible Monarch of the spiritual world, conquering by love that man might live.

The Meaning of Gethsemane for Us

Although Gethsemane was a preparation for death, in its larger sense it was a preparation for life. We must each have our Gethsemane for life's preparation in three things: first, in prayer for divine strength; second, in obedience to the divine will; third, in faith in the divine plan. Out of this preparation can come the larger life that puts God at the center and preserves those values which make life an important and fruitful experience.

While Jesus was praying, Judas was bargaining. His position as one of the twelve had become hopeless, and He hastened to friends with whom he had established liaison in the Sanhedrin. With these he consummated a bargain to deliver Jesus into their hands for a certain amount of money. Judas led the temple authorities and soldiers to the place where he knew Jesus customarily prayed, and there he desecrated the sacred precincts of prayer by his kiss of betrayal. Then he delivered Jesus into the hands of His enemies. With this arrest, Jesus was now on His way to the cross via Gabbatha and its subsequent trial and judgment.

Three things stand out among the many things which have already become apparent in connection with Jesus' prayer and arrest:

THE BLOOD OF AGONY

In His redemptive passion Jesus shed blood, and in the Garden of Gethsemane "his sweat became like great drops of blood falling down upon the ground" (Lk 22:44). This sweat was caused by the violent agony of the conscious sufferings of Jesus for our sin, a foretaste of the shedding of blood on the cross. The blood is related to the atonement because it is described in the Bible as the symbol of life: "The life of the flesh is in the blood." The mental and spiritual agony in the garden was followed by physical agony on the cross when nails, thorns and spear were either pressed, driven or thrust into Jesus' body.

THE KISS OF PERFIDY

Judas had arranged to identify and betray Jesus to His enemies by a kiss. It was a perfidious act, for it was the customary kiss of a disciple to his teacher. It served its purpose and sent two men to their deaths — Jesus who died for all, and Judas who died for himself.

THE SWORD AND THE CUP

The only act of violence attending Jesus' arrest was Peter's impetuous defense of Jesus by the sword when he injured the high priest's servant. He was instantly reprimanded by Jesus and bidden to sheath his sword, and given to understand that Christ's kingdom would not be established by force or violence.

In contrast to the sword was the cup. While the immediate reference of the cup, as Jesus used it here, was to death, it also embraced the cup of communion which Jesus had just shared with His disciples in the upper room. Jesus' conquest would be a redemptive one. He would conquer by nonviolence in a passive way, but also by love in an active way. The sharpest weapon in the arsenal of Christianity is not politics, law or governmental alignment, but love.

As we tread again the winding path of Gethsemane's olive grove we are rediscovering the verities of our faith — the great truths of redemption.

46

The Trial of Jesus

18:15-40

THE CIRCUMSTANCES which surround the trial of Jesus confront us with one of the most anomalous situations of history: the arrest, the trial and the condemnation of a just and perfect man. It was to this trial that the officers of the Sanhedrin and the soldiers of Caesar led Jesus from His prayer rendezvous in Gethsemane.

BEFORE ANNAS

He was first taken to the palace of the high priest Annas because of Annas' superior knowledge of the law and his ability to handle the difficult situation presented by Jesus' presence and influence in the nation. Not much is said in John's account of what took place before Annas. It is limited to two questions. One concerned Peter, who stood in the open court warming himself by an open fire against the cold of that April night. As he stood there dejected and discouraged, the woman doorkeeper (for female porters were not uncommon), recognizing Peter, asked in contempt, "Art not thou also one of this man's disciples?" (v. 17). Something in his face, or great size, or Galilean speech had betrayed him. But Peter said, "I am not" (v. 17).

Peter's denial was not the calculated, premeditated act that was true of Judas' betrayal. It was due to Peter's impulsive nature which responded to circumstances rather than character, and the circumstances here were the alien fire at which Peter warmed himself. While he warmed his hands, his heart grew cold and he defected.

Discipleship is a two-way street which provides strength and comfort for the disciple by the exalted presence of Jesus, and comfort and strength for the Master by the faithful presence of the disciple. In Jesus' case He had not only suffered the indignities of His enemies, but lost the help of His friends, for in the garden they slept and in the courtyard Peter disclaimed Him.

The other recorded question in the palace of Annas was asked of Jesus in order to elicit evidence to be used against Him. The high priest asked Him of His disciples and His doctrine. Why had He gathered so many disciples? What did He mean by sending them throughout Galilee and Judea? Why had He allowed the crowds to hail Him as Messiah? What did He mean by asserting that He would establish the kingdom of God? Jesus gave no answer to this question, but simply referred to His record. He had taught frankly and without reserve, claiming no secret doctrines and professing no seditious purposes. Everything that He said had been said openly. All they needed to do was to ask His auditors; they would be witnesses. But they were not the kind of witnesses the enemies of Jesus wanted, for they desired only that Jesus be handed over to the Romans as quickly as possible.

Before Caiaphas

The scene changed, and Jesus was removed to the palace of the reigning high priest, Caiaphas, who was the only one who could hold official relations with Pilate and ask him to carry out the resolution to put Jesus to death. John omits entirely any record of the trial of Jesus before Caiaphas, so whatever we know of what transpired in this second scene of the trial has been gathered from the other three gospels.

It was not a trial at all, only a mockery, for the tribunal which was called to condemn Jesus was not a legal court but one that was extemporized by the excited and embittered Jews who sought occasion to dispose of Jesus. The rules of jurisprudence condemn the trial of Jesus before Caiaphas as an outrage. No accuser appeared, and the judge himself took the place of the accuser in violation of all laws of judicial procedure. Witnesses against the prisoner were procured by bribery and committed perjury in their testimony. There was not a single witness for the defense, though the law gave such witnesses the preference, and there was no counsel for the defense. From the very moment the court convened, it sought to condemn and not acquit.

There were no written laws to which Caiaphas could appeal, for the Old Testament had not anticipated the case of anyone calling himself the Messiah falsely and maliciously. The only grounds on which the theocracy could demand a capital conviction lay outside the law of Moses, and that is why they were so eager to get Jesus into Pilate's hands and under Roman law.

There remained nothing to do except to feign hypocritical horror that this peasant from Galilee should claim equality with God. Thus, it was Caiaphas' chief concern to establish the crime of blasphemy. So, looking straight at the accused, the mitered prelate in his white robes asked, "I put you on your oath before the living God, art thou the Christ — the anointed One — the King Messiah, the Son of God?"

With kingly dignity in the face of certain death, Jesus calmly replied to the adjuration, "Thou hast said." As if this were not enough, Caiaphas and the judges, rising on their cushions, demanded in loud voices, "Art thou, then, the Son of God?" And Jesus replied, "I am."

This was enough. Quivering with passion, Caiaphas rent the linen bosom of his high-priestly robe and cried "blasphemy," suggesting to his colleagues in this irregular, illegal and self-constituted court that witnesses be dispensed with and sentence be passed. They agreed that on His own confession Jesus was worthy of death. He could therefore be presented to Pilate as a state criminal whose pretentions were a peril to the imperial rights of Caesar.

Before Pilate

About three o'clock in the morning, Jesus was led under escort of the temple police to the residence of Pontius Pilate on Mount Zion. There was a hall in the palace where trials were usually conducted, but the Jews would not enter it for fear of defilement during the Passover. So Pilate had his official seat established in an open-air court.

Upon taking his seat, Pilate formally asked Caiaphas what accusation they had against the prisoner. Caiaphas answered, "If he were not a malefactor [a great offender], we would not have delivered him up unto thee" (18:30). And then he went on to describe the legal dilemma in which they found themselves. He said, "We have power to punish ordinary offenders by our own laws but this man's crimes go beyond our powers, therefore we have handed him over to you to be executed."

"What is his crime?" demanded Pilate. But Caiaphas knew that to accuse Jesus of claiming deity would have been a religious matter to be judged by their own laws. Jesus had to be exposed as a pretender to Caesar's power, and so Caiaphas accused Jesus of stirring up the nation against paying tribute to Caesar.

Before Caiaphas, the chief concern was to establish blasphemy to satisfy the Jews: Did Jesus claim to be the Son of God? Before Pilate, the chief concern was to establish sedition and rebellion: Did Jesus claim to be the King of the Jews and therefore a rival of Caesar? Until this was established, Jesus could not be lawfully executed.

Pilate then took Jesus aside into his private chambers and asked Him, "Art thou the King of the Jews?" "Yes, I am a King," replied Jesus. "To this end was I born, and for this cause came I into the world, that I should bear witness unto the truth. Every one that is of the truth heareth my voice" (18:37). For the second time Jesus sealed His fate; He had claimed to be the Son of God, and now He claimed to be King of the Jews.

Seeing no alternative, Pilate brought Jesus out to the open-air court where he announced that he had examined Him and found nothing in Him worthy of death. But the Jews raised such a clamor and storm of accusation against Jesus that Pilate decided to send Him to Herod Antipas, who resided just a few streets away.

When Herod had nothing to add to the condemnation of Jesus, he sent Him back to Pilate who now had to make some final disposition of the Galilean. But Pilate thought he saw a way out of his dilemma over the disposition of Jesus, and that way out was in the person of one Barabbas. It was the custom to carry out capital sentences at feast times so that the people at large might get a lesson, but it was likewise the custom to release any one prisoner condemned to death whom the people might name in the Passover week. Pilate appealed to this custom in the hope that the people might solve his problem.

Awaiting execution in the prison at Jerusalem was a man by name of Barabbas, a vicious, loathesome criminal. Pilate presumed that when he proposed the release of either Jesus or Barabbas, the people would choose Jesus. But when Pilate proposed Jesus' release, the people, urged on by the priests, cried out, much to Pilate's regret, "Not this man, but Barabbas." By these recriminating accusations Jesus was tried, condemned and sentenced to the cross.

Preparations had been made for three executions on three crosses, which had already been ordered and made. Now at the last minute there was a change, for Barabbas was freed and Jesus condemned to die. On whose cross would Jesus die? Not His own, for none was made for Him. He would die on Barabbas' cross, and if the implication is fully followed, He died on the cross that was fashioned for you and me.

47

Preparation for the Crucifixion
19:1-17

FROM THIS MOMENT there was no doubt of the issue Jesus faced with certainty — the cross on which He would die. That cross is far more than a symbol to adorn our altars and churches or an ornament to be worn upon our persons. Its significance lies in the infinite value of the one who died upon it.

The cross and its Christ are God's remedy for man's sin, God's answer for man's predicament, God's offer for man's peace, God's hope for man's future, and God's promise for man's salvation.

Pilate saw the cross as the symbol of a mistake, the Jews saw it as the symbol of hatred, Mary saw it as the symbol of love, and the disciples saw it as the symbol of disappointment. Today some see it as the symbol of religion while others see it as the symbol of God's salvation. It is in our total biblical perspective to look at the cross in the light of God's eternal love and mercy. "For God so loved the world, that he gave his only begotten Son, that whosoever believeth in him should not perish, but have everlasting life."

The prelude to the crucifixion is confined to two places: the judgment hall and the guard room, where five things occurred:

> the humiliation of Jesus (vv. 1-3)
> the presentation of Jesus (vv. 4-6)
> the identification of Jesus (vv. 7-12)
> the rejection of Jesus (vv. 13-15)
> the procession of Jesus to the cross (vv. 16-17)

THE HUMILIATION OF JESUS (vv. 1-3)

This humiliation consisted of a number of debasing and abu-

sive acts performed at the instigation of the priests and prompt-
ings of the people.

THE SCOURGING

"Then Pilate therefore took Jesus, and scourged him" (v. 1).
Scourging was always inflicted as the first step in carrying out
a capital sentence. In keeping with this practice, Jesus was
seized by some of the soldiers standing near and, after being
stripped to the waist, was beaten with knots of rope, or plaited
leather thongs, armed at the ends with acorn-shaped drops of
lead or small sharp-pointed bones. This continued as long as the
soldiers chose, which in this case must have been a long time,
in order to vent the pent-up wrath of the officials on Jesus.

THE CROWNING

"And the soldiers platted a crown of thorns, and put it on his
head" (v. 2). Jesus was to be arrayed in the caricature of a
king. He was to be mocked in this manner to reveal the extent
of the Jews' rejection of His claims to be their King. The first
emblem of mockery was the thorns, woven together and bent
into the shape of a mocking crown. This was placed on Jesus'
head and pressed down until the long, steellike spines pierced
His head and caused trickles of blood to run down head and
face. Instead of the golden crown encrusted with jewels, this
crown — the emblem of mock sovereignty — was used to heap
indignity and insult upon Jesus.

THE ROBING

"And they put on him a purple robe" (v. 2). This robe was
the emblem of mock royalty with the intention of ridiculing His
claim to be the King of the Jews. When the scourging was over,
Jesus was formally delivered over to a military officer with the
authority to see Him crucified. Upon His quivering, beaten body
they threw the scarlet sagum or robe — as a rough burlesque
of the long and fine purple one worn by the emperor and other
eastern monarchs.

To complete the mockery they thrust a long slender reed into
His hand as an emblem of mock authority. It was a mocking

substitute for the jeweled batons used by kings to indicate imperial authority. Having arrayed Jesus with these mocking emblems, they heaped indignity upon indignity on Him with mocking oaths of allegiance, saluting Him with derision and shouting, "Hail, King of the Jews!" (v. 3). Then they indulged their blasphemous conduct by tearing the reed from His hands, and striking Him with it over face and head. Others struck Him with their fists; some in their contempt spat on Him.

The Presentation of Jesus

> Pilate therefore went forth again, and saith unto them, Behold, I bring him forth to you, that ye may know that I find no fault in him. Then came Jesus forth, wearing the crown of thorns, and the purple robe. And Pilate saith unto them, Behold the man! When the chief priests therefore and officers saw him, they cried out, saying, Crucify him, crucify him. Pilate saith unto them, Take ye him, and crucify him: for I find no fault in him (vv. 4-6).

Pilate, who had apparently retired into the palace for a respite from the howling mob, now reappeared upon the balcony with his wife, Procla, to make one more effort to escape his horrible dilemma. Professing to find no fault in Jesus, Pilate then turned to the figure at his side and said to the people, "Ecce Homo! [Behold the man]!"

It was at this point, no doubt, that Pilate washed his hands in water as a symbol expressive of the repudiation of responsibility. Calling for water, Pilate with significant gestures washed his hands, saying aloud as he did so, "I am innocent of the blood of this just person: see ye to it." Whereupon the people answered, "His blood be on us, and on our children" (Mt 27:24-25). And it was to be so. Before Christ was nailed to the cross, Judas in despair hanged himself. The following year Caiaphas was deposed from his priestly office. Herod, dethroned by Caesar, died in exile and infamy. Pilate, shortly after the crucifixion, was stripped of his authority and banished from his native land. He subsequently committed suicide. The house of Annas was destroyed by a mob of Jews, and his son was dragged through the streets, scourged and murdered. Jerusalem, besieged by the Romans, was almost totally destroyed and tens of thousands of its inhabitants were crucified. The Jews, scattered through every land, have been a nation of outcasts, persecuted, ostracized, and scorned of all men. Truly their prayer has been and is still being answered.

THE IDENTIFICATION OF JESUS

The Jews answered him, We have a law, and by our law he ought to die, because he made himself the Son of God. When Pilate therefore heard that saying, he was the more afraid; and went again into the judgment hall, and saith unto Jesus, Whence art thou? But Jesus gave him no answer. Then saith Pilate unto him, Speakest thou not unto me? Knowest thou not that I have power to crucify thee, and have power to release thee? Jesus answered, Thou couldest have no power at all against me, except it were given thee from above: therefore he that delivered me unto thee hath the greater sin. And from thenceforth Pilate sought to release him: but the Jews cried out, saying, If thou let this man go, thou art not Caesar's friend: whosoever maketh himself a king speaketh against Caesar (vv. 7-12).

Pilate said, "Take ye him, and crucify him: for I find no fault in him." Since the priests were determined to have Jesus' life, they then demanded it upon a new ground. They said that if He had committed no crime worthy of death by Roman law, He had by Jewish law. "We have a law, and by our law he ought to die, because he made himself the Son of God." If He was not guilty of sedition against Roman law, He was guilty of blasphemy against God, according to the Jews.

Frightened at the new turn of events, Pilate took Jesus into the praetorium for a private audience. Could He be the Son of God? "Whence art thou?" was his question, but Jesus was silent. Then Pilate said, "Knowest thou not that I have power to crucify thee, and have power to release thee?" Pilate had the power of man, but Jesus had the power of God. God is supreme, and man is powerless unless given authority by God. Jesus said to Pilate, and all puny men who follow, "Thou couldest have no power at all against me, except it were given thee from above" (v. 11).

THE REJECTION OF JESUS

> When Pilate therefore heard that saying, he brought Jesus forth, and sat down in the judgment seat in a place that is called the Pavement, but in the Hebrew, Gabbatha. And it was the preparation of the passover, and about the sixth hour: and he saith unto the Jews, Behold your King! But they cried out, Away with him, away with him, crucify him. Pilate saith unto them, Shall I crucify your King? The chief priests answered, We have no king but Caesar (vv. 13-15).

It was about nine o'clock. Pilate once more took his official seat in the courtyard of the palace. Turning to Jesus, who was still wearing the crown of thorns and the scarlet cloak, he cried in a burst of unconcealed contempt against the Jews, "Behold your King!" The only answer to their scornful rejection was a hurricane of cries saying, "Away with him, away with him, crucify him. Pilate saith unto them, Shall I crucify your King? The chief priests answered, We have no king but Caesar" (v. 15).

Feeling that he could do no more to save Jesus, Pilate gave the final order for crucifixion: "Then delivered he him therefore unto them to be crucified. And they took Jesus, and led him away" (v. 16).

While everything was being prepared for His execution, Jesus stood in the guardroom of the Praetorium, receiving the insults and physical abuse of the soldiers. His mock purple robe was removed and once more His own linen aba was placed upon Him.

Two things remained for Jesus to bear to Calvary. One was the crown of thorns, the emblem of the curse to be a reminder to all who saw Him die that He was dying for sin. The other was the cross itself which was now laid upon His shoulders.

THE PROCESSION OF JESUS

"Then delivered he him therefore unto them to be crucified. And they took Jesus, and led him away. And he bearing his cross went forth into a place called the place of a skull, which is called in the Hebrew Golgotha" (vv. 16-17).

The sad procession to the place of execution had begun with each prisoner carrying a whitened board suspended from his neck. This board proclaimed in black letters the offenses for which he was about to die. As the procession wound through the streets, a great crowd followed, but quite dissimilar to that crowd which five days before had welcomed Jesus to Jerusalem with "Hosanna – blessed." Today "Hosanna!" was changed to "Crucify!" and the palms became the cross.

Not all who made up that multitude were hostile to Jesus. Once when Jesus faltered under the weight of the cross and impeded the advance of the procession, a soldier seized a man from the crowd and compelled him to bear the cross. This involuntary crossbearer was Simon of Cyrene, who afterward became a Christian with all his family.

It is easy to be a cross-wearer; it is different to be a crossbearer. Are you a follower of Jesus? Have you volunteered to bear His cross? Until you have, none of the fruits of redemption can be yours to enjoy.

It costs something to be a crossbearer. Some time ago Lieutenant Peter Mulgrew of the Royal New Zealand Navy lost both legs and several fingers as he and friends attempted to climb Mount Makalu, a 27,824-foot mountain peak in Nepal. The effort was made without oxygen and other normal aids usually used in mountain climbing, but Lieutenant Mulgrew thought the venture worth the risk and he seemed more than willing to pay the price involved in conquering the mountain. His sole reward was recognition from some scientific society and a modest pension from his government. This was done for a corruptible crown, while the crossbearer's reward will be an incorruptible one.

48

The Execution of Jesus

19:18-42

THE PROCESSION ARRIVED at the place of crucifixion where the crosspieces were nailed to the upright posts of the three crosses. The center cross was set apart for our Lord and He was laid upon it, His arms outstretched along the two crossbeams. Huge nails were driven through the palms of His hands into the wood. Then His legs were bent up until the soles of His feet lay flat against the upright beam, where they were fastened together by two great iron nails driven into the beam. With the body firmly secured to the cross by ropes and nails, it was raised up opposite the place that had been dug out of the rocky surface, and then rudely dropped into its stony socket.

This was the world's most dramatic moment, when Jesus ascended the cross to be a voluntary sacrifice for sin. The title which He bore around His neck was the superscription which was nailed to the top of the upright beam of the cross. Pilate had written it with his own hands in Aramaic, Latin and Greek: THE KING OF THE JEWS. No tribute could have been more fitting or more prophetic than this inscription which linked the cross and its dying Saviour to all the nationalities of the world. Jesus is not a classified and restricted Saviour; He is the Saviour of all mankind.

Meanwhile the fierce heat of the Syrian sun beat down upon the cross and exacted its toll of anguish and suffering from its divine victim, who "endured the cross, despising the shame" for us. What we hear rather than what we see from the cross is important. Last words are always important, especially the last words of the dying. But of all the great words that have ever been uttered, the most significant are the seven sayings of Jesus on the cross.

The first three sayings were uttered in the daylight during the first three hours of the six Jesus was on the cross; the last four sayings were uttered in the last three hours, in darkness. The first three relate to those who stood around the cross and represented His thoughtfulness for others. The last four relate to Himself and represent His travail and triumph in atonement for sin. The seven words of Jesus are formed from a composite from three of the gospel writers:

The Word of Forgiveness

"Father, forgive them; for they know not what they do" (Lk 23:34). The first and last sayings from the cross began with "Father," a designation linking Jesus' redemption with His Father's will and plan. What is being accomplished is not some incidental or accidental emotional achievement to inspire our admiration; this is redemption.

This word, spoken as Jesus was nailed to the cross, expressed His tender feelings toward those who were driving in the nails and, perhaps more significantly, to those religious leaders who were more directly responsible for His death. Yet, most important of all, it expressed Jesus' forgiveness for all humanity. There is a true sense in which our sins, the sins of the whole world, were responsible for Jesus' death. It is with this larger implication in view that Jesus forgives.

A man was preaching to a Jewish audience in New York City's East Side where a crowd of interested listeners had gathered. One obstinate, noisy fellow glared at the speaker as he told of God's redeeming love through Jesus Christ. Making his way to a point in front of the speaker, the heckler blurted out, "Who killed Jesus?" With wise and tender truthfulness, the Christian replied, "I did." The truth is, we all did.

But there can be no forgiveness without repentance. The act of God presumes the act of man. This was a provisional promise from the dying Saviour, that even the sin of crucifixion would be forgiven upon the confession of the crucifiers; that all sin will be forgiven, provided the act of repentance has been initiated.

THE WORD OF SALVATION

"To day shalt thou be with me in paradise" (Lk 23:43). This is the only instance in which Jesus used the word "paradise," which refers to heaven in all its ultimate and consummate bliss and perfection. The same word is used by Paul in describing heaven, and by John in Revelation, where heaven appears in view at the consummation of all God's redemptive events.

When Jesus spoke this word, He distinguished between man and his body, between the physical and the spiritual, between the temporal and the eternal. It was the promise of the immediate survival of the soul in conscious life and the immediate transfer of personality, with all its faculties of intelligence and memory, into divine presence and eternal perpetuity.

THE WORD OF AFFECTION

"When Jesus therefore saw his mother, and the disciple standing by, whom he loved, he saith unto his mother, Woman, behold thy son! Then saith he to the disciple, Behold thy mother! And from that hour that disciple took her unto his own home" (Jn 19:26-27).

Here is evidence of Jesus' human concern for Mary, but it was not in any sense an elevation of Mary to a place of redemptive significance.

This word of affection fits the pattern of Jesus' concern for all the world, for it was love that prompted Calvary. It was love, not the nails, that kept Jesus on the cross, and it is love that draws men to salvation. "Herein is love, not that we loved God, but that he loved us, and sent his Son to be the propitiation for our sins" (1 Jn 4:10).

THE WORD OF ATONEMENT

"My God, my God, why hast thou forsaken me?" (Mt. 27:46). This was the middle saying of the seven words of the cross and the only one in the form of a question. It indicates no skepticism on Jesus' part but records the great burden of sin which He bears for the world, which brought separation from God.

This was the first saying uttered in the darkness of the second half of Jesus' passion. It was the sixth hour, or twelve noon, and Jesus had been on the cross for three hours. This words records the fact of the divine forsaking, when God turns His back on the one on whom was laid "the iniquity of us all." Here is the one who, knowing no sin, is "made him to be sin for us . . . that we might be made the righteousness of God in him" (2 Co 5:21).

At the cross we stand where the fire has burned, and it cannot burn again. Because Jesus died we shall not die, except in body. Because Jesus suffered for sin, we shall not suffer. Because Jesus was judged for sin, we shall not be judged.

THE WORD OF SUFFERING

"After this, Jesus knowing that all things were now accomplished, that the scripture might be fulfilled, saith, I thirst" (Jn 19:28). This thirst was that of a pain-wracked body dehydrated by the sun. It reveals the human nature of Jesus and refutes the Docetic doctrine that Jesus' human nature was only an apparent reality, not a true one. But here the Son of God reacts in an agonizing cry to the pangs of thirst in His physical body of flesh and bone.

THE WORD OF VICTORY

"It is finished" (Jn 19:30). This word proclaimed that the work of salvation was completed. It is "finished" because Jesus had just acknowledged "that all things were now accomplished" (v. 28).

THINGS ACCOMPLISHED BY CHRIST'S DEATH

Christ's death on the cross finished these things:
1. the eternal purposes of God
2. the law

3. the sin question
4. the system of symbol and sacrifice
5. the unchallenged reign of Satan
6. the work of salvation

Many things are finished, but just one thing finished them —
Christ's death. It finished God's side of the work of salvation,
which became an historical fact to which nothing can be added
and from which nothing can be taken away. It finished legalism
and the sacrificial system of priesthood and offering, and ended
all legitimate and valid human effort to attain self-salvation.

With this finishing act we hear Christ's cry of victory and
triumph emerging from the seeming defeat of death on the cross.
The sign that sealed this cry of victory and testified to the finished work of Christ was the rending of the great veil of gold
and purple — sixty feet long and thirty feet broad — before the
inner sanctuary of the temple. At the word of Christ, "It is finished," this veil suddenly was rent in two from the top to the
bottom. The direction of its rending indicates the source of its
destruction to be from the unseen hand of God. This rending
ended the old covenant of law, made Judaism obsolete, and took
God out of the holy of holies and put redeemed man in His
immediate presence.

The Word of Commitment

"And when Jesus had cried with a loud voice, he said, Father,
into thy hands I commend my spirit: and having said thus, he
gave up the ghost" (Lk 23:46). Jesus voluntarily accomplished
His own death by actually and literally dismissing His own life.
Previously He had said to His disciples, "I lay down my life, that
I might take it again. No man taketh it from me, but I lay it
down of myself. I have power to lay it down, and I have power
to take it again" (Jn 10:17-18). Jesus laid down His life and
He said, "Father, into thy hands I commend my spirit." He did
not die from the effects of crucifixion but by self-surrender, as
a voluntary sacrifice for sin.

When the Roman spear pierced Jesus' side there came out
blood and water, the evidence that He was dead. Geikie says,

"Jesus died, literally, of a broken heart. The immediate cause of death appears beyond question, to have been the rupture of His heart, brought about by mental agony." The rupture of Jesus' heart took place when He knew that all things were accomplished in His redemptive ministry, for He said, "It is finished." At this juncture He deliberately "sent forth" (Mt 27:50), "dismissed out of" (Lk 23:46), and "gave over" (Jn 19:30) His life. This dismissal of His life is what is involved in "giving up the ghost."

The great work of salvation was now completed, and the age of the new covenant began. As a witness to the fulfillment of the old and beginning of the new, we have the three rendings: first, the rent and broken heart of Jesus; second, the rent and opened graves of the dead; third, the rent and divided veil of the temple. The remainder of the chapter deals with the preparation of Jesus' body for burial in the garden tomb.

49

The Resurrection of Jesus

20:1-18

THE FIRST DAY OF THE WEEK found faithful women making their way along a rocky path in the early gloom of a Palestinian morning. Their mission was to further embalm the body of Jesus against the ravages of death. Among the Jews the hopes of the future were closely connected with the careful preservation of the body after death. For this reason Jesus' body, stained as it was with blood, was tenderly washed and then wrapped in broad bands of white linen, within which were thickly strewn powdered myrrh and aloes, which had been provided by Nicodemus. The ends of the bandages were secured on the inner side with gum. A white cloth was finally laid over the face after a last kiss, the pledge of undying love. Then the corpse was laid in a niche in the rock and, since there was no stone door as in some tombs, a great stone was rolled against the entrance to protect the body from the designs of enemies or the attacks of wild beasts. As a last precaution of security, a strong cord was passed across the face of the stone and secured at both ends by clay.

Since the embalmment had not been finished, the women were going to the tomb to complete their ministrations. Their problem was how they would roll away the stone from the entrance. Their objective was reached, but the grave was empty. Their mission was useless because their Messiah was alive. Their problem was solved because the stone was already removed and at the tomb face stood angels, instead of soldiers, saying, "He is not here, but is risen" (Mt. 28:6).

Each recurring Easter finds millions of people on their way to hilltops, stadiums and churches all over the world so that they may commemorate the resurrection of Jesus. These millions and those women have one thing in common — they do not expect anything unusual to happen on Easter. They expect choirs to sing, trumpets to blow, lilies to adorn the chancels of the church, and preachers to proclaim the Easter story, but they do not expect anything unusual to happen. They expect to pay their religious respects to the fact that Christ is risen, but they do not expect anything unusual to happen. They expect Easter to be a religious interlude in a year of religious forgetfulness, but they do not expect anything unusual to happen.

What is the unusual thing that happened to the faithful women on the first Easter morning? The stone was removed, the body of Jesus was gone, the burial wrappings were in their place on the ledge cut in the side of the tomb, and Christ was alive. And the unusual thing that can happen today is that Christ can come alive in our hearts, the stone of unbelief can be rolled away, the graveclothes of inertia can be removed, and Easter can become an experience of life for 365 days of the year, rather than an essay of religious tradition.

Easter is no time to give an essay on immortality. It is the time to retell the story of the resurrection and relate life to the risen Lord. Easter is an event, not an essay. The unusual occurred, for a miracle took place. For the first time in history a man was raised from the dead. This does not refute the bringing back to life of the son of the widow of Nain, or of the daughter of Jairus, or of Lazarus. These were resusitations, not resurrections. All three of these people lived to die again, but Jesus lived to die no more. He is the first to live again after death.

Easter is essentially two things: an *event* and an *experience*.

THE EVENT AS SEEN IN THE DISCOVERY OF MARY (vv. 1-10)

The resurrection is something that actually happened. It is the world's best authenticated story.

THE DISCOVERY OF MARY

"The first day of the week cometh Mary Magdalene early, when it was yet dark, unto the sepulchre, and seeth the stone taken away from the sepulchre" (v. 1).

The time was "the first day of the week." It was the new day which would forever commemorate the resurrection. As the seventh rest day was a memorial of creation, so the first rest day is a memorial of the new creation.

The person was Mary Magdalene. In this account Mary makes the discovery of the rolled-away stone and the empty sepulcher. As Jesus had voluntarily died, so now He voluntarily and of His own will silently withdrew from the linen chrysalis in which His body had been wrapped. Now, living again, He had a new body which had powers of appearance and disappearance, of locomotion and levitation, of recognition and imperception. Yes, Jesus Christ was alive.

THE RESURRECTION CONFIRMED

> Then she runneth, and cometh to Simon Peter, and to the other disciple, whom Jesus loved, and saith unto them, They have taken away the Lord out of the sepulchre, and we know not where they have laid him. Peter therefore went forth, and that other disciple, and come to the sepulchre. So they ran both together: and the other disciple did outrun Peter, and came first to the sepulchre. And he stooping down, and looking in, saw the linen clothes lying; yet went he not in. Then cometh Simon Peter following him, and went into the sepulchre, and seeth the linen clothes lie, and the napkin, that was about his head, not lying with the linen clothes, but wrapped together in a place by itself. Then went in also that other disciple, which came first to the sepulchre, and he saw, and believed. For as yet they knew not the scripture, that he must rise again from the dead. Then the disciples went away again unto their own home (vv. 2-10).

Mary of Magdala returned to the disciples' rendezvous and reported what she had discovered. Peter and John hastened to the garden, with Peter leading the way and entering the tomb first. The discovery of the resurrection was confirmed. The tomb was empty. The burial clothes lay carefully in position in the empty niche, with the bands for the body and limbs lying by themselves, and the facecloth folded up in a place by itself.

It was indeed true! The resurrection was a fact. The great

truth flashed on the minds of the two disciples. Neither Peter nor John had as yet realized that it had been foretold in the Scripture. "For as yet they knew not the scripture, that he must rise again from the dead." The previous predictions of Jesus had remained enigmatic to them, but in the light of the empty tomb they understood.

THE EVENT AS SEEN IN MARY'S EXPERIENCE (vv. 11-18)

The event now becomes an experience. In this sense Easter is not something to talk about and read about; it is something to live. Easter did not happen just so that it would be tucked away in some niche of history or shrine of religion. It happened that something might happen to us. Christ lives that we may live, not in a distant day of resurrection, but in the present day of struggle, temptation, sickness and sorrow.

MARY AND THE ANGELS

> But Mary stood without at the sepulchre weeping: and as she wept, she stooped down, and looked into the sepulchre, and seeth two angels in white sitting, the one at the head, and the other at the feet, where the body of Jesus had lain. And they say unto her, Woman, why weepest thou? She saith unto them, Because they have taken away my Lord, and I know not where they have laid him (vv. 11-13).

While the disciples "went away again unto their own home," Mary, still inquisitive and expectant, remained beside the empty tomb, expressing her feelings in tears. Hers was the legitimate sorrow of separation and disappointment.

It is to the glory of woman that she seldom forsakes those she loves, even when things are darkest. And when the disciples returned to their rendezvous on the assumption that nothing more would happen, Mary had the unforgettable experience of seeing the angels and the risen Lord.

The angels inquired, "Why weepest thou?" Mary's sorrow was because of her separation from her Lord: "They have taken away my Lord, and I know not where they have laid him." In the light of the empty tomb, and the confirmation of the resurrec-

tion by the disciples, this does not appear to be skepticism. It
is a form of reply which comes from her deep sorrow, and it is
soon to be dispelled by her experience with the risen Christ.

> And when she had thus said, she turned herself back, and
> saw Jesus standing, and knew not that it was Jesus. Jesus saith
> unto her, Woman, why weepest thou? Whom seekest thou?
> She, supposing him to be the gardener, saith unto him, Sir, if
> thou have borne him hence, tell me where thou hast laid him,
> and I will take him away. Jesus saith unto her, Mary. She
> turned herself, and saith unto him, Rabboni; which is to say,
> Master. Jesus saith unto her, Touch me not; for I am not yet
> ascended to my Father: but go to my brethren, and say unto
> them, I ascend unto my Father, and your Father; and to my
> God, and your God. Mary Magdalene came and told the dis-
> ciples that she had seen the Lord, and that he had spoken
> these things unto her (vv. 14-18).

While Mary conversed with the angels, she was interrupted by
the appearance of a man in the simple dress of the humbler
classes. Being in a garden, she assumed that he was the local
gardener. She was asked by Jesus whom she was seeking, and
her reply was "Sir, if thou have borne him hence, tell me where
thou hast laid him, and I will take him away." The answer she
received was Jesus' familiarly spoken "Mary." She exclaimed in
recognition, "Rabboni" — my teacher. There was no doubt now.
The event had become an experience.

Two Notable Things

MARY'S FAILURE TO IDENTIFY JESUS

When Mary first saw Jesus, her failure to identify Him was
due perhaps to the mysterious nature of His new body. He came
and disappeared. At this moment her experience had run the
gamut of emotional extremes, and she was unprepared for this
appearance of Jesus.

This was the first "spiritual body" ever seen by human eyes.
The corruptible had changed to incorruption; the mortal had

changed to immortality. Her earthly eyes were not yet accustomed to this heavenly sight.

Mary wanted the assurance of the senses, but she had to be content with the assurance of faith. She wanted to retain Jesus for fellowship, but it was not time to retain Jesus in any permanent fellowship because He had to go to His Father. The ascension had to complete the redemptive work of Jesus by His return to the Father in a high-priestly capacity. Fellowship was not to be corporeal, but spiritual.

"Touch me not Mary. Instead, go and bear witness to my brethren of what you have seen." Losing no time, Mary went and reported all her experience.

HOW BELIEVERS CAN HAVE THIS EXPERIENCE

Before this wonderful experience can happen to us, we must understand a few important things:

Life on this earth has meaning. Few of us think of our lives as belonging to God. Failing to acknowledge that He has any claim upon us, we live a materialistic existence — going to work, coming home, eating, sleeping, seeking diversion, and finally filling up a piece of earth's surface six by six by three feet in size. This is existence, but it is not the experience of life when we understand its definition, direction and destination.

The reason Jesus arose from the dead was to be able to meet His disciples in a divine-human confrontation and give them a new concept of life. These men who had despaired of life and had abandoned hope were suddenly faced with new reasons to live. Later they transformed the world.

Death has meaning. The first meaning of death is its relation to sin. Because of sin, man died and has been dying ever since. Somehow we avoid the force of this and feel a false immunity to death, assuming that everyone else but us will die.

Most of us do not include death in our scheme of life, but it is a fact which may either be an ending or a beginning, a conclusion or a commencement. Jesus' resurrection revised the meaning of death, giving us new hope of a continuing life.

There are unusual demands for the unusual things that can

happen to us. Finding the meaning of life and death does not come cheaply. Although Jesus said, "Strait is the gate, and narrow is the way, which leadeth unto life" (Mt. 7:14), we think it is something easy and broad-minded.

Jesus said, "If any man will come after me, let him deny himself, and take up his cross daily, and follow me (Lk 9:23), but we have been saying that a cross-less religion of good works and sporadic church attendance was enough. Jesus said, "Except ye be converted, and become as little children, ye shall not enter into the kingdom of heaven" (Mt. 18:3), but we boast self-sufficiency and self-reliance and feel no need for God.

None can follow Jesus to this new meaning of life and death while remaining in the anonymity of an unconfessed faith and an uncommitted life, because the formula of an Easter faith is, "That if thou shalt confess with thy mouth the Lord Jesus, and shalt believe in thine heart that God hath raised him from the dead, thou shalt be saved. For with the heart man believeth unto righteousness; and with the mouth confession is made unto salvation" (Ro 10:9-10).

50

Peace for Troubled Hearts

20:19-23

THE NEWS OF THE RESURRECTION spread rapidly among the disciples, yet it required time to reach all of them. Even so, the fact was too stupendous and wonderful to be fully comprehended at once. Cut off suddenly from all the hopes of the earthly kingdom they had cherished, and bereft by the loss of their Teacher and Leader, they were in a state of paralytic helplessness.

Even the multiple reports of the empty grave, the vision of angels, and the announcement that Jesus was alive and had been seen were insufficient to break the disciples' gloom. In this spirit of incredulousness, they had gathered that same evening at an appointed rendezvous to eat a simple meal together.

The doors were well secured because they were afraid that the priests and rabbis would discover them and indict them for their identification with Jesus. A human form suddenly appeared, entering the unopened and still-barred doors. Immediately they recognized their unannounced visitor as Jesus and, before they could utter a word, the salutation they had heard so often fell from His lips: "Shalom alechem [peace be unto you]."

What happened in this secret meeting place is the sequel to the resurrection itself and is important to our faith and experience. Six new things are revealed:

THE NEW DAY

"Then the same day at evening, being the first day of the week . . ." (v. 19a). It was on the first day of the week that the women discovered the empty tomb, and it was on the first day of the week when the Lord made His last appearance to His disciples on the day of resurrection. In between were His appearances in the garden and later on the Emmaus road.

The precedent for this new day was due to the new order of redemption based upon the resurrection. Henceforth Jesus' followers would break the bread of communion and worship on what they would call the Lord's Day or Sunday.

The worship of this new day was to be under the new circumstances created by the rent veil of the temple which indicated a new spiritual order. This new order recognized the ending of the Levitical priesthood and the offering of physical sacrifices. On the positive side it recognized the new priesthood of believers who had access to God's presence without benefit of the ministry of a priesthood. It recognized immediate entrance into God's presence without ecclesiastical interposition.

THE NEW BODY

"When the doors were shut where the disciples were assembled for fear of the Jews, came Jesus and stood in the midst, and saith unto them, Peace be unto you" (v. 19*b*). The first meeting of the disciples after the death and resurrection of Jesus was one of self-interest in response to their fears of discovery and detection by the Jews. They were not meeting as a board of directors for the incorporation of a new world order to plan their strategy to carry on their global activities. They were secretly huddled in fear and apprehension. Thomas was absent and missed the exhilarating experience of the presence of the risen Christ.

The account says "the doors were shut." Suddenly Jesus appeared through these closed and barred doors without them being opened. This required a miraculous appearance by the molecular displacement of the properties of the doors, achieved solely by the constitution of His new body. It was corporeal even though it was not material, it could appear and disappear, eat food, defy the law of gravitation, ascend into space and, as here, enter a room through closed doors.

Luke says that when Jesus suddenly appeared in their midst, "they were terrified and affrighted, and supposed that they had seen a spirit" (Lk 24:37). This is understandable, for the normal reaction to any resurrection might be fear and consternation. But when Jesus spoke to them He said, "Peace be unto you," and they were composed and assured.

Coming where His disciples were, Jesus stood in the midst of them and their fears. They did not have to seek Him; He sought them as He will us. As the aggressor to help us in our need, He can enter closed doors and calm fearful hearts.

THE NEW ASSURANCE

"And when he had so said, he shewed unto them his hands and his side. Then were the disciples glad, when they saw the Lord" (v. 20). Notice that the resurrection was not valid until it was based upon crucifixion. He was indeed alive, but the disciples were asked to notice how Jesus died. The final test of the effectiveness of the risen Christ was in His crucifixion. At every phase of Jesus' ministry He was identified as the Saviour whose dying was to take away our sin. If this were not so, His resurrection was to no purpose.

At Jesus' birth He was named Jesus because He would "save his people from their sins" (Mt 1:21). *In His life* He "was in all points tempted like as we are, yet was without sin" (Heb. 4: 15). *At His death* He said, when all the redemptive elements were completed, "It is finished." *At His resurrection* He "shewed unto them his hands and his side" as the marks of crucifixion. Paul said, "I declare unto you the gospel . . . how that Christ died for our sins according to the scriptures; and that he was buried, and that he rose again the third day according to the scriptures" (1 Co 15:1-4).

Having been presented in every phase of life as Saviour, Jesus must be received in this capacity, or else our acceptance of Him is neither valid nor helpful. We may know Jesus historically, intellectually or philosophically without effect, for unless we know Him by "his hands and his side" we do not know Him at all.

The New Provision

"Then said Jesus to them again, Peace be unto you" (v. 21*a*). Three times Jesus conferred the blessing of peace upon the disciples. In verse 19 it was the *peace of forgiveness* for the defections, disbelief and desertion of the disciples; in verse 21 it was the *peace of preparation* for the new role to be played by the disciples in their mission to the world; in verse 26 it was the *peace of reassurance* with Thomas once more present with the Lord and the disciples.

The peace provided was something more than the emotional quality of peaceableness. It was the conferred and committed quality of the peace of Jesus of which He spoke when He said, "Peace I leave with you, my peace I give unto you" (Jn 14:27). It was His peace they were to take into the world.

Personal peace is something more than the *absence of worry, trouble and fear*. It is the *presence* of the person of Christ, a resource of grace upon which we may draw for the process and crisis of life.

World peace is likewise something more than the absence of war. If we had real peace in the world we would not be preparing for war, even if, on our nation's part, it is a defensive measure. Nineteen centuries of progress from the Caesars to the United Nations have clearly proved that we cannot produce lasting peace, and we are seemingly getting farther and farther from the goal. Whether we believe it or not, lasting peace can come only by the formula of peace Jesus gave to His disciples, for He "made peace through the blood of his cross" (Col 1:20).

The New Commission

"As my Father hath sent me, even so send I you" (v. 21*b*). It was in this same connection that Jesus gave His Great Commission: "Go ye into all the world, and preach the gospel to every creature" (Mk 16:15). The disciples' mission is formally ratified. As He was sent, they were being sent. What they would do was what He would do. As He witnessed to the God who sent Him, they were to be witnesses of Jesus Christ.

G. Campbell Morgan explains that in formalizing the disciples'

mission, Jesus used two verbs: "sent" in the past tense, referring
to Jesus, and "send" in the present tense, referring to the disciples. However, they are not the past and present tenses of the
same action verb. The verb "sent" referring to Jesus is *apostello*,
meaning to have delegated authority. The verb "send" referring to the disciples is *pempo*, meaning to dispatch under authority as you would a messenger.

This understanding is very important in the light of the next
verses relating to the breathing upon them of the Holy Spirit,
for it does not confer upon apostles the same authority that Jesus had.

HOW WAS JESUS SENT BY GOD AND HOW ARE WE SENT BY JESUS?

Jesus was sent to redeem the world. We are sent to proclaim
that redemption, but in no sense to preempt the prerogatives of
Christ in redeeming and forgiving.

Jesus was sent to give life. We are sent to propagate life
through preaching and witnessing.

Jesus was sent to be the light of the world. We are sent as
lights in His place and stead.

Jesus was sent to change the world and not be changed by it.
We are sent to do the same thing and to remember that "the
men who move the world are the ones who do not let the world
move them."

Jesus came to represent God. We are sent to represent Jesus,
not as plenipotentiaries but as messengers.

THE NEW ENABLEMENT

"And when he had said this, he breathed on them, and saith
unto them, Receive ye the Holy Ghost: whose soever sins ye remit, they are remitted unto them; and whose soever sins ye retain, they are retained" (vv. 22-23). This is the prelude to Pentecost. In no sense is it the same, nor is it to be considered as
another coming of the Holy Spirit. This could not be true as long
as Jesus was in the world, for the Holy Spirit could only come
after His ascension.

Jesus had just commissioned His disciples to take His place

in the world, and now, in this "breathing" upon them, He was preparing them for their mission by communicating a first-fruits of the Spirit in anticipation of the Pentecostal baptism already promised. He told His disciples that the Holy Spirit would come to take His place, to administer the benefits and blessings of redemption.

This "breathing" upon them was a real communication, but it was in no sense a substitute for the Pentecostal baptism. It was a communication for the interim period of ten days, between the ascension of Jesus and the coming of the Holy Spirit, during which time no Member of the Godhead would be present on earth.

Besides this communication of power through the person of the Holy Spirit breathed upon them, there immediately followed a communication of authority regarding the forgiveness of sins. Jesus said, "Whose soever sins ye remit [loose], they are remitted unto them; and whose soever sins ye retain [hold], they are retained." This was a temporary endowment for the interim of Jesus' absence.

A monstrous perversion of Scripture has been made at this point in claiming that this is the communication of judicial power to the disciples to absolve or condemn sinners, and to open and shut the doors of heaven. But this is a power belonging only to God, and since the Holy Spirit would be the divine Representative on earth, He alone would "reprove the world of sin." Thus the remitting and retention of sins would be in His power alone. But since an interim period of ten days would exist between the ascension of Jesus and the coming of the Holy Spirit at Pentecost, this interim authority was given the disciples through the Holy Spirit whom Jesus breathed upon them.

The disciples (representing the church) have the evangelistic authority, through the Great Commission, to proclaim the gospel and its forgiveness of sins, but only God has the authority to forgive the sins of those who avail themselves of the sin-forgiving benefits of redemption. This understanding of Scripture destroys the ecclesiastical monstrosities that have perverted the simple provisions of the gospel, namely, that by reason of Christ's

death each person in his own right, and without benefit of sacer-
dotal service, can enter God's presence and receive forgiveness.

This upper room appearance is ended, and Jesus demonstrates one of the mysterious facilities of His resurrected body
by disappearing for a whole week. During this week the priests
and rabbis are in great anxiety, while the disciples, in total seclusion, are contemplating the wonderful events of the resurrection and their new position and power as world emissaries of
the risen Christ.

51

Are There Any Thomases Here?

20:24-29

A GREAT VARIETY of people were involved in the events surrounding the resurrection. There was *Mary Magdalene*, the first to observe that Christ was risen. There were the *Emmaus disciples* who unknowingly walked with Jesus until He performed certain familiar things, whereupon they knew Him. There was the *bulk of the disciples* who heard the breathtaking reports of women as if they were "idle tales and they believed them not." And then there was *Thomas*, who unfortunately is called a skeptic and a doubter. Absent when Christ made His first appearance to the disciples, he had demanded proof before he would believe and accept the fact.

A whole week elapsed before the next appearance of Jesus. It was Sunday, to be known henceforth as "the first day of the week," and once more the disciples were assembled. Once more Jesus stood in their midst, and this time Thomas, known as Didymus or "the twin," was present. When the disciples had reported Jesus' other appearance, Thomas had said, "Except I shall see in his hands the print of the nails, and put my finger into the print of the nails, and thrust my hand into his side, I will not believe" (v. 25).

To have demanded physical proof is supposed to be evidence of the skepticism of Thomas, who is almost universally dubbed "Doubting Thomas." But this is not the case. It was not a case of skepticism or unbelief, but rather an evidence of difference in personality and approach to faith. Not all people are constituted the same. While faith is the same, approach to faith may be as different as the divergence in people.

A skeptic is a person "who carries a critical or incredulous attitude into his inquiries." This was not entirely true of Thomas. In an earlier incident recorded in chapter 11, word had come that Lazarus had died and Jesus had announced His intention of going to Bethany. What was the attitude of the disciples to such a dangerous journey? It was not Peter who spoke up, but Thomas who said, "Let us also go, that we may die with him" (11:16). Thomas was willing to risk his life for Christ. This does not look like the profile of a skeptic or a doubter.

There is an irreverent skepticism which has no intention of believing under any circumstance. It says, "I decline to believe what is above reason and understanding; I must see everything before I can believe anything." This state of mind could in no degree of fairness be attributed to Thomas.

Thomas was an individualist. Instead of believing just because others did, on the basis of what they had seen, he wanted to believe because he likewise had seen. When the ten disciples reported that they had seen marks of the crucifixion in the body of Jesus, Thomas wanted the same basis for faith as they had. He was demanding no more than his colleagues had experienced. Doubt, disbelief or skepticism was not involved.

Some can believe because what they are expected to believe is a matter of record in the Bible. Others have no less faith in the Bible, but would like to know how and why. Peter suggests we ought to have "a reason of the hope that is in you."

Some people, like Thomas, honestly defy classification. There are other disciples who are forever demanding that all other disciples fit into their particular mold of thought and inquiry. They insist that they dot their "i's" and cross their "t's" in the prescribed manner, or else they are not acceptable among the purists.

Once we understand Thomas we will be more tolerant and charitable Christian people. The boastful spirit of an easy faith may be the shield of a lazy mind, for perhaps we do not understand what we believe.

The meeting from which Thomas had been absent when Jesus made His first appearance was attended by ten disciples. Why were they there? John says, "The disciples were assembled for fear of the Jews." Why was Thomas absent? Our unthinking reply is "because of his unfaithfulness." But couldn't it have been the opposite? Couldn't it have been proof that Thomas showed lack of fear and may have been doing something tangible about his situation rather than shielding himself from the Jews?

While this fear of the disciples does not necessarily mean the absence of faith, it at least reveals that their fear was more dominant than their faith. They did not go to their rendezvous in expectation of meeting a risen Lord but in their own self-interest because they feared harm from the Jews.

One form of fear may not be any worse than another, and if Thomas feared Jesus was not risen, it was not worse than the other disciples fearing what would happen to them. Furthermore, if Thomas really doubted the resurrection, he was not worse than the other disciples who considered the reports of the women about the rolled-away stone and the empty tomb and undisturbed graveclothes as nothing but "idle tales."

When Thomas found out that Jesus had appeared during his absence, he expressed his own individualistic spirit of inquiry. Perhaps he was aggravated by disappointment at what he had missed and said, "Except I shall see in his hands. . . ."

This sort of inquiry was not new to Thomas. Before the resurrection in the upper room, Jesus had said, "And if I go and prepare. . . . And whither I go ye know, and the way ye know" (Jn 14:3-4). Then Thomas broke in and said, "Lord, we know not whither thou goest; and how can we know the way?" This was no more skeptical than later at the resurrection. Once he asked to be given evidence of the way. The next time he asked for evidences of the resurrection in terms of physical sight. Whatever Thomas was driving at in these two instances, it was not doubt in the sense of unbelief.

WHY THOMAS ACTED AS HE DID

HE WANTED A FIRSTHAND EXPERIENCE

Thomas had been absent when Christ was present and, having missed the experience of seeing Jesus, he wanted the appearance duplicated so he could have it firsthand as had the other disciples. Much of our trouble would disappear in the personal satisfaction of a spiritual experience with the person and presence of Christ.

HE ACTED AS THE OTHER DISCIPLES HAD

Thomas had to get his information about the resurrection secondhand when he wanted it through his own observation and experience. He might have been prodded into this attitude by the doubting of his fellow disciples who had refused to believe the women's resurrection reports. Thomas was acting no differently.

But Thomas discovered that he did not need what he had demanded. He had asked for proof in terms of tangible wounds, but he discovered that all He needed was the person of Jesus. When Jesus appeared and offered the physical evidence for him to investigate and verify, Thomas cried out, "My Lord and my God."

It was a renewed spiritual experience with Jesus which satisfied Thomas, and this came by a personal encounter with Jesus. All Thomas needed was the sight of His Master, and that is all we need. Jesus Christ will be the satisfaction of all our inquiries and the answer to all our doubts.

Jesus was not angry with Thomas, nor did He scold, condemn, or humiliate him before his fellow disciples. He simply said to Thomas, "Reach hither thy finger" (v. 27).

This is not what we would do if there were any suspicion of doubt in a fellow disciple. We would berate, denounce and condemn. Then we would expose and hurt him, hold him up to public contempt, and brand him as a heretic.

There is little tolerance in our judgment of others and little love in our treatment of those who may disagree with us. Our orthodoxy is sometimes Phariseeism that pillories people upon the crosses of our own bigotry.

This incident closes with a beatitude, the "Believer's Beatitude." It says, "Blessed are they that have not seen, and yet have believed" (v. 29).

52

That Ye Might Believe

20:30-31

THE LAST TWO VERSES of chapter 20 without doubt constitute one of the high points of the book, setting forth John's purpose to declare the unique character of Jesus as the Son of God.

The gospel of John is bracketed by two confessions of Christ's deity – one by Nathaniel, "Thou art the Son of God" (1:49); and the other by Thomas, "My Lord and my God" (20:28). At the beginning of John's gospel, he says, "Behold the Lamb of God," while at the end he says, "Believe the Son of God."

We are confronted with two significant statements at the end of this gospel. At the end of chapter 20: "Many other signs truly did Jesus" (v. 30). At the end of chapter 21: "There are also many other things which Jesus did" (v. 25).

The first of these two concluding statements, "Many other signs truly did Jesus," was inspired by the resurrection appearances of Jesus and undoubtedly included many miraculous events which were considered unnecessary to mention. The second statement, "many other things which Jesus did," shows that much more evidence of Jesus' sayings and doings could be presented. But nothing more is necessary to form sufficient evidence to convince anyone of Jesus' divine nature.

Some so-called "unknown sayings of Jesus" are called the Apocrypha, but none of these are found in any of the four gospels. Whatever may be true and important about the unknown sayings of Jesus, the important thing to all of us is the known sayings which are recorded. Mark Twain said, "The things that bother me in the Bible are not the things I do not understand, but the things I do understand."

The most important thing to anyone seeking the ultimate in

life is truth. Too few people are concerned with truth as such. They go to church, not seeking truth, but a lift to make them happy or secure. Yet none of these things can be true in us in the real sense unless we know and receive the truth.

Having approached the end of the fourth gospel, we are confronted with this revealing statement — "Many other signs truly did Jesus in the presence of his disciples, which are not written in this book: But these are written, that ye might believe that Jesus is Christ, the Son of God; and that believing ye might have life through his name." Here are three important things:

The Means of Salvation Is Faith

"These are written that ye might believe." Faith is the means of salvation, and a saving faith is faith in these things that "are written." Generally they are the things written in the Bible, which is God's revelation, and specifically they are the things written in the gospel of John. In this gospel are to be found the things we are asked to believe, such as:

Chapter 1 — The preexistent Christ of whom it says, "But as many as received him, to them gave he power to become the sons of God, even to them that believe on his name" (v. 12).

Chapter 2 — The miracle at Cana of Galilee where Jesus demonstrates His command over nature.

Chapter 3 — The interview with Nicodemus to whom He says, "Marvel not that I said unto thee, Ye must be born again" (v. 7).

Chapter 4 — The visit with the woman of Samaria where Jesus reveals the new worship, for "God is a Spirit: and they that worship him must worship him in spirit and in truth" (v. 24).

Chapter 5 — The healing of the paralytic where Jesus identifies Himself with God: "My Father worketh hitherto, and I work" (v. 17). After this the Jews sought to kill Him for "making himself equal with God" (v. 18).

Chapter 6 — The feeding of the five thousand where the people said, "This is of a truth that prophet that should come into the world" (v. 14), and where Jesus identified Himself as "the bread of life."

Chapter 7 — The living water and Jesus' formula of faith: "If any man will do his will, he shall know of the doctrine, whether it be of God, or whether I speak of myself" (v. 17).

Chapter 8 — The light of the world where Jesus said, "If ye had known me, ye should have known my Father also" (v. 19).

Chapter 9 — The blind man healed, with its evidence of the divine nature of Jesus: "If this man were not of God, he could do nothing" (v. 33).

Chapter 10 — The good Shepherd who said, "I am come that they might have life" (v. 10).

Chapter 11 — The raising of Lazarus and the revelation that Jesus is "the resurrection and the life," to which Martha responds, "Yea, Lord: I believe that thou art the Christ, the Son of God, which should come into the world" (v. 27).

Chapter 12 — The approaching cross where Jesus said, "He that loveth his life shall lose it; and he that hateth his life in this world shall keep it unto life eternal" (v. 25).

Chapter 13 — The Last Supper where Jesus gives the supper of remembrance, the memorial of His death. Here again is the identity of Jesus with the Father: "Jesus knowing that the Father had given all things into his hands, and that he was come from God, and went to God" (v. 3).

Chapter 14 — The Father's house and Jesus' revelation that He is "the way, the truth, and the life" (v. 6).

Chapter 15 — The vine and the branches, with Jesus as the source of the believer's life and the cause of abundant fruitfulness in life.

Chapter 16 — The coming of the Holy Spirit, who is revealed to be like Christ, who in turn is revealed as one like God, thus constituting the Godhead.

Chapter 17 — The prayer for the disciples in which Jesus speaks of His oneness with God and declares the nature of eternal life. "And this is life eternal, that they might know thee the only true God, and Jesus Christ, whom thou hast sent" (v. 3).

Chapters 18-19 — The crucifixion of Jesus and its revelation of Jesus as the Son of God and the King of the Jews.

Chapter 20 — The resurrection of Jesus with its vindication of Jesus' divine nature and Thomas' confession, "My Lord and my God" (v. 28).

All of these contain the essential elements of the gospel. They tell us of the preexistence of Christ, His deity, His spotless life, His ministry among men, His death and resurrection. All of these are for our belief. There is enough to convict and convince anyone of the truth of Jesus. It is incredible that there should be any unbelief in the face of such a record as this.

Salvation, according to the Bible, is the result of *what we believe*. Belief then is the cause of *what we become*, and what we become is the cause of *what we do*.

The Object of Faith Is Jesus Christ

". . . that Jesus is the Christ, the Son of God." The object of faith is Jesus Christ. In this case it is specified "that Jesus is the Christ, the Son of God" — the highest revelation of Jesus. Anything less than this is ineffectual as an act of saving faith.

Twice in John's gospel Jesus identifies Himself as the Son of God in 9:35-37 and 10:30. He did it again in Mark 14:61-62, as well as in many other places, either by direct statement or inference. This gospel opens with the majestic statement equal to Genesis 1:1 which says, "In the beginning was the Word, and the Word was with God, and the Word was God." Again in 1:34 John says, "And I saw, and bare record that this is the Son of God." Nathaniel says in 1:49, "Rabbi, thou art the Son of God." Reference can also be made to 3:16, 18, and 19:7 where Jesus either claimed equality with God or it was ascribed to Him by God or related to Him by man. Even the Roman centurion was forced to say, "Truly this man was the Son of God" (Mk 15:39).

The object of saving faith, as prescribed in the Bible, is not a body of truth called a creed, although creeds are important. The object of faith is a Person — Jesus Christ. This Person is not merely the historical figure known as Jesus Christ, but the prehistorical and posthistorical Person Jesus Christ known as the Son of God.

Can a person be saved without believing in the deity of

Christ? To be consistent with the facts of revelation, the answer is no! There are two reasons for this:

First, Jesus Christ cannot perform His redeeming work in us unless He is the Son of God. When Jesus returned to His home, "he did not many mighty works there because of their unbelief" (Mt 13:58). They believed only that He was the son of Joseph, not the Son of God. They were willing to accept Him as their fellowman, but not as God. As a man, Jesus could only do what man could do. As God, Jesus was able to do what God could do. Salvation is an act of God — initiated by God, wrought by God, and sustained by God.

Second, man cannot be saved unless he believes in Jesus at this level of deity. A saving faith is described here as a faith in Christ as the Son of God, not as a good man or a great man, but as God. This is consistent with the witness of the entire New Testament and with the proclamations of the first preachers of the gospel. All proclaimed the necessity of faith in Jesus Christ as God.

The Effect of Faith in Jesus Christ Is Life

". . . and that believing ye might have life through his name." The result of a well-placed faith is described as *life*. These words are addressed to men who are living physically but not spiritually. Elsewhere they are described as being "dead in trespasses and sins." They are dead to God.

The "life" spoken of here is that with which Adam was created, but lost because he sinned. It is the life that Jesus had as the eternal Son of God and brought into the world through incarnation. It is the life that was subjected in the wilderness temptation to the successive enticements of "the lust of the flesh," "the lust of the eye" and "the pride of life." It is the life that was submitted to the routine of daily life which we live today where Christ was "in all points tempted like as we are, yet without sin" (Heb 4:15).

Finally, this life was made available by Christ's death on the cross, for He said, "I am come that they might have life" (Jn 10:10). Furthermore, He describes how this life is made available to us: "Therefore doth my Father love me, because I lay down my life, that I might take it again. No man taketh it from me, but I lay it down of myself, I have power to lay it down, and I have power to take it again" (10:17-18). Here is the means by which this life is made available to man — the death of Christ.

While death is the divine means by which Christ's life is released to man, faith is revealed as the human means of receiving this life. The object of this faith is the deity of Jesus Christ, and the effect of this faith is life.

Any act of true faith involves three things:

1. It accepts the will of God.
2. It adjusts to the will of God.
3. It acts on the will of God.

A Christian is a person:

1. who believes something
2. who does something
3. who says something

These three things involve the whole person: intellect, emotion and will. The coordination of all three parts of personality will result in an experience of salvation. We are not left to decide for ourselves what such an act of faith is, but are to follow the clearly indicated revelation of Scripture.

53

The Other Side

21:1-14

THIS INCIDENT, which takes place some time after the resurrection, is described as "the third time that Jesus shewed himself to his disciples" (v. 14). Apparently the tomb-side and road-side appearances are not considered and, beginning with the upper room appearance with Thomas absent, there is the second upper room appearance with Thomas present, plus the lakeside appearance to seven disciples.

It is at this Galilee or Tiberias appearance that Jesus showed Himself, or made Himself manifest, in a state of resurrection life in which He could accommodate Himself to all physical circumstances.

None of the appearances of Jesus, as far as we know, were in the temple. They were always in places of everyday life: either a home, a road for travelers and, as in this case, a fishing venture. Jesus always knew where the disciples were, and He was capable of reaching them and meeting their need.

The incident with all its signficance to modern disciples can be put into the following framework:

DEFECTION AND DEFEAT

After these things Jesus shewed himself again to the disciples at the sea of Tiberias; and on this wise shewed he himself. There were together Simon Peter, and Thomas called Didymus, and Nathanael of Cana in Galilee, and the sons of Zebedee, and two other of his disciples. Simon Peter saith unto them, I go a fishing. They say unto him, We also go with thee. They went forth, and entered into a ship immediately; and that night they caught nothing (vv. 1-3).

Peter, the leader of the eleven, said, "I go a fishing." In this intention he was joined by six others — five of the seven were named while two go nameless. This might suggest that they were lesser disciples than the eleven, or it might contain the spiritual lesson that while there are some who serve in prominence, there are always those who go nameless. Their anonymity is not a sign of unimportance, for the unnamed can be as useful as any others.

The decision to "go a fishing" was a choice to return and pursue their earthly employments, a despairing decision to return to their old life. It did not stem from a disbelief in the resurrection of Jesus; of this they were convinced because of Jesus' appearances. It was the failure to believe that the risen Christ could meet the crisis of a lost cause. Their kingdom hopes were shattered, and there was nothing else to do but go fishing.

The disciples gave up too soon. Surveying the life of Abraham Lincoln, one can see many times when he could have settled for what he had. He could have remained a river ferryman on the Ohio, where as a boy he was overwhelmed by earning a dollar a day. He could have taken up the indolent life of a hunter, fisherman or quoter of Shakespeare. He could have remained postmaster or storekeeper or a circuit-riding lawyer. But Lincoln didn't stop to become any of these lesser things, for he had a sense of destiny. The disciples almost missed the boat, but Jesus found them in their despair and failure, pointed them in the right direction, and gave them a sense of destiny.

The disciples failed to reckon with the power of the risen Christ. Christian victory lies on this side of the resurrection. It is the victory that comes to our prayer life, our service, our ministry and our total experience of life. Do not forget the chronology of victory: it is postresurrection.

There is another lesson in this defeat: the influence of unbelief. When Peter said, "I go a fishing," the other disciples said, "We also go with thee." We never doubt privately or singly; our unbelief has its effect on others. Six disciples followed in the wake of defecting Peter. We can scarcely calculate the evil influence of a doubting heart.

It is recorded that "that night they caught nothing" (v. 3).

This was defeat for men who were expert fishermen. They fished at the best time — "at night." They knew the lake in every detail and were skilled in every way to bring in fish, but they failed.

They went out with empty hearts and came back with empty nets. There is unproductiveness in unbelief, for it does not gender success, it cannot inspire confidence, and it is bound to bring failure. Unbelief is a venture without the Master, going it alone in the great business of living. It is unloosing the lifeline from the source of power.

Many Peters are among us today. They give up too soon after toiling and catching nothing. Using human skill without divine power, the consequence is empty nets.

Obedience and Success

> But when the morning was now come, Jesus stood on the shore: but the disciples knew not that it was Jesus. Then Jesus saith unto them, Children, have ye any meat? They answered him, No. And he said unto them, Cast the net on the right side of the ship, and ye shall find. They cast therefore, and now they were not able to draw it for the multitude of fishes (vv. 4-6).

The defecting disciples had stood on the threshold of a new era of world service, having already received a commission and an unction. But now, due to failure, they wallowed in the troughs of defeat and had to be stripped of all self-confidence and self-dependence. They had to know the lessons to be found in failure and had to understand their limitations and their Lord's omnipotence.

It was in "the morning" that Jesus made His appearance. In God's economy of life there is always a morning for every night of failure. Jesus' appearance turns night into morning, failure into success, sadness into gladness, and emptiness into fullness.

Still unrecognized by the disciples as He stood on the shore, Jesus asked, "Have ye any meat?" They confess to total failure. There is progression in unbelief. They failed in their faith, which led to failure in their efforts, and now they failed to recognize Jesus. They looked without seeing. There is no reason to believe in a radically altered appearance of Jesus. The trouble lay with the disciples, for they did not have the same spiritual rapport which would have brought them quick recognition. They were in the impoverished state of being without meat. Unbelief cannot feed itself; it has only husks to offer and empty nets and hearts.

Jesus suggested a very simple corrective maneuver: "Cast the net on the right side of the ship, and ye shall find" (v. 6). Jesus excelled in everything. He was a master teacher and healer, and here He shows Himself to be a master fisherman. He gives a significant direction: "Cast the net on the right side." Why the right side? Peter and his companions had fished from all sides, all night in all parts of the lake, yet took nothing. He had fished with all the finesse of an expert. But it wasn't a question of *where* but *how,* and under whose guidance and blessing. He was asked now to be obedient to the master fisherman and learn a lasting lesson.

Success follows obedience, for "they cast therefore, and now they were not able to draw it for the multitude of fishes" (v. 6). There was really no difference between the right side and the left side of the boat. It was not so much the locality, for both sides of the boat led to the same waters. It wasn't fishing with new skill, but under new auspices — the risen Christ.

Another thing is important here: they achieved success at the place of previous failure. It was the same lake, the same boat, the same nets and the same fisherman, but added to this were a new obedience and a risen Christ.

Under the same circumstances where they had failed, they now found success. It was success out of failure, and victory out of defeat. What was possible for the first-century disciples is possible for us. In the very waters of life where we have labored in fruitless living with empty nets, God can give success and victory. The secret is obedience — "Cast the net on the right side."

They had cast their nets on the "other side." Theoretically this is not a physical or geographical "other side" but the "other side" of prayerlessness, faithless living, joyless experience, indifference and disobedience. Moreover, it is on the "other side" of the resurrection, the side of power and blessing and the side of the risen Christ and Pentecost. This is the side of spiritual growth and progress, of spiritual maturity and growth in grace.

RESTORATION AND FELLOWSHIP

Therefore that disciple whom Jesus loved saith unto Peter, It is the Lord. Now when Simon Peter heard that it was the Lord, he girt his fisher's coat unto him, (for he was naked,) and did cast himself into the sea. And the other disciples came in a little ship; (for they were not far from land, but as it were two hundred cubits,) dragging the net with fishes. As soon as they were come to land, they saw a fire of coals there, and fish laid thereon, and bread. Jesus saith unto them, Bring of the fish which ye have now caught. Simon Peter went up, and drew the net to land full of great fishes, an hundred and fifty and three: and for all there were so many, yet was not the net broken. Jesus saith unto them, Come and dine. And none of the disciples durst ask him, Who art thou? knowing that it was the Lord. Jesus then cometh, and taketh bread, and giveth them, and fish likewise. This is now the third time that Jesus shewed himself to his disciples, after that he was risen from the dead (vv. 7-14).

The purpose of the entire incident was to bring reassurance to the disciples of both the person and power of the Lord. There were many indications of weakness, doubt and indecision on the part of the disciples. They had already looked back to their former interests and employments, and their excursion into this area brought defeat. Then Jesus reentered their lives and experiences, demonstrating His postresurrection power which resulted in abundance and success. They had experienced in all this the joy of restoration.

The recognition of the Lord by the disciples was at the same place and in the same circumstances of a similar miracle earlier in the disciples' career (Lk 5). This was a repetition of a well-remembered miracle of Jesus and with it came recognition. John's exclamation was "It is the Lord."

Although John made the discovery, it was Peter who could not wait until the task of bringing in the fish was over, for he cast himself into the sea to be the first to see if it was the Master. His impetuosity was premature, for he left the other disciples with the work of conserving the miraculous catch.

John stood for love, Thomas for inquiry, and Peter for zeal. There is a time to hurry and follow our investigative inclinations, but this kind of hurry could be wastefulness too. Peter had a task to do, because fishing was a team effort and he should have stayed with the team. There is a time to satisfy curiosity and a time to gather fish; a time to worship and a time to work. Peter's zeal at this point was misguided and out of place, but it is forgivable. An Indian said, "I don't know about having too much zeal, but I think it is better the pot boil over than not to boil at all."

Peter's discovery was "a fire of coals . . . and fish laid thereon, and bread" (v. 9), whereupon Jesus gave all the disciples an invitation to join Him at breakfast: "Come and dine" (v. 12).

The disciples were thoroughly convinced that it was the Lord, and did not need to demand unnecessary proofs. Content with what they had seen and heard, they entered into the wonderful fellowship of their restoration. How Jesus got the fish and the bread and prepared them is not recorded. It is sufficient that the food was there, and He was there, and the disciples were asked to participate.

This event is another evidence of the natural unnaturalness of the new body. Not only could it appear and disappear, be apparent and yet hidden, but it could also take food. Its substance and structure indicated the need of some form of energy similar to that needed by the human body, yet it had powers that far exceeded the abilities of the present body to perform. It had enough likeness to the old body to have familiarity, but it had enough dissimilarity as to make it miraculous and spectacular. It was so substantial and real that it could be touched and felt, for Jesus said, "Handle me, and see; for a spirit hath not flesh and bones, as ye see me have" (Lk 24:39). The only thing missed was the blood left on Calvary, and no longer necessary in a spiritual body.

The happy ending of the incident puts leisure after labor, rest after toil, fulfillment after faith, and dining after fasting. It is a symbol of that kind of fulfillment which comes to discipleship when the crown will succeed the cross, and a full measure of fellowship will be the continued and eternal reward of discipleship.

54

Abiding Love

21:15-25

SITTING TOGETHER in the still early hours of the morning on the white sand of the beach with a brisk fire burning, Jesus divided a breakfast of fish and bread among His seven disciples. When the meal was finished Jesus turned to Peter and began a series of questions which are among the best-known sayings of the Bible.

A new era of life had dawned for the disciples, who would soon bear the responsibilities of worldwide service without their Lord. This was further preparation for those responsibilities.

In Peter's place as the leader of the disciples, he is not cast in the role of the first pope. There are no ecclesiastical rulership and authority in view here. Rather, it is the preparation of Peter and the other disciples that is in the mind of our Lord.

There are two places of preparation for the disciples: *Galilee* with its preparation of love, and *Pentecost* with its preparation of power. In the divine preparation, power is secondary to love, and enabling comes after ennobling, even as Pentecost followed Galilee. Most people, however, pray for power — the strength to do things. Few people pray for love — the quality to be someone.

The Bible puts beauty and strength together as companion virtues, but it puts beauty before strength, being before doing, and love before power. Love is the most powerful and compelling emotion in our being. When it is raised to the divine level, as it is here, it becomes the highest motivation and stimulation in all of life. When this love is possessed, or perhaps more accurately, when it possesses us, it becomes the source of our greatest good, greatest happiness and greatest usefulness.

Love, according to Jesus, is the greatest commandment: "Master, which is the greatest commandment in the law? Jesus said unto him, Thou shalt love the Lord thy God with all thy heart, and with all thy soul, and with all thy mind. This is the first and great commandment" (Mt 22:36-38).

Love, according to the apostle Paul, is the supreme virtue: "And now abideth faith, hope, love, these three; but the greatest of these is love" (1 Co 13:13).

Love, according to Jesus, is the greatest test of discipleship: "By this shall all men know that ye are my disciples, if ye have love one to another" (Jn 13:35).

We need love more than anything else, and it becomes the Saviour's last effort to establish this climate in the relationship between disciple and Lord as well as between disciple and disciple. Jesus does so by addressing a thrice-repeated question to Peter: "Believest thou me?" The disciples had shown a wavering faith through the ordeal of the crucifixion, and even in varying degrees after the resurrection. But apparently Jesus was satisfied now that their faith was well established. Now it was love as the expulsive force of the disciples' lives that concerned Jesus.

Two distinct and separate verbs for love are used by Jesus and Peter. One is the word *phileo* which means the love with which man loves. The other is *agapao* which means the love with which God loves. The distinction between them is what is being revealed in this series of questions to Peter. It is possible to have an emotional love without having a devotional love. A person can have religious emotion which is expressed through architecture, ritual and beauty, without having the total commitment that devotional love demands.

THE FIRST QUESTION

"Simon, son of Jonas, lovest thou me more than these?" (v. 15). When Peter replies, he uses a different word for love than Jesus used. Jesus used the verb *agapao,* but Peter used the verb *phileo.* Simon could not honestly profess the possession of as high a form of love as Jesus indicated. Jesus' *agapao* was to love with the love wherewith God loved us.

The charge or commission with which Jesus responded to Peter's answer was "Feed my lambs." We have tried to give artificial distinctions between lambs and sheep as expressions of various stages of maturity in believers, but all three words actually mean *believing ones.*

THE SECOND QUESTION

"Simon, son of Jonas, lovest thou me?" (v. 16). In this question Jesus used the same high word for love, which is *agapao,* meaning God's love. Peter responds as he did the first time with the same word *phileo,* meaning friendly affection or brotherly love. Apparently Peter realized that he did not possess this highest affection, and properly judges his true feelings with a lesser word. The charge or commission with which Jesus responded to Peter's answer was "Feed my sheep."

THE THIRD QUESTION

"Simon, son of Jonas, lovest thou me?" (v. 17). Now we observe a striking change in the language of Jesus. He changes the verb *agapao* to the verb *phileo,* coming down to Peter's understanding and experience and asking, "Hast thou affection for me?" And Peter, chagrined and hurt by Jesus' probing questions, replies with the same word for love that Jesus had just used, and that he had used in answer to the first two questions. He said, "Lord, thou knowest all things, thou knowest that I love thee [have affection for thee]." Simon appeals to the Lord's unlimited knowledge as the basis of understanding his feelings and affection for Him.

Peter is not on a basis of love where he can fulfill his utmost devotion to Jesus, for he is not God and cannot love as God loves. He is man and withal a new man in Christ, and will love as such a man ought to love — affectionately, devotedly, passionately, wholeheartedly and without a rival.

The charge or commission with which Jesus responded to Peter's answer was "Feed my sheep." In the first charge (v. 15) when Jesus said, "Feed my lambs," He meant to pasture or nourish the Lord's lambs. In the second charge (v. 16) when Jesus said, "Feed my sheep" He meant to tend or shepherd the Lord's sheep with tender, loving care. Now in the third charge (v. 17) when Jesus said, "Feed my sheep" He reverts to the first word He used for feeding the lambs, which meant to pasture or nourish the Lord's own people.

It is erroneously suggested by some that in the third charge of Jesus to Peter He meant to give the oversight of Peter as a primate, entrusting to him, as pope, the whole flock of God. Instead of a ruling activity, the special reference of Jesus is to a nourishing and protective activity such as any shepherd would give to any sheep or lamb under his care. The idea of primacy and ruling does not appear in any sense whatever in Jesus' charge or commission to Peter.

The question addressed to Peter reveals the greatest qualification to serve. Jesus does not ask Peter if he is wise, learned, strong, well-born or eloquent. He asks, "Lovest thou me?" Love is the greatest and most necessary quality, all other qualifications being equal. The possession of true love is likewise proved by service. Love does not seek to get; it gives. Love does not ask what we are to get out of it; it only wants to give through loving.

Involved in what Jesus said about love was something not always considered. We are apt to think too often of the effervescent, happy side of love, apart from the sacrificial side. Loving Jesus meant following Him, and twice Jesus said to Peter, "Follow me" (vv. 19, 22).

This is in effect a prophecy of Peter's martyrdom, and is the price he must pay for the love he professed to hold for Jesus. Loving Him would not be easy; neither would following Him. All of us would be glad to follow Jesus if it meant a peaceful, easy life, free from suffering and sorrow. But worthwhileness in life is only realized through hardship and suffering. "The door to the room of success swings on the hinges of opposition."

If love was the gateway to the larger life and the credential of the highest devotion, then obedience meant a way of life often fraught with opposition, difficulty and sometimes death. This was demonstrated in the lives and deaths of the apostles. Tradition reports the deaths of the apostles and others as follows:

Matthew suffered martyrdom by the sword in Ethiopia.

Mark died at Alexandria, after being dragged through the streets of that city.

Luke was hanged on an olive tree in Greece.

John was put into a caldron of boiling oil, but escaped death and was banished to Patmos.

Peter was crucified at Rome with his head downward.

James was beheaded at Jerusalem.

James the Less was thrown from a pinnacle of the temple and beaten to death below.

Philip was hanged against a pillar in Phrygia.

Bartholomew was flayed alive.

Andrew was bound to a cross, whence he preached to his persecutors until he died.

Thomas was run through the body at Coromandel, India.

Jude was shot to death with arrows.

Matthias was first stoned and then beheaded.

Barnabas was stoned to death by Jews at Salonica.

Paul was beheaded at Rome by Nero.

Before this experience in Galilee, Peter had boldly professed his willingness to die for Jesus, but when the test came he failed and fled before the wagging tongue of a street maiden. Now it was different. The risen Christ would make the difference between weakness and strength, cowardice and courage, failure and success.

Not all the chaff was winnowed from Peter's life. When he saw John following them, Peter turned in petulence to ask how John could escape what he would go through. If John will be allotted a happier goal, this does not concern Peter, and Jesus turned him back to the purposes of his own life, saying, "What is that to thee? Follow thou me" (v. 22).

This is the last view of our Lord in John's gospel — the risen Son of God saying to Peter, "Follow me." It is His challenge to us. If Jesus asked Peter for the sacrifice of his life, it was only because He had something greater to give him. In exchange for an earthly life, He had life everlasting for Peter.

TWO THINGS REMAIN IN THE GOSPEL

The written testimony. "This is the disciple which testifieth of these things, and wrote these things: and we know that his testimony is true" (v. 24). The Bible was not intended to contain all the items of literature, or to be an exhaustive listing of science, or to be a complete record of history. It is concerned only with such literary items, scientific facts and historical data that will give to man a sufficient revelation of God and salvation. Upon the basis of these facts and records rest the redemption and salvation of mankind.

The unwritten testimony. "And there are also many other things which Jesus did, the which, if they should be written every one, I suppose that even the world itself could not contain the books that should be written" (v. 25).

We have already considered this statement at the end of chapter 20. It is quite unlikely that it has reference to a measurable amount of incidents in the life of Christ which were not recorded, as if there were so many things found in the life-span of Jesus that space could not be found for their recording. It does not refer to the quantity of evidence available, but to the quality, since they would not be necessary in order to enhance the record. It also points to the inspiration of selection by which the Holy Spirit guided the reporter of this gospel to include only what was necessary for a saving faith.

What is written is considered sufficient for its purpose — the salvation of its readers. "But these are written, that ye might believe that Jesus is the Christ, the Son of God; and that believing ye might have life through his name" (20:31).

In concluding our consideration of this fourth gospel we notice some items of comparative interest:

Matthew ends with the resurrection.
Mark ends with the ascension.
Luke ends with the promise of the Holy Spirit.
John ends with the promise of the second coming.*
Matthew ends with the words, "With me."
Mark ends with the words, "Go ye."
Luke ends with the words, "Tarry ye."
John ends with the word, "Follow."

*These comparisons are by Arthur Petrie.

Matthew ends with special emphasis on the Lord's presence (28:19-20).

Mark ends with special emphasis on the Lord's power (16:19-20).

Luke ends with special emphasis on the Lord's promise (24:49).

John ends with special emphasis on the Lord's program (21:22).

Jesus has asked a question, "Lovest thou me?" and given a command, "Follow thou me." With these words He walks off the pages of this fourth gospel to reappear on the Mount of Olives from which He ascends to heaven.

Where does Jesus ask us to follow him? To heaven? Yes, because He is going to the Father's house. To the world? Yes, because this is His purpose through those who are His disciples. He has left them to carry His name into all the world.

Jesus asked Peter to follow Him to death. He asks us to follow Him to life.